Charles Oscar Beasley

Those American R's. Rule, ruin, restoration

Charles Oscar Beasley

Those American R's. Rule, ruin, restoration

ISBN/EAN: 9783337157067

Printed in Europe, USA, Canada, Australia, Japan

Cover: Foto ©Andreas Hilbeck / pixelio.de

More available books at **www.hansebooks.com**

THOSE AMERICAN R's.

Rule,
Ruin,
Restoration.

—BY—

ONE WHO HAS BEEN R'd.

"THE hand that warned Belshazzar derived its horrifying influence from the want of a body."

PHILADELPHIA:
EDWARD E. WENSLEY & CO.,
823 FILBERT STREET.
1882.

Entered, according to Act of Congress, in the year 1882, by
EDWARD E. WENSLEY & CO.,
In the office of the Librarian of Congress, at Washington.

ALL RIGHTS RESERVED.

PRESS OF
EDWARD E. WENSLEY,
Electrotyper & Printer,
823 FILBERT STREET, PHILAD'A.

PREFACE.

"To COMBINE profundity with perspicuity, wit with judgment, solidity with vivacity, and *all* of them with liberality —who is sufficient for these things?" once asked a conscientious author. I would not dare to assume that I have accomplished this. The most that I can say is that I have attempted it.

He who has been *ruled* is likely to speak respectfully of *authority;* he who has been *ruined* should have a story of absorbing interest for all. To the fortunate his experience would be a *warning*, and to the ruined a *consolation;* but he who has been *restored* feels a happiness which can only be produced by the sharpest contrast. *Restoration* is the greatest solace that can be given to mortals. We are hopeful because the bloom of the rose, hid by Autumn's gloomy mantle, will be *restored* in the Spring-time. The labors of the day are bearable because we know that at evening "Nature's sweet *restorer*" will come. *Restoration* is nature's law. Let the law be fulfilled!

There are two classes of readers who will find little interest in perusing this volume—those who are very *light*, and those who are very *heavy;* for a "feather and a guinea fall with equal velocity in a *vacuum*," and it is "as difficult to throw a straw any distance as a *ton.*" My reader, I leave the matter entirely with you. Read till you get tired and then stop until you can summon courage to begin again. Don't let *style* obscure truth, nor good matter be lost through a poor style. I have given you the best matter I had or could find in the best style at my command. My only hope is that the old adage may be verified, that "*the men of principle may be the principal men.*"

As regards the romantic part of this story I would say that its object is only to lead you on to more solid things —to truth.

The politics of this volume, I trust, is such that I will be regarded a Republican by the Democrats, and a *Democrat* by the *Republicans*, and by honest men as *neither*.

If I shall rouse you to think of better things than you do now, if I shall awake a single slumbering virtue of the human heart, if I shall flash one mere spark of patriotism, if I shall raise a laugh or wake a tear—I shall feel my labors abundantly rewarded.

ONE WHO HAS BEEN R'D.

CONTENTS.

CHAPTER.		PAGE.
I.	TYRANNY	1
II.	ELMWOOD	2
III.	"THOSE SPLENDID PILLS"	6
IV.	THE STORM BREWING	15
V.	THE STORM BREAKS	23
VI.	BLUE SHADOWS	27
VII.	GENERAL GUION'S HEADQUARTERS	33
VIII.	THE MOUNTAINS	37
IX.	"HURRAH FOR LINCOLN!"	40
X.	NEARING THE END	44
XI.	THE END AT LAST	47
XII.	A WANDERER	52
XIII.	STILL A WANDERER	56
XIV.		63
XV.	FAREWELL TO ELMWOOD	69
XVI.	THREE REMOVES PROVE A FIRE	72
XVII.	THE DAWN OF THE NEW	76
XVIII.	THE GUESTS	81
XIX.	A GEM OF RAREST RAY SERENE	84
XX.	A NEW MOVE	89

CHAPTER.		PAGE.
XXI.	The Tale Told Again	92
XXII.	Another Storm Brewing	95
XXIII.	Scenes of War	102
XXIV.	Home Again	122
XXV.	Patriotism and the Castletons	131
XXVI.	Philopolis	138
XXVII.	Here we Are!	141
XXVIII.	From Fiction to Reality	149
XXIX.	Jenkins in a New Role	160
XXX.	A Few Gallantries	167
XXXI.	Was it Love?	175
XXXII.	Troubles	184
XXXIII.	A Revelation	186
XXXIV.	He called the Wanderer Home	190
XXXV.	A Great Era	195
XXXVI.	Modern Education	208
XXXVII.	Time dulls Hate, but Quickens Love	215
XXXVIII.	The Second Martyr of the Republic	220
XXXIX.	Imprisoned Love	236
XL.	The New President	249
XLI.	In the Toils	256
XLII.	The Great Idea of the North: "Live to Labor."	262
XLIII.	The Leading Idea of the South: "Labor to Live"	268
XLIV.	A Crisis	278
XLV.	A Mystery	283
XLVI.	The Dead Wood Falling Off	289
XLVII.	The Red Cross	308
XLVIII.	Over the Waters	314
XLIX.	Restoration	319
L.	The Story Told	324

CHAPTER I.

TYRANNY.

"WELL, Doc, here we are," said jovial 'Squire Jenkins, as he gave Dr. Castleton a shake of the hand a little more cordially than usual.

"Come in, come in, 'Squire; we are done for now."

"What on arth's the matter with you? Has that last brood of chickens not made out well?" (The 'Squire's mind always turned to important matters first.)

"No, no! How can you trifle with me, 'Squire, in such a crisis as this. Tyranny is afloat, and liberty is dead for seven years at least."

"Have them blasted fellers that are tryin' to ruin the country by either drivin' us out of the Union or stealin' our niggers, got the upper hand up North and fixed things for Abe Lincoln's election?"

During this conversation the unusual activity that pervaded the Castleton house could not but be noticed. The 'Squire saw in everybody's countenance as they passed and re-passed in the hallway, expressions of great cheerfulness. The slaves were singing in that plaintive melody so peculiar to them when they were expressing their joy at some happy event, or some especial good fortune which had befallen their Master or Mistress.—Joy and gladness seemed to fill every heart, save only the Doctor's. The 'Squire was a blunt fellow of little learning and polish, but with keen perception that often served him instead. He eyed the Doctor, who seemed to wince a little under his penetrating glance. The 'Squire thought he could detect a slight undercurrent of mirth in the Doctor's manner, in spite of the serious air he assumed.

"Now look a'here, Doc, (of all things, the 'Squire hated to be worsted in a joke), I'm beginnin' ter have my 'specs 'justed to this bizness." The 'Squire could not restrain a slight smile. "There isn't but one kind o' tyranny that can last for seven year in this here free country. Bring it out, Doc, bring it out." The Doctor had already given a sign to one of the slaves, who disappeared, and was just then entering with a little burden in her arms, which she carried with a step of softness.

"Here, 'Squire, is the first tyrant of the Castleton family." As the Doctor laid the new-born babe in the arms of the sturdy old 'Squire, those of the household who had by this time gathered in the parlor could see that twenty years' severe dispensation of justice had not yet robbed his heart of its tenderness, but had only imprisoned it, and given the keys of the dungeon to some misfortune to the helpless, or some joy to a friend. Real misfortune to anyone would rouse the 'Squire's good heart to action, or some good fortune to one he loved would moisten his shaggy-browed eyes with tears of joy. It was a happy scene. The 'Squire handed back the precious charge to its nurse, at the same time inquiring if Mrs. Castleton was dong well. He was assured she was. "Doc, have you named this monster yet?"

"No, 'Squire. I was waiting for an opportunity to ask you to name him. You have been a lucky man, and I would like to yield sufficiently to superstition to have the mystic charm of luck thrown about the babe by having you name him, 'Squire."

"Well," said the magistrate, "if that's the idea, I'll make the boy's connection with luck as close a possible, so I will call him 'Oscar Jenkins Castleton.'"

"I can beat you, 'Squire. I can make the connection closer than that. He shall be called 'J. Oscar Castleton,' and when we wish to especially invoke the Goddess of Luck, we'll just say or write that 'J.' stands for Jenkins."

"Well, Doc, I see I have a trial at eleven o'clock and so I'm off," and taking one more glance at the babe he had christened with a name, he shook again the Doctor's hand and departed.

CHAPTER II.

ELMWOOD.

THE events of the last chapter occurred in one of our Southern States that border on the Atlantic. Not at the extreme South, nor yet too near the North, its climate and soil were a happy admixture of the virtues of both the tropical and temperate regions. The sands, lowlands and marshes of the eastern portion of the State indicated that ere long the traveller would reach the sea. Over most of this belt, Cotton was king. But he had many powerful vassals in the persons of monster forests of pine, whose trees dropped into the "boxes" cut in them many thousand barrels of turpentine yearly. And finally, when these faithful giants of the forest have never failed, for a single season out of many, to yield their portion of the staple, and as living trees have passed the period of their usefulness, the woodman's axe hews them down and they may then be seen floating as great lumber rafts down the wide and shallow streams of this region.

As you recede from the sea, the flimsy sand gives way to firmer and more cheerful soil. The woods are no longer almost exclusively of pine. The ash, the hickory, the elm and the oak now have a broader field and a chance for life. Cotton, white, swan-like, as if jealous to be thought summer's snow, does not now hold absolute sway. The cereals cover the fields with their golden colors. Here for the first time you see tobacco growing. Going still further from the sea you reach the mountains. Hot and sultry elsewhere, here 'tis cool. The serene arch of the sky never appears more beautiful than when, standing on a mountain summit, you behold one base of the arch invisibly joining with the plains beyond, and, following the vault with the eye, you turn as its graceful curve directs you, and find that the other base kisses the sea.

It was not far from this mountain range that Elmwood, the residence of the Castletons, was situated. The Castleton house was a characteristic southern home. Built of wood, three stories high, with porticos at front and rear on the first two stories; painted white, with bright green blinds, it stood among the trees and flowers about three hundred yards from the roadside. Back stretched the fields and meadows. Not far away the cabins of the slaves stood wrapped in quietness, awaiting the return of their occupants from work. A few houses could be noticed, a good deal better than the log cabins of the slaves, but much inferior to the house of the Master. These were the residences of the "overseers."

CHAPTER III.

"THOSE SPLENDID PILLS."

THE little town of Bethanoth lay at the foot of cloud-capt mountains, some miles from Elmwood. The distinctive Biblical character of this name—Bethanoth—would lead one to suspect that religion or religious persecution had contributed in some way to the founding of this village. So it had. The followers of the great Christian nobleman, Count Zinzendorf, fleeing from their native land, where their prayers to the God that created them could only ascend to heaven when the despot's sceptre permitted, had come to America for conscience' sake, and had settled here to farm the steep hillsides by day and to pray and sing by night.

Among the first of these German Moravian pioneers of a hundred and fifty years ago to break the virgin soil of what was to be Bethanoth, was Josiah Hanzmann. The first house he worked to build was one to protect his wife and children from the storms; the second was the little church where he and generations of his family were destined to worship.

These settlers had subdued by justice and kindness the

savage breast of the Indian, who still roamed in wild liberty among the hills and forests of this region. Uninterrupted by attacks from them, Bethanoth grew and throve. The years went by and Josiah Hanzmann was gathered to his fathers, whither his good wife and mother of his children had gone before. He was laid beside her on the summit of the mountain that overlooked the house in which he had dwelt so long. The simple white head-stone of his grave had greeted many a rising sun at morn and received his latest ray at evening, till as if in acknowledgment of the salutations the stone had changed its whiteness for a bronzed hue. The storms of many winters, the rains of many summers had beaten upon that stone and left their mark in its broken edges and marred features. So by the time of which we speak many Hanzmanns and descendants of Hanzmanns kept silent company with their forefather Josiah, on the cloudy summit.

A few years before the date of the opening of our story Bethanoth was visited by that dreadful scourge—Scarlet Fever. It did not come often, but when it did, fearful havoc followed in its train. It did not fail to enter the Hanzmann family. Four of the seven children, descendants in the fourth generation of old Josiah, were buried in the Hangmann lot on Summit Hill—victims of the dread fever. Old Dr. Joseph Winner, a primitive Allopath from New England, and long a resident in the vicinity of Bethanoth, was the popular doctor. His limited abilities had long been sufficient for the ordinary ailments which afflicted this neighborhood. While the Doctor's good nature, his brusque and lively manner, coupled with the fact that he was not unnecessarily industrious in contending for the peculiar political and moral ideas which then pervaded his native New England, had made Dr. Winner the "old stand-by" of the county. But scarlet fever was an enemy of a different calibre from his usual foe. Caring little for the "fineries" of medicine, his was the old, time-honored "stop practice;"—that is, for the same diseases, he gave in all cases, old or young, the same remedies. The different temperaments and nervous constitutions of individuals were, in the eyes of the Doctor, useless distinctions. So we need not wonder at the effect of this vigorous treatment of the Doctor's upon his scarlet fever patients. To use the phrase in vogue at the time, "he slew them as he went." His skillful hand was to be seen in the management of the cases of the young Hanzmanns—two brothers and two sisters—who had lately died.

Rebecca Hanzmann, the fairest of all the daughters of the Hanzmanns, was now to be stricken by the fell disease. She was in the midst of the blooming beauty that enshrouds the mountain maiden of seventeen summers. The gayest of all the household, when her merry laugh was hushed it left all around dreary indeed. When not roaming over the hills, with gay heart and light, rebounding step, with companions that could hardly match her who never seemed to tire of the playful chase;—when not thus employed she could be seen sitting beneath the shade of her favorite tree, a "sugar-ball," in the apple orchard. It was a magnificent specimen of that variety of tree. Its branches were large and outspreading and it was not far from a romantic little stream which made its tortuous way among the rocks and hills. Just to the right of this inviting tree was the meadow, clover-covered. In front, through the interstices of the orchard trees, glimpses of the house could be had. Rebecca loved to sit here alone and read while eating the golden "sugar balls," plucked by her own hand. The little brook babbled by; the leaves rustled at the gentle touch of the zephyrs; the odor of new mown hay filled the air, and—she herself was there to complete the scene!

A Grecian poet, Pagan though he was, sings regretfully that death loves more dearly the richest, sweetest treasure.

"Oh, she must be saved! Let us send for Dr. Castleton. He may be able to do something."

So spoke in her despair the loving mother of the fast fading flower.

Two trusty slaves were despatched at once for the Doctor whose fame had now reached Bethanoth. He came.

After giving directions about the nursing of the patient,

Dr. Castleton left some pills, which were the consummation of the latest medical research in the treatment of Scarlet Fever. The anxious and gloomy countenance of the young Doctor as he left the Hanzmann home that day struck deep into the hearts of those loved ones that moved about the bedside of the stricken maiden. Rebecca was delirious. She had, however, possession of her faculties sufficiently to see that *Pills* were being left for her to take, and to remember that *Pills* were the dread weapons of old Dr. Winner in his fatal combat with the fever that had killed her father and sisters. So Rebecca resolved that if she must die, she would die by Nature's own processes, unassisted by pills.

Mrs. Hanzmann prepared for carefully administering two of the pills to the patient. With a smile she gave the first pill to Rebecca who, after having placed it on her parched tongue, drank the water that was to "wash it down." The second pill went through a similar process, and so in turn with all the rest. Thus things continued. Dr. Castleton called each day, and expressed himself much gratisfied at the progress of his patient towards recovery. Naturally of a strong constitution, Rebecca's convalescence was more rapid than is usual in such cases. There was a little circumstance connected with Dr. Castleton's visits to his patient which did not fail to be noticed by those about the house experienced in such symptoms.

The Doctor's visits became *more frequent* as his patient grew better.

> No law inexorable of Esculapius' sons
> But that Cupid its mandate shuns.

The wonted bloom returned to Rebecca's cheek; that voice of hers again resounded with its mellowed sweetness; and the day when first she rose from her bed seemed very bright. The rays of that morning's sun shone so beautifully into her room, having snatched additional sweetness from the yellow jessamines that clambered o'er her window-sill. The happiest of all to greet her on this auspicious morning, was young Dr. Castleton. He lingered for quite a while, chatting merrily with Rebecca.

"What in the world is this?" was an exclamation which came from Mrs. Hanzmann, while engaged in superintending the removal of the bedding, carpets, etc., of Rebecca's room, which were now to be thoroughly aired and renovated. The cause of this exclamation on the part of Mrs. Hanzmann was the finding of a number of pills lodged between the wall and the head-board of Rebecca's bedstead! What made this discovery more astounding was the fact that a closer examination showed that they were none other than Dr. Castleton's splendid and efficacious pills! Rebecca had been watching these proceedings from an adjoining room, where she had taken care to have the rocking-chair upon which she was reclining placed in such a position that it would afford her a good view of what was going on in the sick-chamber.

"Rebecca, can you tell me anything about these pills? I found them about your bedstead," said Mrs. Hanzmann as she, with bewildered look, approached Rebecca with the mystic pills placed upon a piece of paper.

Rebecca, ill concealing the smile that lit up her countenance, fondly embraced her mother to reassure her, and then told her all. How she had kept the pills in her mouth until she got a favorable opportunity for throwing them behind the head-board; how often Dr. Castleton's remarks about the virtue of his pills and their splendid effect upon the patient, had amused her in the dullness and dreariness of her sick hours; how, unable to talk with the loving ones around her, she could yet think of this and keep her spirits cheerful.

Mrs. Hanzmann was much affected by the story. She spoke of the great danger Rebecca had risked; but the happy termination of it all made the prudent mother forget this, and without saying more she retired, being in almost as cheerful a mood as Rebecca herself.

How to break the news to Dr. Castleton was the question that perplexed the Hanzmann family the rest of that day. Rebecca requested that she be permitted to manage the important affair herself. This was granted. On the morrow Dr. Castleton called as usual, and received a most hearty welcome from his fair patient. The Doctor was much pleased at her animation and cheerfulness which were the best assurances of her good progress toward recovery.

"Doctor, I have a little package to show you. It has interested us all very much," said Rebecca, handing the Doctor his favorite pills.

"I am gratified, Miss Rebecca, to find that you are kind enough to think that anything which interests you, would also interest me. I will be pleased to examine the package."

As the Doctor carefully unrolled the paper, he soon saw its contents. He looked at Rebecca. Her eyes were cast upon the floor; such an indescribably charming light seemed to beam from the countenance of the half-modest, half-blushing maiden; such a "do not be angry," appreciative look of those eyes which had the mystic, invisible charm which only beauty can give, subdued the Doctor in their first onslaught. Such bravery as this aroused the admiration of the chivalrous, gallant Doctor. A woman of such fair, yet magnificent physique who could brave, unaided by medical skill, the most terrible of diseases and conquer it, was in his eyes a treasure. But her amiable disposition and her great moral courage lent a perennial charm to her character, which to the ardent Castleton was far more precious than all else she had to bestow. And these charms flowed from the rich fountains of beauty and virtue, which, like the mountain rills of her childhood's home, had not as yet reached the turbid stream rushing impatiently on to be lost in the bosom of the boundless ocean, but which coursed down only the gentle currents of her young and virgin life. It was the old, old story that grows sweeter each time it is told.

When Dr. Lawrence Castleton led, two years later, the fair Rebecca to the altar as his bride, the old story seemed to be outdoing itself. Often did Elmwood teem with memories of those "Splendid Pills."

CHAPTER IV.

THE STORM BREWING.

MOST of the Southern mansions had one especially trusted, good-natured house-servant, usually an old negro slave. She was much loved by the household, and no more happy relations could exist anywhere between persons than often existed between this slave and those whom she served. "Aunt Dinah" was the servant that occupied this peculiar position in the Castleton family.

Among the systems brought about by the existence of slavery was that of "patrolling." No slave could leave his master's grounds at night or on Sundays, without a "pass" signed by his master. Mounted patrolmen paraded the roads at night, entered the premises of the various owners, and searched among the cabins for any strange slaves. If they happened upon some unlucky negro who was trying to steal a visit to some fellow-bondsman or bondswoman, and who could not show a "pass," he was taken by the patrolmen and roundly flogged. This rigorous system was thought necessary in those times for the preservation of order and for the preventing of negro insurrections.

The usual "pass" was given Aunt Dinah, one evening, to visit a neighboring plantation. The next morning, Mrs. Castleton was much astonished to hear Aunt Dinah speak of her visit in the following terms, which, at the same time, were so characteristic of the simplicity and confidence of many of the slaves in their masters:

"Missis, what's dat I hear 'bout las' night down on Mister Slocum's plantation? De black folks dah was talkin' 'bout a man dat come from way up Norf; he sed de white folks up dah was all a'comin' down here 'fo long and take us away from our massas and missises. I wants, Missis, to know what dem folks mean."

Mrs. Castleton was much aroused. She told Aunt Dinah that it was only the talk of wicked people who were trying to stir up strife, and that she must not pay any attention to it.

Mrs. Castleton made haste to disclose the news to her husband. Dr. Castleton was one of those who firmly and conscientiously believed the preservation of the institution of slavery necessary for the prosperity and existence of the South. It was a flagrant violation of the law for any one to attempt to talk to the slaves about freedom, or to in any way do anything which would lead to the disturbing of the institution, or interfere with the social order. In cases, however, where persons violated this law, the slow legal methods of the magistrates were generally dispensed with, and the citizens themselves would summarily dispose of the offender by giving him notice to quit the country within twenty-four hours, and woe be to him, if he failed to heed the warning!

Dr. Castleton lost no time in communicating to the neighboring planters the intelligence he had received. Instantly bodies of men were in motion, searching the country for any strangers. Happily for him, the messenger of Northern Liberty could not be found, and so in a few days the accustomed quietness reigned in and around Elmwood.

"The citizens of Binghampton county are respectfully invited to assemble at the Court House in Ardenton on Saturday evening [afternoon] August 13th, to assert anew the great constitutional principles upon which our Government is founded, and to rally to the support of the chosen representatives of these principles, John C. Breckinridge, and Joseph Lane, candidates for President and Vice President of the United States."

This notice appeared in "The Binghampton County Messenger" a few days previous to the event which happened on the occasion of Aunt Dinah's visit to the plantation of Mr. Millard Slocum.

Saturday, August 13th, came; and on that day many carriages might be seen coming into Ardenton, bearing the majority of the citizens of Binghampton county. The meeting was held in the large, shady grove in front of the Court House.

Dr. Castleton, who, as before intimated, was quite active in all political matters, presided.

A*

Hon. James L. Harpurton was the first speaker. Mr. Harpurton was a lawyer and a politician of the Calhoun school.

"Fellow citizens," he began, "it gives me great pleasure to have the privilege to-day of renewing my fidelity to those wise and beneficent principles of government with which my political forefathers baptized me in my infancy, and by the grace of which my young manhood was cherished, and which, I trust, in my old age, I may be permitted to carry with me to the grave."

Then Mr. Harpurton began a learned and exhaustive review of the foundation and structure of the government. The States Rights doctrine was thus summarized:

"The States are the nurturing mother of the Federal Government; upon them it depends for its very existence. The states made the Federal Government, they can destroy it; they gave it power, they can take that power away."

When the applause which greeted this sentiment had subsided, a slight sensation was caused by a strong voice from the crowd calling out "How about 'We, the people,' in the preamble of the constitution, if the *States* made it?" This question came from a man well known in Binghampton county. He was one of those who believed in the maintenance of that Union which Washington and his compatriots had labored to form. James Freeman was not a man of the schools. Intelligence and strong common-

AN EXPLANATION.

sense was his foundation for political principles, and bravery to speak them, was the way he spread his doctrines among his neighbors.

The question of James Freeman was abstruse, but one often considered by the States Rights men ; so it gave Mr. Harpurton little trouble to promptly answer: "I am glad, Mr. Chairman, that we have an answer—a crushing answer —to all those who, though living in the South, with all their property, their hopes and aspirations centered in the South, yet import the vicious principles of Northern politics, with which they may despoil and destroy their own native firesides.

"The Preamble to the constitution of the United States does not say '*We, the people.*' It says, 'We the people of the *United States.*'

"It is, sir, an undisputed historical fact that the Constitutional Convention of 1787 originally adopted that peramble in the form of 'We the people of the States of Massachusetts, Providence Plantations, New York, Pennsylvania, etc., etc.,' and that the convention changed it to 'We the people of the United States' only when it was pointed out that if any of the states enumerated in the Preamble failed to adopt the Constitution, it would make it appear in a somewhat ridiculous light.

"It was, sir, for this and only this, that it was ever changed. This forever proves that the Constitution emanated from the people of the several states, *as states*, and not from the people in the aggregate. Men speak of the use of the word 'shall' in the Constitution, as if it indicated *inferiority* on the part of that to which the word is applied. That it is, as Webster says, ' the language of command, of a *superior* to an *inferior !* ' If this reasoning be true, then nearly every power granted by the Constitution is degraded. For it reads ' Congress *shall;* ' ' No State *shall!* ' This, if it be a degradation, is not more a degradation of the States than of the Federal Government. It is simply an *equality* of degradations.

" ' Shall ' is, sir, the universal language of treaties between independent nations. It is the language of the old confederation. Would men as exact in the use of English as our fathers were apply the language of confederacy to one system, and then apply that same language to another system of government of a totally different nature?

"We live under a confederacy of States. Our fathers before 1787 lived under a confederacy. There is nothing in the Constitution of the United States destroying its confederal nature."

The strictest attention was given to, and great interest was shown in, this part of the orator's speech. His hearers regarded it as conclusive. James Freeman, notwithstanding, was still unconverted. He was always for the Union, because he believed that there were no ills *within* the Union which would not be greater *out* of the Union. He thought he could detect Secession lurking, like a spectre, beneath the flowery periods of Mr. Harpurton. James Freeman was unconvinced.

Dr. Castleton, the chairman, introduced Mr. Leonard Miltoner as the closing speaker.

Mr. Miltoner was a son of Southern chivalry. His was the fire of the South, which should burn unimpeded —not even its *shadow* should be in the least dimmed. It must shine to its full or be extinguished utterly and forever.

"Mr. Chairman, and fellow citizens of my native state, it is fitting that this meeting should be closed by the vigor and hope of youth addressing it, having already listened to the sober judgment of experience.

"Fellow citizens, the crisis is at hand. The minions of the North are closing in their lines; the vassals of sedition have been sent among us. Even the peaceful shade of Elmwood, the residence of our honored chairman, has not escaped their blighting, withering influence.

"Having nothing themselves, they are very solicitous to snatch the property of others from them. It is easy to be sanctimonious when you can be so at another's expense.

"They are striving day and night to steal your property. The South acquired its property, and, by heaven, *it can preserve it!*"

This aroused the audience to the highest pitch of enthusiasm. The resolutions were in the spirit of the speeches. If the enemy of the South were elected President, the South would protect and assert its rights with the last man and the last dollar.—These were the times in which Jenkins Castleton was cradled!

CHAPTER V.

THE STORM BREAKS.

" * * * O, that we might ken
The end of this day's business, ere it come!
But it sufficeth, that the day will end,
And *then*, the end is known."

THE billows of the sea of politics ran high; the old Ship of State, which had weathered many a storm, plunged to and fro, vexed by Pilots striving to steer her in different directions.

"The dying throes of the infant Hercules," said some who viewed the battle of the elements from afar.

The following extract from the "New Cretonia Trident," the great political organ of the North, was secretly sent to every known supporter of Bell and Everett for President and Vice President in the South, as most of these were opposed to secession. James Freeman received this extract; and its words sank deep into his patriotic heart. He carefully folded it and placed it in his pocket. Passers-by often wondered why it was that they saw James Freeman, with his plough-share stopped in an unfinished furrow, while he himself was absorbed in reading a small pamphlet.

"Many years ago a bark sailed from Liverpool for America. Its name was the 'Old Ocean Monarch!' This was its hundred and thirteenth voyage across the Atlantic.

"The owners of this vessel had long noticed that its great anchor and chain were becoming unfit for use by reason of the ravages made upon them by rust. Especially was this true of the chain.

"So they ordered a new anchor and chain, which were put on board on the day she sailed; and the old anchor and chain were piled up on the wharf. The Captain was unaware of this change.

"It was only after the vessel had left her moorings, and was sailing down the stream, that he noticed his old and trusty anchor lying on the wharf.

"It might have been superstition. However, the veteran of the sea said he had made many voyages safely. Never yet had he been without his old anchor. It had never failed to serve him well. No storm had ever raged so fiercely that this anchor had not held the ship securely. He would not now sail with such a trusty servant left behind.

"So the captain ordered a boat to go back and bring on board again the anchor of the 'Old Ocean Monarch!'

"It was brought and laid beside the new one that had displaced it.

'On the vessel sailed, out of the mouth of the Mersey into the sea and up the Irish coast.

"The captain now noticed a single dark speck in the sky. His experienced eye told of what this was the premonitor.

"Not far off were the terrible rocks of the Irish coast. He made every preparation for the coming storm. He ordered the sails to be reefed, and the anchor to be made ready.

'The storm came in all its fury. '*Drop the anchor!*' was the captain's order.

"Down, down, a hundred fathoms down, went the new anchor, which was to hold fast the ship and prevent her from being washed upon the cruel rocks.

"The ship sank into the valley of water between two giant, raging billows; up with terrific violence the waves tore her again. The chain snapped asunder! The vessel was wild upon the mad waters!

WAR!

"With a voice that sounded above the roar of the plunging sea, the captain shouted: "*Now,* let down the anchor of the 'Old Ocean Monarch!'

"Down, down, a hundred fathoms down, went the tried old anchor. It cut its way among the sands and rocks of the bottom, and sank deep into them.

"The ship plunged down and up again as before.

"The chain received the shock unbroken. The storm spent itself; and when the waters were still once more, there, at its post; was the anchor of the 'Old Ocean Monarch!'"

"Eighty years ago the ship of the United States set sail upon the sea of nations. In the midst of the storms that have beset her, the old anchor of the *Union* has ever held her safely.

"When every other chain has snapped, throw out the cable of the Union! Try the trusty servant! With this anchored in the hearts of patriots North and South, the storms of destruction will beat upon our country in vain."

The time of sore trial for the anchor of the Union came at last, and all was on the hazard of the die.

The beat of drums and martial sounds were heard around the quiet shades of Elmwood. War! war! war!

" Let 'em smell fire, Doc." This was 'Squire Jenkins' greeting to Dr. Castleton one fine morning. The 'Squire, old as he was, had donned a Confederate captain's uniform, and was about starting off for the front.

" Why, 'Squire, I never thought you could look half so handsome. Why, here's Len Miltoner, too."

" The finest looking kunnel in the sarvice," ejuaculated the 'Squire.

Colonel Miltoner and Dr. Castleton exchanged courtesies, and began at once to discuss the situation.

"Look a'here, Doc., I come to tell you good-bye, and to take a kind of a last peep at little Jenk. It's best to talk about the situation and those things *after* the battle."

Mrs. Caslteton now appeared with little Jenkins in her arms. The old 'Squire took him, and while the tyrant lost his fingers in the full beard of his namesake, the new captain kissed the little lips and hurried away, lest some one should detect a tear in his stern eye

Mrs. Castleton and the Doctor too were much affected, and felt that they might not see their true old friend again. Even the fiery Colonel Miltoner was softened for a while by the scene. He, however, made haste to bid the Castleton family farewell. His regiment was to leave for the lines that day.

"I hopes de kunnel will git back safe," said Aunt Dinah, as Colonel Leonard Miltoner disappeared among the trees which shaded the Castleton grounds.

CHAPTER VI.

BLUE SHADOWS.

EVENTS hasten on, and Elmwood has strange bed-fellows.

By a law of the Confederate Government physicians were exempted from military service, except such of them as were especially appointed surgeons of the army. This was a humane measure, and it alleviated the suffering of many homes.

Dr. Castleton longed to be in the ranks of those who were defending Southern homes from invasion and destruction. Daily, by letters and by newspapers, he learned of some friend and neighbor who had died a hero's death. —But his love for the helpless held him back. He ministered to the sick, cared for the dying, and comforted the comfortless. Little Jenkins was now a rollicking boy, and often accompanied the Doctor in his travels round the country.

Rebecca's fortitude, her cheerful spirits, the utter absence of that weak sentimentalism which characterizes many women under such circumstances, served Dr. Castleton well in these times of trouble. Often for days Elmwood would be under the sole charge of Rebecca. Every "overseer" and white man connected with the plantation were off to the war, except one. She had little trouble with the slaves. They continued diligently at their work. Faithful to the last, no more noble example of devotion can be found in all history than the spectacle of these slaves laboring to feed the families of those who were fighting to keep them in bondage.

There was commotion at Elmwood. News was spreading to the effect that General Guion, with the Union army, was nearing Ardenton. Wagons containing fleeing women and children were passing on their way to a place of safety from the dread Yankees. The refugees were hastening toward the mountains. Each wagon stopped a moment at the gate of Elmwood long enough for some one to run in and see if the household had been warned. Dr. Castleton was away on a professional visit. He however soon heard the gloomy tidings, and hastened homeward. In the meantime Rebecca ordered all the valuables to be packed up, and the wagons to be loaded. The slaves were terrified— more so than were Mrs. Castleton and the solitary "overseer." What they could not take in the wagons, the slaves buried in various secluded places. One mule and a horse were left standing in the stables as a blind, while the rest of the stock was hurried to a ravine about four miles distant, and haltered behind the rocks and thick undergrowth. Four hardy mules were reserved to draw the wagons to the mountains. It was thought best to send them on one at a time. The first wagon had already gone when Dr. Castleton came riding up at full speed. He was much surprised at the nerve Rebecca had displayed, and at finding everything so well attended to. Consultations were quick and hurried. No time was to be lost. Jim Black, the "overseer," was left in charge, with all the slaves except Aunt Dinah and three others,—the hostler, body-servant of Dr. Castleton, and one of the field slaves.

Some one suggested that Dr. Castleton himself had better leave the main road and ride through the woods and strike the road again about twenty miles above Elmwood. If the Yankees should happen upon them Dr. Castleton would be likely to be taken prisoner. They would hardly stop to consider whether he was a civilian or a soldier. Dr. Castleton hesitated, for he feared to leave Rebecca and Jenkins. But a glance from brave wife told him to go, and with a hasty embrace and kiss he shot through the woods, and was soon out of sight.

The wagons went as hastily as possible on their way. Aunt Dinah sat in the second wagon with little Jenkins on her lap. Rebecca sat beside them. Fearing little the dangers that might beset herself, she was very anxious about Jenkins and Dr. Castleton. Jenkins, however, was never so frisky as now. "Ma, don't dose mules go nice!" he would often say. So the day passed, and night came and found them still on their way. Rebecca was looking anxiously for the point where Dr. Castleton was to join them.

So far there had been no sign of the approaching Yankees. They hoped to reach the by-road which branched off from the main highway and led to the mountains, before the advanced guard of the enemy reached that point.

"Dis is de place whar Mas' Cas'leton was to be," said Jake the driver.

Concealed behind the hedges of the roadside was Dr. Castleton. Peering out carefully he satisfied himself that the wagons in sight were his. When they came abreast of him he silently rode out and joined the party. He had to make some very vigorous gestures to prevent the sportive Jenkins from holloing out. Rebecca's relieved and thankful look met the doctor. She comforted herself for the loss of the expected caress by thinking that it would have caused some delay of the wagons, and every moment was most precious.

It was a very silent company. Little else was heard save the rustling of the wind through the trees, and the sound of the steady tread of the mules. Jenkins, however, relieved the monotony every now and then.

Dr. Castleton came riding back in a somewhat quick

pace. The refugees knew that something had happened. The Doctor, leaning over the side of the wagon-body, told them in a subdued tone that they had now reached the by-road which led to their place of retreat. A sigh of relief escaped them all. "No sign yet of the Yankees?" asked Rebecca. Dr. Castleton told her that there were none, but no one could tell how soon they would appear.

They had now reached the place of turning, and the wagons were soon on theirway up the long looked-for road. It was very winding, and hid from view by the thick growth of underwood.

Hardly had the wagon train gotten a half-mile from the main road when Aunt Dinah exclaimed that she heard a drum-beat. She was not mistaken. This was the advance guard of the Union army.

General Guion was marching on. He found no one to oppose him. So he expected an easy and triumphal entry into Ardenton.

We have not time to relate many of the particulars of the march. The following little incident is a characteristic one, and will give some idea of the general occurrences of such an advance.

Sam Hoskins, one of the "Poor Whites," who owned no slaves, and who farmed a few acres for a livelihood, happened at the time of General Guion's approach to be driving the gray mare which constituted his only property, with a load of wood. Sam had not heard about "the Yanks." Even if he had, it was not to be supposed that he would be very much frightened. Not Sam Hoskins, who was a survivor of the war of 1812, who was a soldier of the Mexican War, and who also had served in the second Seminole War! "A hero of three wars, and had never been in a battle," was the way Sam's warlike achievements were described by those who knew him well.

On the occasion in question, as before stated, Sam was leisurely hauling a load of wood over the road he had travelled many times before.

Suddenly, much to the astonishment of Sam, a Blue-coated cavalryman appeared. Then another and another.

"Whoa! whoa!" cried Sam to the gray mare.

"You have just stopped her in time. How long, Cap, do you think it will take you to unhitch?" said the first cavalryman to the bewildered Sam. The latter, however, seemed to have lost his confidence in his skill in unhitching an animal quickly. " Men, assist this fellow to loose that mare." They suited the action to the word. Sam, who had not spoken during all these proceedings, stood gazing down the road at his gray mare as she joined the equine band to be henceforth in the service of her "country."

All this had been so quickly and so quietly done that Sam declared to a neighbor a short while afterward that he would yet get even with those "hankerin' blue shadders."

CHAPTER VII.

GENERAL GUION'S HEADQUARTERS.

"THIS is an attractive place" said General Guion, as he was riding past Elmwood. On the side of the road, and nearly in front of Elmwood was a pump which Dr. Castleton had provided for the convenience of travellers and teamsters. At this pump the horses of the army were now being watered. While this was going on, General Guion and some of his officers concluded they would go in and make an inspection of the premises of Elmwood. Just as they were entering the portico, Jim Black, the "overseer," appeared. He had prudence enough to salute the officers, who at once inquired the name of the owner of the property. They were told. A glance around satisfied the General that the family had fled, and the comparative emptiness of the rooms assured him also that the valuables and other property had been removed or secreted.

The General also learned that Elmwood was almost in the centre of the county, and was accessible by several different roads. This suggested to the officers that perhaps Elmwood would be a more suitable place for headquarters during the stay of the army in this neighborhood than Ardenton. The large, airy rooms of the Castleton house and the convenient surroundings determined General Guion to select this place for his headquarters.

The officers found Jim Black very accomodating. Probably it was in return for this that so little damage was done, during General Guion's stay, to the Castleton property.

It must be said to the honor of these Union officers that they took nothing the necessities of the army did not require. Forage and stock were among these necessities. Of course, if the men or officers wanted a little something extra for "mess," they did not hesitate to ask Jim Black to procure it for them. As the slaves were not interrupted much in their work (except some who were put around the house for assistance when needed), he was able to meet these demands upon him.

A thing which troubled Jim somewhat was attending to those horses and mules which he had haltered in the ravine. A permanent occupancy of Elmwood by Yankee officers had not been contemplated by Jim. Some of the soldiers were addicted to roving habits, and there was no telling when they might run upon the hidden animals. Besides, the quantity of fodder and corn which would often be carried in that direction might awaken suspicions. These supplies, of course, were always taken over in the night. But the moon often shone brightly then. Jim's natural shrewdness served him in this perplexity. He concluded to fence off this ravine, so that if the stock was discovered there, it would appear to belong to the next plantation, and thus no blame could fall to Jim for concealing from the officers that which they needed so badly.

This Jim had done. He kept four of the most trusted slaves in the ravine all the time. To ward off suspicion the mule and horse which Dr. Castleton had ordered to be left in the stable as a blind were used by Jim in the field; and he would now and then ask for the loan of a horse for a day or so from some of the officers. Thus Jim pretty well secured the safety of the ravine animals.

It was the custom of the Union Generals whenever they took possession of a county or district to endeavor to get accurate information concerning the prominent residents of the various places they occupied. This information was gotten in various ways, often from the slaves, sometimes from some well known Union man. General Guion was not long in learning the desired facts about Ardenton and vicinity. The residences of Colonel Leonard Miltoner and the Hon. James L. Harpurton received his careful attention. The Miltoner place was burned, and everything of value taken away from it. The residence of Mr. Harpurton was used as a store house. But strict orders were given that no one should touch a thing which belonged to *James Freeman!*

When the news of the occupancy of Ardenton by the Union troops had spread abroad, it was long before James Freeman heard of it in the dreary cave, whence he had fled for his life—fled not from the Yankees, but from his own countrymen, who looked upon him as a cowardly traitor to his country, because he would not take up arms against that Union he loved so well. When his little girl, thirteen years of age, came one Saturday afternoon to his lurking place with the morsels which were to serve him as food until she could get a chance to bring him a new supply, told him of the arrival of the Union troops, James Freeman snatched his faithful child in his arms, and rushed out, like a bird caged for many weeks, happy to greet the air once more. He hurried homeward. Never was man more joyed to behold his deliverers than James Freeman. He was not long in calling upon General Guion at Elmwood, and he was given a royal welcome.

CHAPTER VIII.

THE MOUNTAINS.

WE left the Castletons on their way to a place of retreat. From a knoll the refugees viewed the passing of the army.

For the first time Dr. Castleton realized the horrors of war. Visions of the lonely cabin, which he was as anxious to reach as ever king was his palace, loomed up before him. To see his wife and child in their wretchedness touched him to the quick.

"Has it come to this?"

It had.

Still the wagons kept on their journey.

The place of their destination was a little hut in the deep recesses of the mountains: It belonged to a man whom Dr. Castleton had often befriended, and one that he could trust.

Having approached within seven miles of their place of refuge, they alighted, and began to unload the wagons. The road was no longer accessible. The hut must now be reached by winding paths. The mules must be loaded to carry as much as possible. The wagons were carefully concealed not far away. What they could not put on the backs of the mules, the slaves themselves carried.

Dr. Castleton dismounted, and in the most comfortable way it could be done, he placed Rebecca upon his horse. Aunt Dinah carried Jenkins in her arms. Dr. Castleton led the horse, and the refugees again started on their journey.

No events worth noting occurred until they reached the hut. Here the doctor saw his friend, who had everything prepared for the expected party, and who met them at the door.

It was a hut with, of course, a single room and loft overhead. Dr. Castleton was not long in making his dispositions.

Rebecca, himself, Aunt Dinah and Jenkins were to occupy the room below. The slaves were to sleep in the loft above. It was more of a camp than anything else. A kind of tent was erected outside, where the cooking (which, by the way, was quite limited) and the eating were done.

Rebecca bore all this with that heroic fortitude of which she had given proof before. Far better the pure mountain air, her faithful servants around her, Dr. Castleton her protector by her side, little Jenkins her pride with her every moment—far better all this than being at Elmwood, where she would be liable at any moment to the grossest insults and indignities. Life at the hut did not vary much from day to day. The little communication which was kept up with Jim Black at Elmwood furnished food for thought and conversation. It was next to impossible to get hold of a newspaper, but the news of the great battles, however, reached them finally by some means.

This absence of information about the progress of the war caused the Castleton camp much uneasiness. They were in a continued state of suspense because they knew not the movements of the great armies.

The knowledge which Jim Black had given them of the condition of Elmwood seemed to please the refugees much. —But those who knew him well could see that a great change had come over Lawrence Castleton!

CHAPTER IX.

"HURRAH FOR LINCOLN!"

UNDER the Conscript Laws of the Confederacy during the latter years of the war, all able-bodied men, except such as were especially exempt by law, between the ages of eighteen and thirty-five, were compelled to enter the service.

In the last year of the war this limit was extended to forty-five years of age, and finally to fifty.

It will thus be seen that in the early part of the conflict a great many men were at their homes.

In many localities "Vigilance Committees" were formed to see that no sentiments disloyal to the Confederacy should be expressed. The "committee" always expected and generally received the earnest co-operation of the residents. Any lukewarm conversation was generally reported at once to the "chairman," and an investigation commenced immediately. In case of conviction judgment was decisive, and punishment sure.

We must now revert to a short while before the entrance of the Union army into Ardenton.

Dr. Castleton was the chairman of the "Binghampton County Vigilance Committee."

All Ardenton was astonished one morning at finding the following on a board stuck up in front of the house of one of Ardenton's most prominent confederates :

"We've had enuf of Jef Davises foolishness. hes all fer himself and he's ruinin the South. all who want this war stopped are invited to tend a meetin at the smokehouse near Jack Hortons X on Friday nite.

(sined)   One who kin stand his ground."

An excited crowd was gathered around this pine board. Many and loud were the threats.

A message was at once dispatched to Dr. Castleton informing him of what had occurred, and requesting his instant attendance.

By the time the doctor arrived, a number of the "vigilants" were on the scene. A "jury" was at once drawn and they commenced their investigation.

A good many suspected James Freeman. "It's just like him," said one.

"If he didn't do it, he would want to do it. So he ought to be fixed, anyway," said another angered patriot.

One thing seemed evident. Whoever put the notice up came upon horseback or else in a wagon, for a spot in the road showed that a horse had been standing there by the fact that the animal had stamped quite a hole in the ground.

"I think that horse was a mule, if I'm any judge of tracks," declared one of the "jurymen." All the owners of mules in the neighborhood were then named and considered.

It seemed to rage some of them that James Freeman owned no mule.

It came out in this connection that the owner of the "smokehouse near Jack Hortons X," was the possessor of a mule.

The fact of his smokehouse being mentioned as the place of meeting of conspirators was almost sufficient evidence to show that he was privy to the deed, as the perpetrators would hardly have named his smokehouse as a place of meeting without his consent.

The fact also that he was not present at the investigation, though he had been seen in town that morning, was suspicious. • The "jury" found, therefore, that "Josh Henderson, the owner of said smokehouse mentioned on the traitorous pine-board found stuck up in front of Major Seaton's house, is hereby summoned to show cause why he should not be put under discipline for having his smokehouse appear so conspicuously in this dirty business." Dr. Castleton signed the "summons" which three of the "jury" were sent at once to serve.

"I'll be durned if this here smuttin' of pine boards round here isn't got to stop, an'·the roads had better be picketed" roared an excited "Vigilant."

"That infernel smokehouse shall be burned," sung out another. This was received with wild shouts of applause.

By this time the summoning posse appeared with Josh Henderson, the accused.

"Mr. Henderson, what have you to say to this grave charge?" asked Dr. Castleton. Henderson denied everything, but it made no impression. He was sentenced to receive thirty-nine; and this having been given with a will by the posse, who used Henderson's own mule whip in the operation, the crowd hastened to finish up by burning the smokehouse. Several jugs were emptied as they viewed it burning. When nothing of the former building remained but embers, the crowd dispersed, satisfied that a more healthy patriotic spirit would thereafter prevail.

The next case which attracted the attention of the committee was that of a man who, it was alleged, had halloed "Hurrah for Lincoln!" He was summoned; when he declared that he had said "Hurrah for Lincoln!"—but he meant *Lincoln County!* (This was an adjoining county.) This neat turn of affairs caused a little merriment, and the "committee" was contented with allowing the Lincoln enthusiast to publish his explanation in the "Binghampton Messenger," and let the matter drop.

CHAPTER X.

NEARING THE END.

TIME passed on. War raged his worst. The Aurora Borealis of the heavens found itself reflected on the earth made red with the blood of brothers.

"The noblest men that ever lived in tide of times!"

Did ever soil receive such richness? Did ever lands behold such heroes as North and South beheld in their respective sons, each proving his devotion to his cause in the splendid agony of battle!

General Guion had long since marched from Elmwood to other fields. He left two companies only of soldiers to occupy the place while he continued the conquest of the country. The news of General Guion's departure and of other matters of interest was sent to the refugees in the mountains by the ever faithful Jim Black. A copy of the "Binghampton County Messenger" was among the other papers and letters sent them. Dr. Castleton read his familiar paper with eagerness. Almost the first thing that met his eye was a double-leaded column reading thus:

REPORT OF THE BATTLE.

"DECISIVE BATTLE!
WONDERFUL HEROISM OF THE ARDENTON TROOPS!
FULL PARTICULARS!
LIST OF THE KILLED AND WOUNDED."

Dr. Castleton's eyes went hastily down the column. He read aloud to the little company gathered under the tent in front of the hut. As he read how the brave boys rushed to the charge; how the cannon mowed them down like the scythe the grass; how the gap would be instantly refilled by others, only to be likewise mowed down; how the battle raged; how they fought; how they died,—as Dr. Castleton read all this he could see now and then a tear in Rebecca's eye.

"A Binghampton county regiment goes in twelve hundred strong, and only two hundred and twenty men answer to the roll-call after the battle."

A breathless silence was on all around.
Doctor Castleton continued:

"The regiment occupied the right of the line. The enemy were strongly posted on a hill in front, from whence they poured a deadly artillery fire.

"Colonel Miltoner was ordered to storm the height.

"As the men, the heroic colonel at their head, charged up that hill of death, they presented a sublime and terrible spectacle.

"They were soon lost amid the fire and smoke of carnage.

"On they went. Soon the artillery of the enemy seemed to grow less from that hill. 'They fly! they fly!' was a cry that went through the lines.

"The day was won. The Yankees were in full retreat, a portion of our forces pursuing. Colonel Miltoner's men halted only when twenty cannon and the hill the enemy occupied were theirs.—But at what a fearful cost! There, pale and ghastly in the sunlight lay the hero of Ardenton—Colonel Miltoner—*dead*. His noble physique and fine-cut features were not completely marred, even by death.

"With sad hearts his brave comrades tenderly placed the body in an ambulance, and removed it from the field. It was sent to Ardenton and arrived here day before yesterday.

"The funeral took place yesterday afternoon.

"The county was in mourning, and rarely has the churchyard at Ardenton seen so many gathered within its enclosure.

"Mrs. Miltoner, mother of the dead hero, was completely overcome with grief. 'He died for his country,' she was at times heard to murmur.

"'Earth to earth, ashes to ashes, dust to dust,' and Colonel Miltoner was committed to Mother Earth. The little mound and his resplendent memory were all that we had left us to tell that he once was ours.

>"'How sleep the brave, who sink to rest
>By all their country's wishes blest!
>When Spring, with dewy fingers cold,
>Returns to deck their hallowed mould,
>She there shall dress a sweeter sod
>Than Fancy's feet have ever trod.
>By fairy hands their knell is rung;
>By forms unseen their dirge is sung;
>There honor comes, a pilgrim gray,
>To bless the turf that wraps their clay;
>And Freedom shall awhile repair,
>To dwell a weeping hermit there."

CHAPTER XI.

THE END AT LAST.

THERE was other news in some of the letters concerning the great battle.

In one of them it was stated that General Guion commanded the Federal forces on that occasion, and also that he displayed great bravery, and was severely wounded in the action.

The days of the Confederacy were numbered. The heart of its territory had been pierced by hostile armies; it was drained of its men and money; it was cut off from communication with the outside world; it had no food for its men in the field or their wives and children at home.

Thinking men now saw that the struggle was hopeless.

There was, one afternoon about this time, an excited crowd around the office of the " Messenger " in Ardenton. Evidently something of unusual interest had taken place.

A strange mingling of sadness and joy was noticeable in the countenances of the men as they were earnestly conversing together in groups of three and four.

"I don't believe it," said one.

" He never surrendered alive," declared another.

"I'm glad it's over," was the feeling of a third.

"What will become of the poor South?"

We cannot give more of the sentiments expressed by the group of Ardenton's residents on this interesting occasion. Suffice it to say that it was the surrender of General Robert E. Lee which was the subject of discussion in front of the "Messenger" office on that day.

It was not long before a notice appeared in the "Messenger" informing the people of the "Binghampton military district" that "they would be required to take the oath of allegiance to the United States and to abide by the Proclamation of President Abraham Lincoln abolishing the institution of Slavery." The notice was signed by the captain in command of the companies of Federal troops stationed at Elmwood. Some of the remnant of Southern chivalry which remained about Ardenton bowed to the inevitable with the grace that became men as wise as brave. Others were more obdurate, and took occasion to show their mortification in many ways.

One of those who could not understand that the Old had passed away and the New come about was Dr. Lawrence Castleton. When the chairman of the "Binghampton County Vigilance Committee" presented himself at the Captain's headquarters to take the required oath swearing away the property his ancestors' money had honestly bought, and which was his main reliance for obtaining bread for

TAKING THE OATH.

his wife and children, he thought it was a bitter cup indeed.
He had few friends left to console him in his affliction. Most of them were dead. The God of War had indeed spared to him his tried old friend, 'Squire Jenkins, who had returned to offer him his left hand—his other one lay on some battle-field. He now stood beside Dr Castleton as he took the oath. The scarred veteran was still the same jovial fellow of other times. He had not aged much in these four years. He was, of course, a little pale from loss of blood, but that was all.

"Hello, Cap! How do you do?" said 'Squire Jenkins to the blue-coated chieftain.

The Captain shook the extended left hand with generous cordialty.

"What's the use, Cap, of growling about this oath bizness. When the Doctor has surgeoned a man and cut off the mortifying flesh, and then wants to give him a pill to settle him down, why he might as well take her down without gasping, hey, Cap?"

This was the humor in which the 'Squire kissed the book.

While the Doctor and 'Squire Jenkins were conversing with the Captain (who, by the way, was a pretty good natured fellow), a laconic looking individual came sauntering along the road. "Say, have you taken the oath!" cried out the assiduous blue-coat.

B*

"What ar you drivin' at now?" replied Sam Hoskins, who had lost a gray mare in the service of his country.

The Captain politely informed him of the requirements of the military law, and began at once to hand the book to the ever backward Sam.

"Do you mean by that to ask me to swar anything fer you Yanks? I wouldn't let my yaller dog, let alone meself, swar anything to the blasted varmints thet stole my mare in broad daylight!" roared the indignant Hoskins, as he turned to walk away in disgust.

"Arrest that man!" ordered the Captain.

A corporal and two soldiers soon placed Mr. Hoskins upon the hospitalities of the guard-house.

We have refrained from reminding the reader that Dr. Castleton was taking this oath beneath the shade of those Elms that once warded off the sun's hot rays from his happy home. We wished to spare the reader this if possible. It had best be unwritten the remorse and sorrow the pen is unable to picture.

Dr. Castleton had just returned from his exile in the mountains. He found his home desolated, friends gone, his country devastated—all lost, save honor. The slaves who had served him long and well were scattered he knew not where. Aunt Dinah and two of the three servants he had carried away were still with him, but they were no longer *his*. They were thenceforth Freedom's.

THE NEW HOME.

Dr. Castleton's spirit would not brook to bring Rebecca and Jenkins and the babe which had been born to them amid these terrible scenes of war,—he could not bring them back to this coffin of an Elmwood.

Dr. Castleton hastened from this place of saddest memories, and going into Ardenton, he secured a modest frame dwelling which would henceforth be the home of himself and his.

Rebecca now showed what a true woman she was. No word of hers breathed discontent. Her smile was just as sweet, her voice as ringing as before. Had Dr. Castleton ushered her into Elmwood with all its beauties, its flowers, its comforts, with its wealth increased tenfold, he would not have found Rebecca more loving or more the light of his household than he found her now.

"Lawrence dear," she would often laughingly say, "you know how the loss of 'those splendid pills' turned out. It may be all this loss will turn out as well for us."

—These were the times when Jenkins Castleton was first a school-boy.

CHAPTER XII:

A WANDERER.

WE will not linger over the scenes in and around the camp of the refugees in the mountains; nor will we speak particularly of the events of their journey back to Ardenton after hearing of the surrender. One incident only will be worth our while to relate.

The Southern people said little or nothing to the negroes about the theory of the war or the causes which led to it. The slaves had, however, a general idea about it. They knew that upon the issue of the war depended their continued enslavement or emancipation. But this was about all they did know about it. There was hardly one slave in a thousand that could read. There were laws restricting the teaching of slaves to read. This, of course, was a prudential measure to prevent insurrections—those terrors to the Southern mind. If there must be slavery it was, in their estimation, necessary to have peaceful slavery. Intelligence could never be kept in bondage. This the South well knew. When every black man in the South can read he carries with him his everlasting freedom, even if the law did not secure it to him.

BREAKING THE NEWS. 53

Aunt Dinah was sitting by Rebecca in the seat of the wagon on their return from their exile. "Aunt Dinah, do you know that you are not mine any more?" said Rebecca to the good slave.

"Missis, what's dat you say about me? Has yer *sold* me?"

"No, Aunt Dinah, I have not sold you. The war is now over, and the President of the United States at Washington has declared all the slaves free, and they no longer belong to their masters."

"You don't mean, missis, to tell me dat man from de Norf who was at Mister Slocum's a long time ago a'talkin' to us dah has come back agin to take us away like he sed. How dey goin' to fix us if dey don't sell us, Missis?"

"Why, they can't sell you. Nobody would be allowed to buy you. I suppose that your former masters will have to hire you and pay you money, and let you buy your own rations. You will probably have to pay rent for your cabins, too," continued Rebecca. Aunt Dinah seemed much troubled and perplexed at this news.

"Is dis what dose people up Norf have been comin' down here for, to kill our young massas, and to drive us from our homes, tryin' to take us away, and make us pay for all dese things ourselves?" queried Aunt Dinah again.

"That seems to be the way it will turn out," answered the once mistress. "I am very sorry for some of you.

The planters may not have money enough to hire you all, and provisions cannot be bought without money. I cannot see, Aunt Dinah, what those of you who are thus unfortunate will do. And then, too, when you get sick, how you will get doctors and medicines I cannot see."

"De Lord help us!" devoutly said the troubled servant, who felt like a bird let out from long confinement, to find only the desert for a resting place.

"But I will keep you, Aunt Dinah, if you want to stay with me," said Rebecca tenderly, as she looked at Aunt Dinah with that glance others had felt before.

The grateful servant fell on her knees, and, as she took the hand of the woman she loved so well—a woman who had always treated her with the greatest kindness—her good old heart overflowed in tears.

Rebecca wept.

Little Jenkins knew not what to make of it all. He put his arms around his mother's neck, and fondly asked what was the matter.

"Mamma, is Aunt Dinah sick?" said the child.

"No, dear, she is only troubled," answered his mother, when she had composed herself sufficiently to speak.

Nothing more was said. Aunt Dinah seemed to be praying.

Almost before they knew it, they were in sight of Elmwood; and such a sight! On the front portico were

ELMWOOD. 55

lounging half a dozen soldiers; from the window of her once bed-chamber floated triumphantly the Stars and Stripes; the flowers and the green sward which always greeted her eye as she entered the gate were now all gone —trampled out by the tread of guards and pickets. Everything reminded her of desolation and degradation. She bade the driver to urge the mules to a quicker pace. They were not long in reaching Ardenton. In other times people whom Rebecca met in the road would have wondered much at seeing her riding behind such a team and in such a vehicle. But the neighbors wondered not. This was now a common, every-day sight to them. Dr. Castleton met the party as they entered the village and conducted them to the house of their future residence.

Dr. Castleton would often say to Rebecca that without Elmwood he felt himself to be a wanderer indeed.

"The sun seemed shorn of his beams."

CHAPTER XIII.

STILL A WANDERER.

IT would seem that Time, commonly called most regular and immutable, often belies itself and will accomplish the work of years in a moment. Let everything of man's perish around him, yet if he can but save his spirit from the general ruin, he will still possess much. But when the spirit goes with the rest, it leaves him without hope. Dr. Castleton's spirit was gone. It was wrapt up in the flowers and shades of Elmwood; it vanished with his home. God had been merciful to him.—Rebecca was his.

There was much sickness about Ardenton now. Returning soldiers brought the seeds of disease from the camps of the army; lack of proper medicinal supplies aggravated and increased sickness. Especially was the want of quinine, without which life could hardly be sustained, sorely felt. Little of this most necessary drug was manufactured in the South. Most of it that was received was usually smuggled through the lines. This prohibition of quinine was a cruel though possibly necessary regulation of the U. S. Government. It brought death to the innocent slave, whom an ounce of the forbidden panacea might have saved to live Freedom's child; mother and babe perished sighing for it. But what was this to the success of the Federal arms and the preservation of the Union? When war is not cruel, it is not war.

Dr. Castleton did not look at things in this light. He felt; he did not think.

Events hasten on. The spirit of change gradually spread itself over everything and all.

There was nothing now to attract Dr. Castleton in the neighborhood of Binghampton county. Would not new fields, new associations, give him some relief? So thought Dr. Castleton, as he rode along the road one day on a professional visit.

He awaited a favorable opportunity of proposing the idea to Rebecca. He did not know how it would be received, still he would try the results. It was a pleasant afternoon a few days after the meditation of the Doctor upon the subject of removing from Ardenton, that he found Rebecca alone in the little parlor. Jenkins was playing in the yard; Aunt Dinah was busy in the kitchen.

"Rebecca, what do you think of Ardenton?" cautiously asked the Doctor.

"It has few attractions for me," replied the wife. "But why do you ask?" she said, looking inquiringly at him.

"I have been thinking seriously of removing from this part of the country. I have long wished for a change of scene. If our property is not all to be confiscated, we might sell Elmwood for a little something. How do you like the idea?"

Rebecca was in a very contemplative mood during this talk of Dr. Castleton's. She said nothing for some time. Finally she asked if he had thought of any particular place to which it might be desirable to remove. He said he had not.

"Then would it not be better to wait awhile and see what situation the South will be placed in, and what will be the policy of the Federal Government towards the conquered states? Everything is at sea now."

This prudent advice convinced Dr. Castleton that for the present he had better make no change, but await the future. Here the conversation dropped. Soon the Doctor was mounted, and away to answer a call.

"Who is it that is sick?" inquired Dr. Castleton of the negro boy that had come for him.

"It's old Aunt Jane Cas'leton," the boy replied. (The slaves always bore the name of their master.)

Jane was an old woman of nearly eighty years of age. She had originally belonged to the grandfather of Dr. Lawrence Castleton, and had never been sold out of the Castleton family. She was now blind and very much bent

THE BURIED TREASURE. 59

under the weight of years. She would sit in her cabin door and plait straw for hours. This she could do with wonderful facility—to plait, and sing the old hymns was her only occupation.

It was during the war of 1812 that two travellers stopped at the house of John Castleton, grandfather of Dr. Lawrence Castleton, and desired accomodation for the night. It was cold and dreary, and in those days houses of any size were few and far between in that region. John Castleton took the strangers in and gave them shelter.

It was not long after this night that old John Castleton died. In his will it was found that he had two large chests of gold and silver buried in the right hand corner of the cellar of the house. This cellar was not used for anything except as a storing place for rubbish.

This clause in the will was a great surprise, as no one knew of the old man having any such amount of money.

The cellar was at once entered. The cobwebs were cleared away, the obstructions removed, and the right hand corner reached. Here, behold, there was a great hole, apparently recently dug ! No chests were there !

The amazed company returned to the room above in the greatest consternation. Many and varied were the theories advanced by the astonished heirs. Presently some one mentioned the two strangers who had not long ago stopped at the house. That seemed to clear up the mystery.

Descriptions of the two men were published far and wide. They were traced to the borders of the adjoining state, but there all traces of the men were lost. Time passed on, and the incident was almost forgotten, except that it became one of the traditional stories of Binghampton county.

Let us now return to Dr. Castleton.

When he got to Jane's cabin he found her at the point of death, but conscious.

"Mas Larance, I wants to tell you something before I goes. On de—de—de (she was growing weaker) path to de Brown place, under de big poplar tree, I buried old Mas' Cas'leton's money. I—I—I—" She said no more, for death prevented.

This was heard by all in the cabin, and for some moments no one could speak. Dr. Castleton asked if he had heard aright. The negroes who had assembled around the bedside declared that they certainly heard her speak of "old mas' Cas'leton's money."

The report was spread abroad by the negroes. Binghampton was aroused. Spades and shovels were in demand, and the path to "the Brown place," which was about three miles from Elmwood, was traversed by an unusual number of foot travelers.

Dr. Castleton gave notice that he would claim the money if found. This somewhat lessened the activity, but the hope of secretly finding it was sufficient to keep the curious astir. Sam Hoskins was on the ground early and late. He told them that he was the freest man in the place, as he had never taken "that blasted oath."

Every tree that grew near the path was almost dug up by the roots.—But no chests were found.

There was on one day an unusual stampede of the money diggers from their base of operations. A report had spread that Sam Hoskins had said that "thar used to be another path to the 'Brown place,' which wasn't much used of late." As soon as this was mentioned the old residents recollected that there was once another path to the "Brown place." The old path was soon found. But alas! Some new earth thrown up at the foot of an old poplar told a mournful tale! Pieces of rusty money here and there, and the finger prints which could be seen in the bottom of the hole told how the finder had raked up the pieces that fell out of the jars as he drew them out. The bottoms of seven earthen jars were lying near.

"Sam Hoskins got this yere money," said the chagrined diggers.

The volatile Sam was closely watched. He was not observed to use any rusty money. Still his place began to look better. He astonished the people of Ardenton one day by driving in with a pair of fine grays. Everybody believed that Sam was the lucky man, but they had no proof.

"It's a good thing to strike the right path," the lucky Hoskins would often say in reply to questions concerning the money-finding matter.

CHAPTER XIV.

THIS chapter shall be nameless. Would that we could leave the pages also blank and let the reader in silence fill them up with meditations upon the direst calamity that ever bevel a nation.

Cicero's death; the condemnation of Socrates; the murder of Cæsar; Napoleon at St. Helena—terrible tales these all.—But wait.

"And the vale of Siddim was full of slime-pits; and the Kings of Sodom and Gomorrah fled and fell there and they that remained fled to the mountains.

"And they took all the goods of Sodom and Gomorrah, and all their victuals, and went their way.

" And they took Lot, Abram's brother's son, who dwelt in Sodom, and his goods, and departed.

"And there came one that had escaped and told Abram the Hebrew.

* * * * * * * * * * *

"And when Abram heard that his *brother* was taken captive, he armed his trained servants, born in his own house, three hundred and eighteen, and pursued them unto Dan.

"And he *divided* himself *against* them, he and his servants by night, and smote them and pursued them unto Hobah which is on the left hand of Damascus.

"*And he brought back all the goods, and also brought again his brother Lot, and his goods, and the women also, and the people.*"

This was the text a negro preacher took in speaking to a

great crowd of men and women who had gathered in front of their cabins one Sunday morning. He was a very intelligent negro. He had been a slave, but belonged to a somewhat indulgent master, and had thus learned to read better than the average slave preacher. When the war commenced he was often seen with James Freeman, and when the latter was driven to seek a cave that he might save his life, Uncle Daniel often in the night visited him. At these visits James Freeman talked long and freely with the slave about the war and its probable effects upon the condition of the blacks. He read to him from old copies of the " New Cretonia Trident." He told him much about the history of Abraham Lincoln. Uncle Daniel had become so affected by the stories of the great Lincoln's life that he regarded him with an awe and reverence that bordered upon superstition.

The war was over and the slaves were free on the Sunday morning upon which Uncle Daniel read the text we have given. With the vivid imagery which alone characterizes the black race, the fervid preacher began:

"My brudders, dis is a mos' beautiful Sunday mornin', but when I went to bed las' night I nebber saw de clouds so heavy nor de heavens so dark. But dis mornin' look at dat glorious sun! So brite we kin not bear to look at it fur more dan a glance! Its glory shines on all around.

"So, my breddering, was you a short while ago. De

THE SERMON.

clouds hung over you thick and heavy. Your heaven was blacker and darker dan eber night was; but thank de Lord, everything is now so bright. De glorious light of Freedom shines in your black faces an' makes dem brighter dan de angels!

"But how did all dis kum about? Why I will tell you. Dat Sodom an' Gomorrah I was readin' to you bout from my tex' was Affrikay, whar our forefathers kum from. I will call our fust home Sodom and Gomorrah, kase dey say we was free over dah; den we mus' hab bin good. But we got made slaves; den we mus' hab bin wicked or de Lord would not hab let us been made slaves.

"Sodom an' Gomorrah seems to me, my bruddering, to be a good name fur de black man's home in mos' cases.

"Dese Kings of Sodom, our fust home, was not allus born in dat country; but dey kum over dah in ships, an' made demselves Kings of it. Sometimes dey was different color frum what we was.

"De tex' says, 'Dey took all de *goods* of Sodom an' Gomorrah an' all deir vittles, an' went deir way.' Dat was all right, for de *goods* may hev bin theirn. But *dey took Lot, Abram's brudder's son*, who dwelt in Sodom, an' departed. Dis was wrong. For, in de fust place, *Lot* was not *goods*. He was a man, an' dey had no right to take him dat way.

"'An' dar kum one dat had 'scaped an' tole Abram de
c

Hebrew. An' Abram heard dat his brudder was taken captive. He armed his trained sarvants, born in his own house, three hundred and eighteen, an' pursued dem unto Dan."

"Bruddering, whar's dis Abraham dat listened to de story of ' one dat 'scaped?' Ah, Mister Jim Freeman tole me all 'bout him when I used to go see him in his cave. He libs up Norf. He is de great master who heard 'bout us, an' armed his trained sarvants an' for four yeahs has bin leadin' dem to our rescue. He has taken de Kings of Sodom an' Gomorrah an' pursued dem unto Dan.

"He has 'vided himself agin 'dem; he has smoten dem by night an' pursued dem into Hobah, which I b'lieves is a wuss place dan Dan.

"But dat is not all. O bruddering, listen." His hearers were now looking up with staring eyes. They were completely carried away by the deep emotion of the speaker.

"O bruddering, listen! Hear de rest.

"'*He brought back all de goods.*'

"De wheel keep rollin'.

"'*An'. also brought agin his brudder Lot* an'*his* goods and de women also and de people.' De wheel had rolled all de way roun'! Father Abraham (I calls it by de longer word kase I luvs to linger on de heavenly sound) Father Abraham is now rollin' on de wheel. De Kings of Sodom and Gomorrah are become as chaff.

"I sometimes think I see our Father Abraham among his dark children. Sometimes when a ray of light suddenly comes in my cabin winder, I thinks its him or his spirct. Glory be to de Lord. Let us pray fur our great father who has freed us ; who has drowned de shouts of blood-hounds runnin' us down wid de glorious shouts of de delivered captive; who has hung de 'seers' whip up to rot, an' given us de staff of freedom."

This touching reference with which Uncle Daniel closed his sermon reached the untutored hearts of his simple minded hearers. They fell on their knees while Uncle Daniel offered up a fervent prayer for "Abraham Lincoln, our great father."

The scene was indescribable. The silence of all, save the fervent voice of the preacher was terrible, and made the effect doubly felt.

Uncle Daniel went away when they had finished singing a hymn. Many of the other negroes remained, and it was long before they engaged in their usual Sunday afternoon occupations.

That sermon was one never to be forgotten by any who heard it. For two or three days it was all the blacks talked about.

One day, a short while after dinner-time, uncle Daniel was seen running toward the cabins in great agitation.

"It's done, it's done," he cried as he approached.

"'They've killed Father Abraham! they've killed Father Abraham!'"

He had just heard of the assassination of President Lincoln. It was long before he could make the terror-stricken negroes realize the truth. When they did, a regular panic seized them. They thought they would be put back into slavery again, and untold evils, they imagined, threatened them.

No work was done the rest of that day by any negro who heard the dreadful news. There was almost equal consternation among the whites.

Among some, however, there was a feeling expressed in the exclamation: " Well, his successor, though a Republican, is nevertheless a *Southern* man."

Among the great majority of the whites, however, there was a far different feeling.

A silent monitor within told them that the South had lost a friend who had for her no malice and all charity, who towered above those who surrounded him in greatness and goodness as the sun towers above the earth. He alone stood between the fanatics and avengers and their victim, the stricken South. His big heart beat for all. Untold the woes the hand that shed his costly blood brought upon an already afflicted country!

Will ever
"Danger's troubled night be o'er,
And the Star of Peace return?"

CHAPTER XV.

FAREWELL TO ELMWOOD.

"WE learn that Dr. Lawrence Castleton, the well known and popular physician, intends to remove from Ardenton. Our readers will learn of this with great regret, as Dr. Castleton has many friends in this county who will miss his professional skill in times of sickness, and his courteous and genial company in times of health. We wish the Doctor every success in his new field, and we also wish health and happiness to Mrs. Castleton and the boys."

This little article appeared one day in the "Messenger," and created no little surprise.

The old people said Ardenton would seem an unnatural place without a single person bearing the name of Castleton. But the Old was passing away and the New was replacing it. Elmwood was sold for a respectable sum—a large sum for those times—but at a price far below its value.

The day of departure came. No one desired to take a farewell look at Elmwood. All declared that they preferred to remember it as a thing of beauty and not as a wreck.

Dr. Castleton had selected Marbleburgh, a town more in the interior of the State, as the place of his future residence.

The country around Marbleburgh was rich and productive. It was on the line of one of the great railroads, and was altogether quite an attractive locality.

About the only relic of Elmwood that remained with them was Aunt Dinah. The good old servant never once thought of ever leaving "Mas' Cas'leton's."

The new doctor was not altogether unknown in Marbleburg. Several prominent men there had met Dr. Castleton in other times.

Rebecca was still the faithful wife of former years. Her time was taken up in making her husband and children more happy. She watched over the daily lives of the boys whom change tossed about from place to place.

Dr. Castleton saw the temple of the States being gradually rebuilt. He watched the progress of reconstruction. But he himself was not reconstructable.

The South in a new garb did not appear to him to be the South. He was a stranger in a strange land!

Next door to Dr. Castleton's house in Marbleburg lived Stephen Floyd—a Union man during the war, and a Radical [Republican] since—that then despised class of men. For a native Southerner to be a Republican or a supporter of "nigger equality" was looked upon as traitorous, and as an insult to the public distress—regarded thus by the old unreconstructed *regime!* Stephen Floyd was a brave, bold man. He was the leader of the negroes of the county. He organized them; he disciplined them and made their votes effective. They looked upon him as the pilot of their ship, without whom they could not weather the storm.

Dr. Castleton had little communication with Stephen Floyd. There was much talk among the people of Marbleburg because Dr. Castleton had attended the wife of Floyd during an illness.

"He should let the d— Radicals and all their breed die out," was often said by the fiery.

But Dr. Castleton was a man of feeling if nothing more. He responded to a call from Stephen Floyd, he said, as he responded to a call from a negro. Nobody thought he recognized an equal in the negro because the blacks were doctored by him, and why should his doctoring Floyd's family make him their social equal? Such was the logic of the time.

Dr. Castleton did not like Marbleburg as well as he expected. Besides the fact that it was a very *healthy* locality, which, in the strange economy of human affairs, is not always desirable, it was a perfect hot-bed of Radicalism, and the negroes formed a majority of the voters of the county. This was a most serious objection to Marbleburg.

CHAPTER XVI.

THREE REMOVES PROVE A FIRE.

THE spirit of the wanderer, like that of the lover, is ever restless. It was hardly possible to be in a worse condition than he was now, thought Dr. Castleton, and it might be possible to gain a better situation by some of his rambles.

Rebecca was a great reader. She read of the surging world around her. She longed to be in the whirlwind. She preferred the boisterous sea of the world to the calm of undisturbed poverty. She often looked at Jenkins as he wended his way to the little log school-house where his first lessons were taught him. "Where, after he's through with the log school-house?" thought the anxious mother.

She saw no prospect of educating her children at Marbleburg. To give Jenkins that education which his unusual brightness demanded—for he was indeed a bright boy— was the one great wish of her heart.

We have already said that Rebecca bore these gathering clouds of misfortune with heroic nobleness. Dr. Castleton made little money with his practice. Rebecca did not complain that she had to wear a single dress a whole year. Aunt Dinah was getting old and feeble. Rebecca wielded the dread broom and the house-cleaning brush with as good a will as if she were sitting under her orchard tree of years before eating the luscious "sugar-ball." But she felt it after all. The good will was forced by stern necessity. "What is the use," Rebecca would sometimes say, "to make bad worse by vain and foolish regrets and whinings? It costs nothing to be cheerful, and it makes things so much better."

"Shall we go and try to live in that beautiful city, the capital of our State?" said Dr. Castleton one day to Rebecca.

Before she had time to answer, the postmaster came by and told Rebecca that he had a big envelope full of papers and documents directed to her at the postoffice. Dr. Castleton sent for it at once. It proved to contain a notice of the death of Rebecca's father, and also a copy of his will. It was found that her third part of fifteen thousand dollars in silver awaited her at Bethanoth! This joyful news made her feel herself once more. Dr. Castleton felt as if a great burden had fallen from his weary shoulders.

Fervent and grateful were the prayers the little family offered up that night.

"Ho for Burleigh!" said Rebecca the morning they started for the depot.

Stephen Floyd had kindly tendered the use of two of his

wagons to Dr. Castleton. These were accepted, and Stephen Floyd offered his hand and wished the Doctor every success. Dr. Castleton shook the proffered hand, and thanked Mr. Floyd for his good wishes.

Burleigh was about one hundred miles distant.

They arrived safely at the depot and took the train for Burleigh.

"DARING ROBBERY.
THE MARBLEBURG TRAIN ATTACKED!
MANY PASSENGERS ROBBED."

This was the startling announcement in the Burleigh papers the morning after Dr. Castleton left Marbleburg.

The train was boarded about thirty miles from Marbleburg by a noted band of outlaws who had terrorized the country ever since the war. They were led by a mulatto negro.

They did not use much violence, as everybody submitted because they knew the uselessness of resistance. Dr. Castleton's heart sank within him as he handed over the God-send which had been just left to Rebecca from her father's estate, and which was his hope for the future. Rebecca for once lost her equanimity, and was so much frightened that she did not know what was happening to her husband.

The robbers let the train move on undisturbed.

When Dr. Castleton found that Rebecca had recovered from her fright he told her what had happened. It was a fearful blow.

A great crowd was at the depot in Burleigh to meet the robbed train, and indignation at the daring deed was great.

Some one was seen rushing through the crowd, apparently endeavoring to reach Dr. Castleton, who had just emerged from the train.

It was none other than Jim Black, the faithful overseer!

Dr. Castleton was overjoyed to meet him. Rebecca also greeted him most kindly.

"Hello, Jim, you here?" sung out the sportive Jenkins, as he saw the familiar form of the once master of Elmwood.

"Doctor, how yu're fixed!" inquired Jim at once.

"Very poorly indeed. I lost my all," replied Dr. Castleton.

"Well, jis come with me," said Jim again.

They followed him to the edge of the platform, where they took the hack Jim had brought down for them, and were soon wheeling into town.

CHAPTER XVII.

THE DAWN OF THE NEW.

THERE was a curious assemblage about to be called together at Burleigh at this time. It was the realization of the dream of many philanthropists. It was terrible evidence that the Old had passed away, and that the New was at hand.

It was the first State Legislature which assembled under the new Constitution which Reconstruction had brought about. We will not tire the reader with a minute description of this strange body of men. We will content ourselves with learning its general character.

The black man was there! The "Scalawag" was there (By this term was meant a native Southerner who was a Republican)! The ubiquitous "Carpet-bagger" was there; the unreconstructed Democrat was there; the conservative Democrat was there; ex-Confederate, Federal, and deserter from both, found a place in the curious medley.

We will introduce the reader into the gallery of the Legislative Chamber during a day in the early part of the session and let him feast at the banquet there offered.

CONSISTENCY. 77

"Mr. President," the Hon. John M. Butler, carpet-bagger from one of the upper counties, arose and said, "The Old has passed away and the New has come about. The Old way of paying Legislators was to give them *three* dollars a day. In order to suit the new state of things, I move our salary be *seven* dollars a day."

This was received with that enthusiasm which should ever greet such a patriotic proposition. But the general satisfaction was all at once disturbed by Hon. Ab. Magab, colored member from the Marbleburg district, rising in his seat and saying:

"Mister Bresident, I'se jis got one word of remark to offer regardin' dis moshun of de honorable member who has jis risen and tuk his seat.

"I'se a great lover of de ole times, an' de ole price of a day's hard labor, sich as we has here, seems tur me to be very refreshin,; 'sides, Mr. Bresident, de honorable gemmen forgits what a dollar or so will buy dese days. Why sir, I 'specks to do wunders wid even one day's grab.

"'Cordin' to las' counts steers kuld be bought fur four and a quarter a head.

"Sir, two or three days heah, will stock, sir, to my very satisfaxshun my five acres an' put em in time fur de next crop.

"Sir, I'm fur de old price and shill vote thereto."

Financial indignation greeted these injudicious remarks.

"Mr. President," said the angered Hon. Mr. Butler, " from what accounts I can gather from persons who know the gentleman well who has just taken his seat, I infer that he is the last man to make objections to this very prudent measure.

"Magistrate Larkins, who sits near me, has just informed me that the honorable member from Marbleburg is, according to the record of the Justice's office, more of a success at stealing hoes than at opposing good and wise motions." [Great laughter.]

"Mister Bresident, I thinks de member who has jes spoken is gettin' a little too 'ticler in bringin' up furrin' matters.

" Dat hoe affair of mine has nuthin' ter do wid dis bill: 'sides, Mr. Bresident, when I tuk sich a likin' to dat hoe, it war a square open-frunted likin'. I din'nt go through de State treasury doah to git dat hoe, like de honorable gemmen seems to be doin'."

This sally was received with a good deal of merriment, especially among the Democratic members. It is unnecessary to add that the bill passed by a large majority.

About this time there were a number of outrages perpetrated by the Ku Klux Klan upon negroes who had made themselves obnoxious by taking too active an interest in politics; and also some "Scalawags," and now and then a "Carpet Bagger," would suffer similar treatment.

These outrages were often terrible and cruel. They were the last desperate means of men who felt themselves insulted and degraded by a set of Northern adventurers who did not settle in the South because they loved the Southern people, or because they wanted to benefit the stricken States by their advice and industry, but who came there for the express purpose of gaining office by the negro vote, and draining the already impoverished land of what they could. Against such men, and such men *only*, did these conquered men of the South take desperate and unholy measures. It was wrong fighting wrong; and the fact that the moment the carpet-bagger could no longer get office he left at once the land of his adoption, seems to prove his mercenary motives. Those Northern men who settled there for the purpose of making the South their *home*, are there to-day, and are respected.

To put a stop to these outrages a measure was introduced in the Legislature, and passed, giving the Governor power to declare any county in a state of insurrection, and to order out the militia to keep the peace.

Governor W. W. Hodges, the official upon whom this extraordinary power was granted, was a peculiar figure. He was a man of eminent ability and his influence before the war was very great. He was the editor of the principal paper in the State, and did as much to make his State secede from the Union as any man in it. He was a member of the Secessional Convention, and the morning after he had signed the famous ordinance he declared in his paper that "he would transmit the pen with which he signed the ordinance of secession from despotism to the dominion of constitutional liberty, as the greatest legacy he could leave to his posterity; and our noble State will make good that declaration with the last man and the last dollar." But when he saw that the war would be a failure on the part of the South, he all at once turned a rabid Union man, wanted the war stopped and the State restored again to the Union. For this sudden change he was, after the surrender, appointed Military Governor of the State by the President; and then at the first election under the reconstructed constitution, he was chosen Governor of the State, chiefly by the negro vote.

CHAPTER XVIII.

THE GUESTS.

"MISTER Castleton, I'm very glad yu're come," said Jim Black, as he drove the Doctor into the city of Burleigh. "I heard that you had left Marbleburg, and I kum down to meet you.

"I tell you, Doctor, I have a plan for you. Doctoring is played out. People have got no money to invest in that sort of thing. There's a big building here that we could rent cheap, and we kin jes make the biggest haul boarding these members of the new Legislature you ever saw.

"Won't need much fixing up, fur the fellers arn't used to much, and they'll think a chinay wash-bowl and a little strip of flowered carpet a big thing.

"They say they're goin' to have big pay, and their hotel bills are a small matter. Doctor, how's this strike yur?"

Dr. Castleton was quite amazed at the proposition, but a moment's reflection caused him to regard it with some little favor. He asked Jim if he could raise any money. He replied, he "had a friend or so."

By this time they had arrived at the house of a gentleman of Dr. Castleton's acquaintance, where he thought of calling first.

He was very glad to see the Doctor and his family, and kindly offered the hospitalities of his house until the Doctor could make some definite arrangements.

At the earliest opportunity Dr. Castleton mentioned the proposal of Jim, Black to Rebecca. The plan, to his astonishment, pleased her much. "I like it," she said, "because it will give me an opportunity to offer you some practical assistance."

So it was arranged. The Dickens House was secured, and by the aid of the friends of Jim Black, and also of Dr. Castleton the hotel was soon well fitted out.

When it became known that Dr. Castleton had opened the Dickens House, among the first to call there and ask for accomodations was *Stephen Floyd*, Senator from Marbleburg. He told Dr. Castleton that some twenty or thirty other members would take apartments at the Dickens House if arrangements could be made. The new-fledged proprietor inquired who they were. Mr. Floyd informed him, and mentioned that they were also Republican members.

This did not at all please Dr. Castleton. But Rebecca, remarking that the hotel was a public house, and any one who paid his bills could get board there, she did not think it made any difference about their politics. Dr. Castleton's strong and positive sentiments were so well known that he did not think any one would question his fidelity to the old cause because he boarded Radical members.

He therefore told Mr. Floyd that his house was open for the reception of guests. The next day about thirty members of the Legislature registered at the Dickens House, among whom was Stephen Floyd.

Some six Democratic members—personal friends of Dr. Castleton's—registered also.

There were some remarks of surprise made to the effect that Dr. Castleton was "keeping a Radical House," but it did not damage Dr. Castleton in the estimation of his friends who knew his circumstances and his sentiments.

Jim Black proved himself a splendid manager.

Rebecca's courtesy and affability made it very pleasant to those men, who now rarely received a kindly look from a Southern woman. So affairs were going on among the Castletons. Jenkins was started to school, where he made fine progress. He was sent to the Parochial School connected with one of the churches in Burleigh. No sectarian doctrines were taught, and it was the best school in the city.

CHAPTER XIX.

A GEM OF RAREST RAY SERENE.

SO THE session passed on, and was nearing its close. The guests of the Dickens House were getting fewer every day.

While Dr. Castleton had made a good living for his family he had not made much money. What he should do when the Legislature adjourned he did not know. There was scarcely the barest possibility of his gaining any competency by his profession.

In his dilemma he, as usual, consulted Rebecca. But for once she could come to no conclusion as to what she thought best.

We will have to leave Rebecca and Dr. Castleton in earnest conversation for a moment, and digress a little:

General S. L. Littletoney was a Union General who had deposited his carpet-bag in the State, and had at once gained a prominent position among the ruling powers.

General Littletoney was a financier. He was reputed to be engaged in extensive speculations in State bonds and railroad stock. He was the head of a kind of syndicate, and the accounts of his enormous operations, and of the great amount of money he was accumulating were almost incredible.

"Lawrence, do you know much about this General Littletoney, who is making so much money in bonds and stocks?" asked Rebecca of Dr. Castleton.

"I hear a good deal about him, but I cannot see what interest I should have in him or his stocks," continued the Doctor.

"I am told that he is a very kind-hearted, generous man. Do you think it probable that some of your Republican friends would mention our situation to him, and interest him in our behalf?"

If it was possible for Dr. Lawrence Castleton to be indignant at any proposition Rebecca should make, he was so now. What! Go to the man who helped to drive him from his happy home, and who now flourished over his misfortune —go to such a one for assistance? His rejection of the proposal was so positive that Rebecca was loth to even refer to the matter again. She managed to change the conversation, and for the time the matter dropped.

Rebecca and Dr. Castleton knew not that some one was overhearing their confidential conversation. The ever-alert Jim Black happened to be removing some marketing from the wagon into the side gate, which opened into the kitchen yard.

It was on the back porch that the conversation between husband and wife was taking place. Jim heard the name of General Littletoney mentioned.

Jim, out of simple curiosity, listened to what was said about the famous General. The whole conversation we have narrated was heard by the astonished ex-overseer. It touched even his rough-hearted nature to know that his old employer and friend had come to such distress.

Jim Black walked away from the Dickens House the next morning at an unusual hour. No one knew of his departure.

Those employed about the State Capitol wondered much as to what business such a rustic-looking individual as Jim Black could be transacting with the high officials of the State. Stephen Floyd was also at the Capitol that day. He and Jim Black were old acquaintances, and the two were engaged in conversation for a long time. When they had ceased talking, they were seen to approach the office of General Littletoney. They remained some moments there, and when they had finished their business with the General they separated, having engagements to meet again at an early date.

A few days after these occurrences, Dr. Castleton received the following note:

"STATE CAPITOL, JUNE 10, 187—.
"DR. LAWRENCE CASLTETON,
"Dear Sir :—
"I am directed by Gen. S. M. Littletoney to say to you that he would be pleased to have an interview with you at your earliest convenience upon private matters.
"This is done at the instance of Mr. Stephen Floyd, of Marbleburg.
"I am
"Very Respectfully,
"T. R. BROWN,
"Private Sec."

Dr. Castleton was somewhat surprised at this note. He could not but think that Rebecca was instrumental in having it sent to him.

He showed it to her, but she was more surprised than he. Rebecca declared that she had no doubt it was something that would be of interest to attend to, and she advised Dr. Castleton to call upon the General. He did·so.

General Littletoney said that he had been waited upon by Mr. Stephen Floyd, Senator from Marbleburg, in company with another gentleman, and had been informed by them that he might be of assistance to Dr. Castleton. He had heard of the courtesy of Dr. Castleton and of Mrs. Castleton to some members of the Legislature—friends of the General's—and the latter would be pleased to return it in any manner he was able. General Littletoney then learned in the course of the conversation what were the needs and circumstances of Dr. Castleton.

The General wrote a check for a sum that ran up into the thousands, and handed it to Dr. Castleton, at the same time informing him that he had no intention of exhibiting his liberality or of bringing up any unpleasant thoughts upon the changed condition of affairs. He simply wished Dr. Castleton to accept this little amount as an acknowledgment of the appreciation in which he was held by those who had enjoyed his hospitality, and whose stay in Burleigh had been made pleasant by the affability and kindness of Mrs. Castleton.

Dr. Castleton was much moved by this exhibition of generosity. It was so frank, and had such an appearance of sincerity about it, that he could not but accept it. There was again a feeling of great relief manifested by the Castletons.

Rebecca was very outspoken in her praise of the kind-hearted general.

"I told you so," was her comment to her husband.

CHAPTER XX.

A NEW MOVE.

"WHAT shall we do with this money," said Rebecca, a few days after the reception of the general's gift.

This was a most perplexing question. "Would it be best for me to invest it in fitting out an office with a view of resuming the practice of my profession?" suggested Dr. Castleton.

Rebecca had learned a good deal about the ways of business during the time she was assisting Dr. Castleton in the capacity of host. She had much faith in money invested among the *living*, and very little faith in it when invested among the dead and the dying. In earlier years she had shown traces of this feeling.

Rececca was very expert with the needle. The parlor, the bed-chamber and the dress of her children were evidences of her handiwork in this respect.

"Lawrence." she said, "I do not think practicing medicine agrees with your health at all. Being called up at all times of the night, travelling in every kind of weather and having irregular meals will tell upon you as they have done in the past, if you resume your practice.

"Besides there is so little to be made at it, and you are expected to keep your family in a style befitting the situation of a city physician."

"Well, what do you suggest? I am at a loss to decide," replied Dr. Castleton.

"I went up street yesterday," replied Rebecca, "to purchase for myself a new bonnet. I am sure that I could trim a bonnet much better than many of those I saw. There are few millinery establishments in Burleigh. Do you not think we might be successful in the millinery business?"

"Who will be the milliner?" inquired Dr. Casleton.

"Why, *I* will." said Rebecca.

They continued discussing the pro's and con's of the new scheme. It seemed venturesome, but the most expedient. Everything was venturesome in those times.

It was decided.

Rebecca should leave for New Cretonia, the great commercial city of the North, early in September to purchase the stock of millinery. Dr. Castleton would, in the meantime, rent the storehouse and get it in order for the reception of the stock.

There was a good deal of anxiety on the part of Dr. Castleton, concerning Rebecca's proposed trip to the great city. He had, however, an abiding confidence in Rebecca's tact and ability. He found that it would be endangering the success of the new enterprise for them both to leave together. Nothing else seemed left to do but for her to go.

The day of parting came.

It was the first time husband and wife had been separated by any great distance. The many dangers of the traveller loomed up before them.

Jenkins seemed most distressed. He could not realize that he would be without "Mamma."

A warm embrace and farewell kiss to her loved ones, and brave Rebecca was flying on her great journey.

CHAPTER XXI.

THE TALE TOLD AGAIN.

"THE Court House at Marbleburg, Plant county, was yesterday crowded with citizens in attendance upon the political meeting called in support of the Democratic candidates for the various offices to be filled at the coming election in August.

"Hon. John Long, Gen. James Driscom, and others, addressed the meeting. There was much excitement and every indication given that the coming contest will be a bitter one.

"Great comment was made upon the presence at the meeting of Stephen Floyd, the Scalawag leader of the negroes of this county.

"Many regarded his presence as an insult and flagrant act of defiance.

"But when it was understood that he had come to consult with the Democratic leaders about a compromise in some of the county offices, it somwhat allayed the indignation of the citizens.

"The meeting adjourned and the crowd dispersed.

"Stephen Floyd left the meeting a few moments before it adjourned, in company with some of the prominent Democrats, and was apparently going to hold the proposed conference with them about the compromise.

"It was dark, and Stephen Floyd had not yet returned home. He lived only a few hundred yards from the Court House. Mrs. Floyd sent up to inquire about him, but he could not be found. Some of the negroes who were Floyd's chief lieutenants came to his house to see him. They were much frightened to learn that he had not yet returned. They knew he had gone to a place where he was not too dearly loved.

"The Court House by seven o'clock was surrounded by a great crowd of negroes, who were almost crazy with fear and alarm. The Court House was searched, but no trace of Floyd could be found. During the night they searched. Negroes were pouring in from one end of the county to the other. No one was allowed by the negroes to go in or out of the Court House. They were determined to find their great leader if he was in that building.

"All kinds of reports spread as to his whereabouts. As he could not be found, it gave color to the report that the Democrats had spirited him away, or that he had been murdered. The alarm and excitement continued. Armed bands of negroes paraded through town, evidently prepared to use every means to rescue, if possible, the much-loved-by-them Floyd.

"About three o'clock in the morning of the following day it was found that a room used for keeping wood in had not been searched. They went at once for the keys, *but they could not be found.*

"A great rush was all at once made for the door of the wood-room. It was broken down in a moment, and there, upon a pile of wood was Stephen Floyd, with his throat cut from ear to ear, and a rope dangling from his neck! It was a ghastly sight.

"The news of the finding of Floyd's dead body spread like wild-fire. The negroes threatened to kill every man who was at the meeting. There was consternation everywhere.

"Sheriff Henderson summoned a posse to protect the lives and property of the citizens. At this writing things here are in a terrible state.

"This is a cruel and horrible deed, but the county and the State are no doubt greatly benefitted by being rid of this blackest of Republicans —Floyd."

This was the startling news which Dr. Castleton read one morning shortly after Rebecca had started on her journey. He was filled with grief as he read the terrible story. Stephen Floyd had just befriended him, had always done him a good turn when he could, and now for him to be so cruelly murdered was a great blow to Dr. Castleton.

The murder of Floyd created the greatest excitement throughout the whole State. The Radicals were loud in condemnation of the supposed assassinating Democrats.

They believed it was the Ku Klux; they thought it was the Democratic candidates; every Radical paper took up the sound, wafted it further on, adding what of horror and of force it could to it.

Vengeance and Justice was the cry!

CHAPTER XXII.

ANOTHER STORM BREWING.

A CORONER'S jury was summoned, consisting of both blacks and whites, to hold an inquest on the body of Stephen Floyd.

No clue to the murderer or murderers could be found. The unfortunate man had many enemies, some within his own party. Some Radicals felt him in their way and were jealous of his power and influence over the negroes. On the other hand the Democrats hated him with all the vigor of their natures. Some of them were often bold in their threats against him. He was at a meeting where his fiercest enemies were out in great numbers. It was probable that the Democrats had killed him, but no proof against any one could be found. Whether it was a private enemy, an dignant Democrat, or a jealous Radical that killed Stephen Floyd will probably never be known.

Shortly after the Floyd murder there occurred a number of outrages by the Ku Klux. Some negroes were taken out in the dead hour of night and whipped, because they were "getting too smart." One prominent negro, who was very insolent and boasted of the power and "equality" of the negroes, was given notice to leave. He disobeyed, and on a beautiful moonlight night some silent horsemen, disguised in black, called at his cabin and awoke him. They took him into the town, and with but a few minutes to prepare himself for death, swung him by the neck to a limb of a tree, and left his lifeless body swinging in the air to greet the morning sun and the early rising citizens.

These outrages were denounced by all good men; but they were regarded as the work of the Democrats. and brought great condemnation from the Radicals upon that party.

Some outrages were perpetrated about this time which attracted more than usual attention. An anonymous letter was published in the "Marbleburg Democrat," saying that certain outrages upon some negroes had not been perpetrated by order of the Ku Klux Klan, and that some other organization must be at work within Plant county.

This little notice caused an investigation to be made in the cases specified. To the amazement of everybody, strong evidence was brought out showing that the outrages had been perpetrated by *negroes disguised as Ku Klux upon other negroes!* The cases were brought into Court and six negroes were sent to the penitentiary for the offence. The outrages of which these negroes were convicted had been the most cruel of all.

Shortly after these trials Gov. Hodges issued a proclamation declaring Plant county in a state of insurrection, and ordering one Colonel George W. Cox to raise a regiment of State militia to keep the peace.

The reader's earnest attention is invited to the character of this Colonel Cox and the army he raised.

Few people knew much about Cox, beyond the fact that he was a native of the adjoining State, who during the war commanded a band of deserters from both armies, composed of natives of his own and the State he sometimes lived in. He alternately played the Union or the Confederate *rôle* as occasion warranted, subsisting by plundering the people of the mountain districts, to whom he was a terror. He committed many acts of violence in the border counties of both States, for which he continued amenable to the laws, but his band of desperadoes was too large to admit of the Sheriff's arresting him.

It was said that because he was a man of this character, Gov. Hodges employed him to do the scandalous work he had in hand. The Governor's high-sounding proclamation appealing "to all able-bodied, patriotic men to respond to the call for troops," and informing them that " we are nearing a condition of things which will end in civil war, unless stern measures are taken to prevent it;" and "The signs of the times are more ominous of civil strife than they were in June, 1860." This fulmination of the

D

peace-loving Governor, so it was then declared, followed too closely upon the outrages the people had good evidence to believe had been instigated and perpetrated by the "Loyal Leagues," and by the negroes themselves, who were controlled by the leading men of the Radical party, to have much effect on respectable people. It was only the idlers and most abandoned part of the population that enlisted under the Banner of the notorious Cox. Vagrants, vagabonds, escaped cut-throats and rowdies of the mountain districts hastened to respond to the call.

But in spite of all the promises of prompt pay, good clothing, excellent rations, the "chances to make," and the prospect of having a good time, Cox could only succeed in enlisting four hundred and twenty worthless fellows under his banner. Some of them were former followers of Cox, old in infamy as well as in years. Many of them were youths under twenty.

Thus collected together this band commenced its march from the mountains to the interior of the State.

These military movements of Gov. Hodges caused the greatest alarm and excitement among the people of the State. They could see no cause or necessity for any such arbitrary and unheard-of proceedings.

The movement, however, was justified on the part of the Governor, on the ground that it was necessary to arrest and punish the Ku Klux, and to stop lawlessness.

A REIGN OF TERROR. 99

But others said that there was no resistance to the officials of the law in any county of the State; that the Courts were open and untrammeled in the adjudication of all matters coming under their jurisdiction, and that there was not a sheriff in the whole State who could not arrest and commit or secure any known criminal in their respective counties. So the people marvelled at a band of freebooters being thus turned upon them.

Cox and his men were most insolent in all they said and did on their march to the Capital. They threatened to kill anyone who by word, look, or gesture insulted them.

They committed many outrages upon unoffending citizens. Every town through which they passed afforded the freebooters an opportunity for committing some outrage.

They gathered, too, as they went, all the released chain gangs and outcasts like themselves, and enlisted them under the banner of Cox.

Time will not permit a recital of all the acts of violence these men committed upon the homes of peaceful and law-abiding citizens.

At Clintonbury they gave a characteristic performance, which will give the reader a general idea of their mode of action.

On the evening of the day the band arrived at Clintonbury, while supper was being served at the Trevelaine House, the principal hotel of the place, a number of this command were promenading the pavement of the dining hall. Suddenly they began to fire off their pistols and carbines, exclaiming as they did it, "They're firing into us. That shot came from the dining room!" and immediately they rushed to the doors and windows of the dining room, with sabres drawn, guns and pistols cocked, and levelled upon the unoffending ladies and gentlemen seated around the table.

A general stampede ensued, of course, and the dining room was soon cleared.

In the crowd that indulged in this pastime were some high officers of Cox's staff.

The famed Cox himself soon made his appearance, and although not a citizen had fired a gun or offered the least resistance to a single one of the militia, the latter insisted that they had been fired upon.

It was with the greatest difficulty that a number of respectable citizens, who had witnessed the whole affair, were enabled to satisfy Cox that not a gun had been fired, except by his own men.

Though satisfied that the guests were perfectly innocent, Cox did not rebuke his men for their disgraceful and unsoldierly conduct. But, on the other hand, he drew himself up and boastfully said, "If a gun is fired into my men to-night, I will not leave a house in this town. I will burn them all to the ground."

Men could not but feel alarmed at such proceedings. It looked as though the Governor wanted to goad the people to civil war.

The "New Cretonia Mercury," the great newspaper of the country, published these actions also, substantially as given above, but often pictured the scenes more terribly. It remarked about this time, that "The people of that State are quiet and law-abiding. There is no earthly need of troops. Truly outrages have been committed there upon the negroes and some Radicals, but those who perpetrated them do not belong to any particular party, nor are the outrages more common there than in other States."

One of the first acts of Cox was to pass a sentence of outlawry against a Colonel, a prominent citizen of one of the towns he passed through. One of Cox's men alleged that this man had threatened "to kill Cox at sight." The order was at once issued to the command that "any one was at liberty to shoot Colonel ——— at sight."

Fortunately for the doomed man the regiment was called away before he could be found. The charge against this man, as events afterwards showed, was utterly unfounded.

CHAPTER XXIII.

SCENES OF WAR.

WHEN Cox and his men arrived in the counties where the Ku Klux and supposed Ku Klux outrages had been committed, he at once seized and arrested nearly all the prominent citizens. No warrants were sworn out for them, and it was not known what charges were made against them.

The prisoners who were among the first citizens of the State, applied to the Chief Justice of the State for protection under the sacred right of *habeas corpus*. The Chief Justice granted the writs which were at once served on Cox. But he refused to obey them, saying: "That sort of thing is played out."

This tyrant continued his march, and when he arrived at Marbleburg—the place in which Stephen Floyd was murdered—he at once declared it under martial law.

A public meeting was in progress in the Court House at the time. It was a joint discussion between the Congressional and Legislative candidates of both political parties.

THE SIEGE. 103

The Republican candidates had spoken, and Gen. J. M. Long was about to reply, when the Court House was surrounded by a large body of armed men, over two hundred strong, commanded by Cox. Unable to comprehend such proceedings, and as if some panic had seized them, the crowd rushed for the doors and endeavored to pass the cordon of soldiers who had hemmed them in, but they were forced back at the point of the bayonet.

Several men attempted to escape, but were knocked down, clubbed and kicked in a fearful manner. Two of the victims had to be carried off on a litter. After order was restored, Colonel Cox entered the Court House, and permitted all those who "were not wanted" to pass out. Eight of the most prominent citizens of the county were then arrested, among them being the Democratic candidate for Congress for the Marbleburg District.

The prisoners were conveyed to Cox's Camp and placed in custody.

Another outrage was added to the last about two hours afterward.

Cox sent a squad of soldiers under command of a Lieutenant to the residence of Col. Jones, the former Sheriff of the county, which place was about five miles distant.

When the soldiers arrived, Jones was plowing in a field, whither the squad repaired. Without explaining the cause of their visit, Jones was at once seized in a rough manner.

A mule was taken from the plough, and he was ordered to mount. Upon his inquiring the cause of his arrest, he was answered by curses and threats. Mr. Jones objected to being arrested without seeing counsel. At this, one of the soldiers knocked him down with a piece of a fence rail, and ordered him to mount the mule. When he recovered from the blow, he did so, and was tied, and whipped with hickory switches all the way to Marbleburg.

As Cox refused to recognize the writs of *habeas corpus*, he was asked what he proposed to do with the prisoners, of whom he had more than twenty languishing in his camp. He replied that he had organized a court-martial, composed mainly of himself and officers, to try them.

Among the prisoners in the hands of Cox and his freebooters, were Ex-Judges, members of Congress, of the State Legislature, Sheriffs and others—all prominent and respectable citizens. The arrest of each was always accompanied by some insult or indignity. An eminent citizen, who was arrested in the Court House while the speaking was going on, ventured to inquire for the second time what he was arrested for, when the officer presented his pistol to the man's face and tried to fire, but the cap exploded and the pistol did not go off. Cries of "Shoot the d—— rascal" went up from some of the other soldiers. The same kind of threats were heard outside.

Cox arrested, too, all the Coroner's jury that sat on the

case of Stephen Floyd, except *the negro jurymen*. It was understood that the charges against the prisoners was Ku Kluxing. But this was not known for a certainty. It was thought, however, that they would be convicted of this charge upon the evidence of the same negroes who had been Ku Kluxing in the county. It was also rumored that Cox would execute, in a summary manner, any of the parties against whom they could get this evidence, and that he would be sustained in such action by Governor Hodges.

The "New Cretonia Mercury" graphically describes the fearful situation of affairs:

"A civil war is in progress in this State. Everywhere you go, people are intensely excited over the high-handed, war-like measures of Gov. Hodges, in sending a band of armed cut-throats and fugitives from justice over the State, invested with the extraordinary power of an army of invasion.

"In some places the people appear so panic-stricken and so completely taken aback by the outrages of Colonel Cox's unlawful rabble, that they can scarcely believe that they live in a free country in time of peace.

"The worst terrors of the civil war are again realized in this peaceful State in a most fearful and alarming manner. Spies, informers, and unscrupulous detectives everywhere precede the Governor's army of terrorism, the advent of which, in each neighborhood, is followed by the arrest of the most honorable and respectable citizens living there.

"Midnight, too, is the hour selected for perpetrating the most unjustifiable and unwarrantable outrages. Homes are surrounded by Cox's armed band; the inmates are threatened with instant death if resistance is made, and citizens are dragged, in the presence of their wives and daughters, from their beds and homes to the imprisonment of a camp, subject to the wild curses, horrible jeers, and infamous threats of a band of assassins. If such acts are not calculated to produce war and blood-shed, then human endurance is great indeed. Many an unsophisticated traveller from the North innocently and indignantly asks the cause of this infamous war-like programme.

"But beyond the fact that an *election* takes place next month, in which the prospects of Gov. Hodges and *his party* are not very bright, he learns nothing.

"The beginning of it was fully stated in the 'Mercury' over a month since, when several negroes were sent to the penitentiary for six years each, for committing midnight outrages on their sable brethren, while disguised and representing themselves as members of the Ku Klux Klan.

"When through the instrumentality of Loyal Leagues (composed of Radicals and negroes) there are perpetrated a number of outrages, mostly on colored men and all on Radicals in the name of the Ku Klux, Gov. Hodges then declares certain counties in a state of insurrection; calls out the militia; appeals to the President of the United States for troops, and lastly authorizes Cox to raise a regiment of men to carry the election by terror!

"This is now the programme, and it is being carried out without regard to law, order or the sacred rights of citizens. * * *

"Writs of *habeas corpus* issued by the Chief Justice, requiring Cox to produce the bodies of the prisoners, are treated with utter disrespect, and the Chief Justice finds his authority set at defiance by this illiterate, ignorant desperado who is backed by the Governor.

"It is openly alleged that the Governor has no idea that a tyrant of Cox's blood-thirsty disposition can live long among the people.

"He wishes to provoke a civil war, and if Cox does not survive his Plant county campaign, Hodges will be grateful.

"If the people can be driven to desperation, and a conflict with Cox's free-booters provoked, then Hodges could say rebellion did exist, and in a few days he would have a corps of such men as Cox's, and a commander infamous enough to lead them, if one could be found."

A few days after this additional facts satisfied the "Mercury" that: "Hodges would be successful in driving the people to desperation, and in precipitating a civil conflict.

"This is the whole aim of the Governor in view of the approaching election in August. He is strengthened by all the leading Radical office-holders in the State, and by the two Senators who represent the State in the Senate at Washington.

"If the citizens in any of these counties should arm themselves to resist Cox's free-booters and bandits, and a serious conflict should ensue, Hodges would then declare the entire State in insurrection, martial law would follow, and the August elections for the Congressional delegations and the State Legislature would be conducted under the supervision of Cox and his set, and would be carried for the Radical candidates at the point of the militia bayonets. Such is the conduct of Hodges.

"Under any circumstances the fate of the Radical party in this State is sealed.

"An election in the ordinary way would result in an overwhelming defeat for that party, and it is to overcome this foregone conclusion that Hodges at first plotted outrages in the name of the Ku Klux, and afterwards declared certain counties in a state of insurrection, and lastly sends a herd of banditti to accomplish his ends."

Now, as we have one side clearly and forcibly stated, let Governor Hodges himself be heard.

When the Chief Justice learned that Cox had refused to give up the prisoners, and had declared that he held them under orders from Gov. Hodges, the Chief Justice wrote a letter to the Governor, to which he received the following reply:

"EXECUTIVE OFFICE, }
BURLEIGH, July 19, 187–}

"*The Honorable, the Chief Justice of the Supreme Court:*

"Your communication of yesterday, concerning the arrests made by Geo. W. Cox, together with the enclosed, is received.

"I respectfully reply, that Geo. W. Cox made the arrests and holds the prisoners by my order. He was instructed firmly, but respectfully, to decline to deliver the prisoners.

"No one goes before me in respect for the civil law, or for those whose duty it is to enforce it, but the condition of Plant county and some other portions of the State has been such, that though, reluctant to use the strong power invested in me by law, I have been forced to declare them in a state of insurrection.

"For months past there has been maturing in these localities, under the guidance of bad and disloyal men, a dangerous spirit of insurrection.

I have invoked public opinion to aid me in suppress'ng this treason. I have issued proclamation after proclamation to the people of the State to break up these unlawful combinations,

"I have brought to bear every civil authority to restore peace and order, but all in vain.

"The Constitution and laws of the United States and of this State, are set at naught; the civil courts are no longer a protection to life, liberty or property; insurrection and outrage go unpunished, and the civil magistrates are intimidated and afraid to perform their functions.

"To a majority of the people of those sections, the approach of night is like the entrance to the Valley of the Shadow of Death; the men dare not sleep beneath their roofs at night, but, abandoning their wives and little ones, wander in the woods 'till day. The civil government was crumbling around me.

"I determined to nip this new treason in the bud.

"By virtue of the power vested in me by the constitution and the laws, and by that inherent right of self-preservation that belongs to all governments, I proclaimed Plant county in a state of insurrection.

"Col. Geo. W. Cox, commanding the military forces in that county, made the arrests referred in the writs of *habeas corpus*, and he now detains the prisoners by my order.

"At this time I am satisfied the public interest requires that these prisoners shall not be delivered up to the civil authorities.

"I devoutly hope that the time may be short when a restoration of peace and order may relieve Plant county from the pressure of military force, and the enforcement of military law.

"When that time shall arrive, I will promptly restore the civil authority.

"WM. W. HODGES."

This piteous and eloquent appeal did not seem to convince the Chief Justice that the prisoners should be held by the Governor, and the judicial authority so summarily disregarded.

Meanwhile, the arrests continued. The Court House at Marbleburg, where Cox had his prisoners incarcerated, was becoming daily more crowded.

Squads of soldiers were sent to make raids into adjoining counties—counties which had never been declared in a state of insurrection. It was a noticeable fact that it was always some prominent politician who was seized ; and also that he always happened to belong to the political party opposite to the one to which the Governor belonged.

Probably the most implacable political enemy the heroic Governor had was one Josiah Hofner, editor of the "Burleigh Sentry." He ridiculed the Executive with a pen of fire. His sarcasm was withering and his store of epithets unlimited. The irate editor did not reside in Burleigh, but lived in one of the interior counties. People remarked that the old-time liberty of speech was now a thing of the past, and that Josiah Hofner had better look out for himself.

A report spread that the Governor's troops were raiding in the neighborhood of Hofner's place of residence, and that threats had been made with a view of arresting him.

The following open letter settled the Governor's wayward decision, and brought about prompt action:

HUNTSBORO, August 5, 187—

"GOV. HODGES:

"You say you will handle me in due time. You white-livered miscreant, do it now. You dared me to *resist* you. I dare you to *arrest* me. I am here to protect my family. The Jacobins of your club, after shooting powder in Mrs. Hofner's face, threw a five-pound rock in her window, which struck near one of my children. Your ignorant Jacobins are incited to this by lying charges against me—that I am King of the Ku Klux.

"You villain, come and arrest a man, and order your clubs not to arrest women and children.

"Yours with contempt and defiance, *habeas corpus* or no *habeas corpus*.

"JOSIAH HOFNER,
"Editor of the 'Burleigh Sentry.'"

A day or so after this epistle was received, a Lieutenant in command of a squad of the Governor's militia met Mr. Hofner in the road about five miles from his home, and informed him that he was a prisoner. He was marched to Marbleburg, but the Court House was now so crowded that the jail was thought the most appropriate place for the suppressed editor. Thither he was conveyed. Some vile prisoners were removed from the dungeon in order to make room for their new comrade. When he was safely lodged there, the keys were turned in the great lock and our editor was left alone in his glory. Suddenly he bethought himself that after such a fatiguing march, he was very thirsty. He knocked at the iron door. A gruff voice asked "What do you want?"

"I would like to have a drink of water," replied the prisoner.

"Look in the corner of your cell an' you'll see some water that was fresh *dis mornin'* when it was brought." With this the keeper walked away. Hofner gazed at the bucket from which the former occupants of his cell had quenched their thirst for a whole day, and discovered a new thought for an editorial against the executive head of the State.

The next morning the thirsty prisoner called for buttermilk. The amazed turnkey began such an animated discussion about the enormity of such a demand on the part of the prisoner, that it attracted the attention of one of Cox's officers who was just then making an inspection of the prison. He came up and ordered the turnkey away and commanded the editor *not to talk*, as it was against positive orders. Before long the door of the prisoner's cell opened again and the before-mentioned bucket was refilled with water. Nothing was said by anyone. The turnkey disappeared and the great door was again locked.

When dinner was brought it was observed that Hofner had not yet drunk a drop of water.

"Do you want a silver mug to drink out er?" growled the keeper.

Not a word came from the knight of the quill.

"You're gittin on a hoss altogether too high fur the small gullies you're got to cross," again spoke the man with the keys.

Hofner was all taciturnity. When the turnkey came back for the dishes, the cabbage pile on the solitary dish was smaller, and there were no traces at all of the little slice of bacon which accompanied the said cabbage.

But no water had been drunk by the thirsty prisoner. The nonplussed keeper retired and presently returned with a big mug of buttermilk. The prisoner drank it with great gusto, and bowed obsequiously in acknowledgment. Josiah Hofner drank nothing but buttermilk during the rest of his imprisonment.

AN INSULT.

"Colonel Cox, commanding the forces at this place, has ordered me to ask you, Mr. Hofner, if you desire him to deliver any message to anyone concerning the procuring of counsel to defend you at the approaching trials?"

Thus spoke an officer to our editor one morning. No answer on the part of the addressed.

"Mr. Hofner, it is necessary for me to return some answer to Colonel Cox," said the astonished officer. A comprehensive yawn was all he received from the stoical prisoner in reply.

"You seem, sir, not to understand the rank of the officer who addresses you, or of our commander. I will give you one more opportunity to reply," said the indignant soldier.

A twitched movement of misery on the part of the prisoner greeted the flashing eyes of the warrior. Josiah Hofner had been ordered "*not to talk*," and he intended to be obedient.

The officer slammed the cell door and muttered: "That d——d rascal must be put down!"

When Cox heard of how his officer had been treated by the insolent prisoner the commander was furious. He ordered Hofner to be put on half diet, and other measures to be taken for taming him.

As the attentive turnkey came in a few days after these occurrences with the "half meal" for his prisoner, he asked the latter if he would not write a letter for him to his mother, as he himself was unable to write. Our editor nodded assent, because he recollected that this was the young fellow who had supplied him with buttermilk at a time when he needed it very badly.

Paper and ink were procured and the knight of the quill took the pen in hand, bent over the paper and looked up as if waiting for the turnkey to begin the dictation.

"Tell Mammy that I set myself to write a few lines which find me well, and I hopes to discover her the same."

This was a sufficient cue for the man of taciturnity, and he wrote:

"JAIL, Marbleburg, August 6, 187—
DEAR MAMMA:
"I am in the jail here guarding the great King of the Ku Klux! He is a fine fellow, and makes things lively for Colonel Cox. He makes the warrior howl, though he says not a word to him.

"The great King says that if his *silence* in prison works up the boss so, what on earth will his *speech* do when he gets out of prison?

"He drinks buttermilk which I get for him every day. He likes it.

"This place is so full that I hav'nt got room to sweep without brushing over somebody.

"I haven't time to write more. I send you a dollar which the great King gave me for you.

"Write soon to your affectionate
his
"JACK X HALLOWAY."
mark.

With this the prisoner put a dollar bill into the letter, folded it, sealed the envelope and directed it.

The turnkey was in high glee and did not slam the door quite so hard as he left.

The important State prisoners were kept in solitary confinement. Cox's Lieutenant was ordered to extort confessions from those who were suspected of belonging to the Ku Klux. One Patterson was taken and hung up by the thumbs three times in succession to make him confess to belonging to the Ku Klux.

When the man rallied sufficiently after each hanging up to speak, he denied belonging to the organization. He was then hustled back to his cell.

Another prisoner who was strongly suspected, was swung up by the *neck*, but when he was cut down it was found that he did not rally. For about an hour they were pretty active in trying to resuscitate the prisoner. He finally recovered a little, but was too weak to speak. The next morning he was asked if he belonged to the Ku Klux. He said he did not.

The people heard of these cruelties and were aroused. The Chief Justice issued more writs of *habeas corpus*, but Cox treated them with utter contempt; said he would use the paper for gun wadding and threatened to shoot the marshal who served them if he did not leave the camp at once.

When he heard of this, the Chief Justice declared the "Judiciary was exhausted and could do no more."

In the midst of this excitement the elections were held. Governor Hodges was rebuked.

In spite of the terrorism and intimidation of his military, the people voted against them.

A Democratic Legislature was elected; all the Congressional delegations except two from the Negro districts were Democratic, and the Radicals found themselves defeated on every hand.

Then came relief for the oppressed.

The strong arm of the Government of the United States came to the rescue. Judge Leighton of the United States District Court issued writs of *habeas corpus* for the production of the prisoners before him on a fixed day at Clintonburg. Governor Hodges and Cox were dismayed.

But they thought discretion the better part of valor, and on the day named produced the prisoners before Judge Leighton in the United States Court.

Cox was marching them into the court room under strong guard of his men. But when Judge Leighton caught the first glimpse of a bayonet coming within the sacred precincts of the Temple of Justice, he delivered this stinging rebuke to the presumptuous Cox:

"*No soldiers allowed in this Court.* When wanted I will send for them. Clerk, stop those men at the door and clear this building of every armed man!"

When order was restored the Court proceeded with the

hearing, the prisoners being in charge of the United States Marshals. Not a militia blue coat was visible. Not even the insolent Cox put in an appearance.

The Judge discharged all the prisoners except five, and not a shadow of evidence was brought against even these. These five were held on suspicion for the murder of Stephen Floyd. They also were released after a short time, having given bail for their appearance at Court. They were never brought to trial, as no evidence could be obtained.

A grand reception was arranged for the released prisoners when they arrived at Burleigh. The whole city was in holiday attire. At the depot a procession was formed.

A mounted escort of citizens headed the line. Then followed the released prisoners in carriages. The people who crowded the streets along the line of march gave hearty cheers to the ransomed. Especially did the familiar figure of Josiah Hofner receive an enthusiastic greeting. Arriving at the Court House they found a platform gaily festooned with flags. They were conducted to seats upon this platform. A great concourse of people had assembled here.

Hon. Samuel Dunkin presided and delivered the address of welcome. The distinguished prisoners responded.

Hon. John ———, an ex-Judge, member of Congress, and an orator of national reputation, was the first speaker.

As he graphically described the scenes and incidents of his long confinement, he was listened to with great attention. The recital of the indignities and insults he had suffered aroused the anger of the multitude, but as often did the funny incidents and the ridiculous scenes he had gone through awake their merriment, and make the whole ground a perfect sea of grins.

Major Robinson, the next speaker, appeared, waving the Stars and Stripes. This tribute to the emblem of the power that had wrenched them from the hand of tyranny was greeted with loud and long-continued applause. Three cheers were then given for the Stars and Stripes, for Judge Leighton and for the prisoners.

The man of the hour was Josiah Hofner. His introduction was the signal for wild shouts. The boys in the trees whistled, the men halloed, the ladies waved their handkerchiefs. Everybody made some demonstration. When he could be heard, Mr. Hofner began a recital of his experience. The crowd relished it greatly. His manner of telling about the buttermilk, the taciturnity and other prison incidents was witty in the extreme. His sarcasm, his epithets, his irony never left him. Never was poor man torn in tatters as was Governor Hodges. He touched up, too, the heroic soldiers, and did full justice to their prowess. The great meeting adjourned and the editorials of the "Sentry" assumed their wonted fire and force

Meanwhile, the newly elected Legislature met. One of its first acts was to repeal the odious Military Bill, under the authority of which all the enormities of Gov. Hodges had been committed.

The House of Representatives at once appointed a Committee to draw up articles of impeachment against Gov. Hodges "for high crimes and misdemeanors in office."

The Committee drew up eight articles against the Governor, charging him with attempted subversion of the liberties of the people, for suspending the sacred right of *habeas corpus*, for illegal arrests and false imprisonment, for allowing grave cruelties and indignities to prisoners, and lastly for applying moneys appropriated for other purposes to the paying of his troops.

When these articles were adopted by a large majority of the House, the Senate was informed of the action, and the House of Representatives proceeded in a body to the Senate chamber. When they were announced, the Senators rose and the presiding officer invited them to seats on his right. The Chairman of the House Committee of Impeachment then presented the articles, arraigned Governor W. W. Hodges at the Bar of the Senate and demanded of the Senate a High Court of Impeachment.

The presiding officer then commanded the Sergeant-at-Arms to make proclamation, which he did by crying: "O yes, O yes! Let all keep silence! Gov. W. W. Hodges is impeached by the House of Representatives!"

From that moment the official functions of Gov. Hodges were suspended until the termination of the trial.

It was a very dignified and solemn scene, and during all the proceedings there was perfect silence. The members seemed to think that they were performing a great and solemn duty. There seemed to be no spirit of exultation over a conquered enemy, or any feeling of revenge or malice.

The Lieutenant-Governor, who was the presiding officer then took farewell of the Senators, thanking them for their courtesy to him while discharging his official duties and informing them that he now went to assume the duties of another department of the State Government.

The Chief Justice was then conducted to the chair to preside during the trial.

The Lieutenant-Governor and the Impeachment Committee then proceeded to the Executive office, where they found Gov. Hodges. They informed him of what had taken place. He merely asked an hour for packing papers, which was granted. He then retired, leaving the Lieutenant-Governor in possession.

The great trial was proceeded with. Gov. Hodges was defended by the most eminent counsel in the State, but the case was too strong against him. The acts of the Governor, as they have already been depicted in the foregoing pages, were proven. Two-thirds of the Senators found him guilty, and impeached him for "high crimes and misdemeanors in office," some of his own party voting for his condemnation. Many sympathized with the unfortunate Governor. Personally he was much liked. He was a self-made man and one of great ability. Without doubt he was conscientious in all he did, but he was misled by those about him.

When his native state discarded him, the Government at Washington took him up; and few people grumbled when the President of the United States appointed him to the lucrative position of postmaster of Burleigh. Here he received a larger salary than he did as Governor. He has made a good officer and has continued to hold the position through three Presidential terms, and if he lives, he will have held it through another, for the succeeding Presidents have continued him in office.

CHAPTER XXIV.

HOME AGAIN.

THESE stirring scenes of turmoil were being transacted while Rebecca was in the great Northern city purchasing her stock of millinery. She did remarkably well for one who had never travelled so far from home before. She had no mishaps, and in September she returned again to Burleigh. The household was overjoyed at her return. Young Jenkins declared he would celebrate the event by staying away from school on that day. Dr. Castleton had everything prepared in the way of a suitable storehouse and dwelling. It was on the main street of the city, only a few squares from the Capitol. Rebecca had secured the services of two milliners from New Cretonia to assist her. A good business was done the first season. Many of Dr. Castleton's old legislative friends patronized Rebecca. Ex-Gov. Hodges would often step in on his way to the post office and chat with the family. He had always been very friendly to Dr. Castleton, and it seemed to remind him of other and better times to talk without official restraint on these occasions.

The first Fall and Winter season closed and Rebecca found herself a woman of business. Dr. Castleton kept her accounts and attended to all outside business matters.

As Spring returned again it brought with it another affliction for the now prospering family. It has been said previously in these pages, that Dr. Castleton was not himself any more, and that he had lost his former vim and enterprise. He had become listless and indifferent. Whether this had anything to do with the sickness that now overtook him, we know not; but he was taken with Typhoid Fever about this time. His illness was long and lingering, and for a time grave doubts of his recovery were entertained. But with the aid of the best medical skill the city afforded, and the careful and unswerving attention of Rebecca, he recovered. Dr. Castleton's illness had, of course, prevented Rebecca from giving that attention to her business it demanded, and her interests in that direction had suffered accordingly. But still she did as well as could have been expected under the circumstances.

The course of true love is not the only thing in this life which does not run smoothly. Business also presents its rough roads and balky ups and downs. Rebecca was destined to have some experience in the stony paths of business. One of her milliners whom she had brought from the North was a fair blonde. She was tall and graceful of figure, and possessed a number of very entertaining qualities. The beaux of the city were correspondingly exercised.

On Sundays the number of gloved hands that covered the knob of the Castleton door-bell would often amount to several more than one person used. The gallant who was first on the ground generally secured the pleasure of escorting the fair one to church.

The unlucky ones who happened in too late, would often inquire of Dr. Castleton what church the pair had gone to attend. They would be informed, but the doctor would afterwards learn that the disappointed *always* attended some other place of worship than the one at which was the object of their adoration.

Our blonde put various interpretations upon this fact when she would be informed of it. She usually attributed it to the rivals' generosity toward each other, every one of whom seemed to yield very gracefully to defeat.

Rebecca, who was more searching in her analysis, would declare that she was of the opinion that the actions of the young men should be traced to a very different cause. She believed they went to a different church because they did not desire to see the living, moving reminder of their disappointment constantly before them. It would tend to distract their minds from attending properly to the sermon and their spiritual duties, which was the main object of their going to church! Rebecca's irony was a powerful weapon. She, however, always used it discreetly, and while she made it tell, it did not leave that sting which usually lingers after them when the pleasing aspect of ironical expressions have passed away. It should be remarked that the above would, in a majority of cases, be the tenor of the Sunday dinner conversation after the sermon had been briefly touched upon, and any new bonnets that had made their appearance described and discussed. Some metaphysical and psycological questions that would sometimes come up in the course of these conversations could only arise from such a source as beauxdom, with the fair blonde for its queen, handsome young fellows for her subjects and courtiers, and such acute ones as the Castletons, young Jenkins included, for the diplomats of her Court.

The Court was much vexed one Sunday evening by the embarrassment presented by two of Her Majesty's subjects calling at the same time. Evidence was clear that they had reached the door step together, one coming from up the street and the other from down. Several that called in a few moments later had their claims set aside at once. They neither expected, nor did they receive, much consideration, and in a few moments they courteously took their leave, a kind invitation from the blonde to call again, being a slight panacea for their misfortune.

A "Council of State" was hastily assembled to consider the case presented by the callers who had made their appearance conjointly.

"You had better not attend church at all this evening," was the opinion of Sir Lawrence Castleton, Minister Plenipotentiary and Envoy Extraordinary to Her Majesty's Court from the Kingdom of Matrimony, "I think the matter could be settled by the Queen declining to accept the services of either of the noble lords in attendance, and by her selecting Master Jenkins Castleton, an *attacle* of our Legation, as the proper one to escort Her Majesty to church."

The eagerness of the *attache* for this proposition assured all present that it would meet with no opposition from that quarter. In fact, Master Jenkins began to prepare himself for the great event even before the Council had come to any definite conclusion in the premises. Thus hastened to their decision by the vigorous action of young Jenkins, the Council decided upon the plan suggested by Minister Castleton.

When the queen announced herself as ready to receive the lords, they came in arm in arm. They found Her Majesty leaning upon the arm of the young *attache*, and apparently in readiness to attend divine service. She politely informed the lords of her intention and the reasons of impartiality which had induced her to decide upon the course she was about to take. Simply asking what church Her Majesty would attend, they bowed and retired, companions in each other's woe.

Master Jenkins stood erect and unmoved during this scene. To the conquered lords his countenance bore neither an air of boasted triumph nor haughty disdain. Nor did he seem to be a blind adulator of Her Majesty. He won simply a plainly visible (though not distasteful) air of superiority. He was a fitting king for such a queen.

Their entrance into church that evening created quite a stir. A number of ladies moved their broad-brimmed Spring hats so quickly around that the rims scraped the cheeks of the gentlemen sitting beside them. A saint, who should have been interested in more heavenly matters, moved his feet in the wrong direction as he suddenly turned his head to behold the apparition coming up the middle aisle. The offended female whose delicate toes had suffered from the misdirection of the aforesaid feet, gave the saint such a look that it caused him to find the hymn more quickly than usual. Master Jenkins perceived all this excitement; but he was as cool as the best of them.

He approached the Castleton pew, and a little opposition to the opening of the pew door being occasioned by the button having been turned, Master Jenkins, unable to brook this restraint, gave the door a pull, to the equal power of which many a fence paling had succumbed. A little creaking noise and the button landed a few feet within the pew, and Her Majesty entered, followed by the *attache*. The door closed and so remained as best it could without a button. The young gallant, leaning back, gazed towards the pulpit, looking neither to the right nor to the left, as unmindful of the laugh and excitement his tearing off the pew door button (which proceeding was witnessed by the whole congregation) had created, as one could possibly be. He was equally disdainfully unconscious of the blushes of mortification which fairly lit up the cheeks of his queen.

This church affair furnished food for gossip in the Court circles all the following week. Rebecca observed that the eagerness with which Master Jenkins had accepted the position of gallant was a somewhat portentious sign.

Thereafter, when two lords called at once, they, out of mercy to the queen, settled it between them as to who should enter. The unlucky man would then take his leave, the other one remaining in possession of the doorstep. But even he rarely wore a look of satisfaction, because he did not know who had been before him. The fact that the blonde would make no decided preference for any particular one of her numerous courtiers, kept a host of them always on the *qui vive.*

Things came to such a pass that the Castleton door bell would be rung unseasonably early on Sunday mornings; often, too, in the evening a number of gallants would be in the parlor waiting for tea to be over.

Some of the devotees finally struck upon the plan of

calling at the store, or writing, during week days, to make an engagement with Her Majesty for the following Sunday. This was getting to be a little too romantic for Rebecca. She had no particular objection to the admirers of her New Cretonia milliner calling on Sundays, but when it came to interfering with her business on week days, it was another matter entirely. Rebecca uttered a mild remonstrance, but it was not very well taken on the part of the blonde. Dr. Castleton observed to her that the number of callers upon the milliner was being the subject of much comment around the town.

This determined Rebecca. She resolved to dethrone the queen at once. She gave her blonde notice a few days after this that her services would no longer be required after the end of the month.

This was a great surprise, as the blonde had no idea that Rebecca was serious in her remonstrance, which had been disregarded. The discharged lady at once proceeded to the office of a young lawyer—one of her admirers—and asked his advice. He told her to refuse to leave Castleton's establishment, and offer to work the rest of the season according to contract.

She did this. Rebecca was firm, however, and informed her she must quit her house at the end of the month. This was reported to the admiring lawyer and he at once sent notice to Dr. Lawrence Castleton that suit

E

would be brought against him for the salary due the blonde for the two months that remained of the season. She had been, declared the counsellor, engaged for the season, and Mrs. Castleton had no right to discharge her until the end of said season. Rebecca replied that she was ready to defend her position.

She then, in company with Dr. Castleton, called upon a well known lawyer in the city and told him she would give him the full amount of salary alleged to be due the plaintiff, if he would prevent her from getting it.

The shrewd lawyer declared that it would be no trouble for him to do that.

The trial came off and Rebecca won her case. Men who worship the rising rather than the setting sun did not all live in the age of Pompey. Our queen of beauxdom had lost her prestige. Her sun rapidly declined. She returned to her native Cretonia, and Burleigh knew her no more.

CHAPTER XXV.

PATRIOTISM AND THE CASTLETONS.

SEVERAL years after the occurrences narrated in the last chapter, the countenance of Rebecca one day again bore an uncommonly grave look. "Lawrence, I have observed Jenkins of late. He is grown to be a big boy. He is rapidly approaching the time when he should be sent to college. Our State University, which was interrupted in its career by the war, has not since been re-opened. We are scarcely able to send him to the old traditional Southern Colleges which have survived the war, and where his ancestors were educated.

"Jenkins is now sixteen years of age, and he has received what academical education is afforded here. We must soon do something in his case."

This was the opening of a conversation between Rebecca and Dr. Castleton one winter's afternoon, when no customers were in the store, and when Jenkins was at school and his two brothers were at play.

"I have often thought of that very thing," said Dr. Castleton. "I have never been able to see much hope for a young man at the South.

"There is little or no foundation for him to build a career upon.

"None but desolating memories cluster around him here, and if he goes up North he only feels himself an exile from his home, driven forth by disaster and misfortune.

"Altogether I do not regard the prospects of Jenkins' future as very bright."

"Why Lawrence, I think you take entirely too gloomy a view of things.

"I believe we now have a New North as well as a New South. I believe the country is more nearly one now than it ever was before, and I see no real reason why a young man should not feel at home anywhere in the Union.

"The South may remind you, Lawrence, and me of desolation and destruction. But what of us! We will soon be in our graves.

"Jenkins and his two brothers should be our care. To them the South is not a land of despair. The South they know is the New South, covered with its mantle of green verdure and snowy cotton—not the South red with blood.

"If Jenkins were to go up North the companions he would mingle with would be young like himself,—would belong to the New North.

"No hatred developed from Anti-Slavery and war times would animate them. They have no personal sufferings of war with which they can charge the South.

"Besides look at the business interests of the South, how they are progressing, and how they are making the present generation of the South a practical one.

"Who would ever have thought a few years ago that *I* would have opened a business and trimmed bonnets? And yet I have done so and cannot complain of my success. There are many other families about us who have done the same and are now being successful in their business. This I think is the New South."

Dr. Castleton evidently did not agree with all the sentiments of his wife.

"This may all be very well, Rebecca, but it will take generations for the South to ever get on its feet again. What will all the youth do without the means and men to guide and educate them properly? The present generation is being raised up loosely, the old-time honor which should be taught the youth in order to make them fit descendents of their sires is not, and cannot be instilled into them.

"The 'New South' you speak so much about is a slipshod South—a conglomeration of ignorant negroes who have as much power in the government as the wisest citizen, and young white men who are working with their hands when they ought to be toiling with their minds and educating themselves. To these add the one-armed and the one-legged and those who have lost all their property.

"And you might close up the list by adding on the widows and orphans. This is a 'New South' indeed!"

Rebecca was a little taken aback by this forcible presentation of the situation, but after a moment's reflection she said:

"I do not think your last objection will hold good either. I don't think the young men of to-day need to be taught by the men of the old time.

"The circumstances which required the peculiar education you refer to have changed. We don't want the old ideas now.

"As regards the sentiment of honor, it is as high now in the breast of every Southern youth as it ever was. It is born in him; and he will develope it and follow naturally its dictations.

"Those negroes, who seem to frighten you so much, I am not a bit afraid of. The old slave negroes are fast dying out, and the younger ones are of a different sort. Many of them will be able to read and will become better citizens year by year.

"These negroes will be *Southerners;* they will have property in the South; they will have all their interests in the South and as soon as they get their eyes open they will differ in politics just like the whites, and they will vote for the interest of the place where they have their homes rather than for the interest of politicians thousands of miles away.

"About the young men who are working I have this to say. They will still leave a sufficient number of more fortunate young men who will receive an education adequate for ruling the politics of the South and for being lawyers, ministers and doctors.

"If we can have an industrious white population with a sufficiency of those engaged in the professions the South will be on the high road to wealth."

Having spoken this much Rebecca picked up a newspaper and read about the elaborate preparations which were being made for the celebration of a great American Anniversary. "Look," she said, "there are commissioners from every state in the Union.

"Jenkins will know also that it was men of the North, and of the South who side by side and shoulder to shoulder achieved the final victory. I would like much for him to see this great exhibition. I think he should be taught its lessons, should imbibe its spirit."

The accounts of the magnificent preparations that were being made for the great celebration interested Dr. Castleton.

The words Rebecca had spoken made a deep impression upon him notwithstanding his strong prejudices. "Rebecca" at length spoke Dr. Castleton, "I think myself it would be a good thing for us to see this great exhibition. But how? That is the great question with me. I sometimes think we might go to Philopolis the city where it is to be held, and open a hotel as we did when we came to Burleigh. We would advertise it to be opened specially for the entertainment of guests from our native State.

"If we found that we succeeded reasonably well and we liked the people of Philopolis, we might remain there, for some years at least, and then in that great city there would be many business opportunities.

"Now is a chance for trying your theory that you can feel at home in any part of the Union."

Rebecca was agreeably surprised at these practical suggestions of her husband. She flattered herself that she had scored a victory. She thought this the first step towards the reconstruction of Dr. Castleton.

"Lawrence, I am much pleased at the tone of your proposition. But it is a matter of such great importance that I think we had better pause awhile and think it over for several days."

At this point of their conversation Jenkins came in book-bag on shoulder.

"Jenkins how do you stand in Geography?" asked his mother, of the school-boy. "I just tell you, mamma, I can see the maps in my mind so clearly that I can put my finger on almost any place you name," was the confidential reply.

"Well, where is Philopolis," asked Rebecca. She was answered promptly and correctly.

"How would you like to go to Philopolis," inquired the mother. "I would like it very much. There is a picture of Philopolis in my Geography and it looks to be a big and beautiful place," said Jenkins.

"Perhaps we will visit it before long," Rebecca answered.

CHAPTER XXVI.

PHILOPOLIS.

NOT long after the events narrated in the last chapter a notice appeared in the "Burleigh Sentry," stating that Mrs. Rebecca Castleton was closing out her large and well selected stock of millinery at very reduced rates, preparatory to removing from the city.

After long and mature consideration, the Castletons had decided upon another important step, and one which was destined to affect greatly the fortunes of the Castleton family.

When Dr. Castleton left Burleigh for Philopolis to make arrangements for the opening of his hotel, many friends called to wish him success and to tell him they would stop with him when they visited the great exhibition. This was very encouraging and seemed to augur well for the future.

Rebecca, having closed out her stock, gave up her storehouse, and took up her residence in the family of one of her neighbors and awaited information from Dr. Castleton.

A short while after this Rebecca received a letter postmarked "Philopolis." It ran thus:

"MY DEAR REBECCA: I arrived here safely yesterday evening. I took a street car at the depot and rode to the hotel.

"I have been around the city a good deal this morning, and I must say that my first impressions of Philopolis are quite favorable, but I do not know what later observations may bring forth.

"I find the people here very courteous and obliging. Everything seems to be on a rush—so different from the easy-going way we have of doing things.

"I am struck also with the sameness of architecture which characterizes all the houses, except those in the business portions of the city.

"I have found several buildings which might be suitable for the hotel—one of them on a principal street.

"I will, however, have to look further, as the selection of a suitable location is very important.

"I have not time to write more now. I hope you are not oppressively lonely. Take the boys with you and visit our friends.

"I will write you daily, and I would be most glad if you could do the same.

"I cannot tell how long it will take me to finish up the arrangements. I will be as brisk as possible.

"Good by till I write again.

"Give my love to the boys and accept the same, and more from
"Your Husband,
"LAWRENCE CASTLETON."

Rebecca was pleased at the cheerful tone of this letter, and it gave her grounds for hope.

She had already taken advantage of the suggestion of Dr. Castleton's letter. Her close application to business had prevented her from giving that attention to social matters she would have liked. Her freedom now from the heavy cares of busy life was a delightful recreation for her. So when she had finished her daily letters to Dr. Castleton, she would indulge herself freely in the pleasure of visiting her friends.

Rebecca was a fine conversationalist, and she had such a fund of general information gathered both from her intercourse with the business world and from reading, that she scarcely ever failed to make herself interesting.

Every one to whom she broached the subject seemed pleased with her idea of moving up North. Rebecca developed more fully her ideas of things in general, which she had imparted to Dr. Castleton on numerous occasions, and she seemed to impress many with the soundness of her views.

At length word came from Dr. Castleton that he had secured a suitable building for the new hotel, and everything was in readiness for the reception of Rebecca and the boys.

Farewells were taken, the good wishes of many friends received, and once more Rebecca Castleton was speeding towards the great North.

> Home of my youth, fare thee well;
> Dearest spot of earth e'er I trod,
> Living, I loved with thee to dwell;
> Dead—rest me 'neath thy sod!

CHAPTER XXVII.

HERE WE ARE!

THE adventures of Rebecca and the boys on their way to Philopolis were few. They had, however, a little relief from the usual monotony of travelling.

The trains were crowded with those who were going early to the great exhibition in order to secure good accomodations. As they neared Philopolis the passengers increased greatly, and the cars were crowded almost to suffocation.

At Cringemore, the nearest large city to Philopolis, the party had several hours to lie over; and as Jenkins was quivering to see everything within range, he requested of his mother that she take a hasty trip around the city. Although it was excessively warm, and while Rebecca's judgment told her that it was best for the boys to remain out of the sun's scorching rays, yet to gratify them she started on a hasty tour of the city. They had a little over three hours to spend in this way.

They visited the new City Hall and other places of interest in the heart of the city, and then took the street cars and started for the great Washington monument. Arriving there, Jenkins' curiosity was excited by seeing some gentlemen and ladies, with lanterns in their hands, entering a door which seemed to lead into the base of the monument. He at once inquired what these strange lights signified. Rebecca was unable to inform him. He was all the more aroused by this, and rushed up to the door and asked the man in charge to give him the desired information. He was told that those lanterns were used to guide the people in ascending the winding stair-case which was erected inside the shaft, and which lead to its top, where a magnificent view of the city and surrounding country could be had.

Jenkins rushed over to his mother and was all eagerness to make the journey upwards to the top of the high monument.

Rebecca did not feel like climbing up several hundred steps in a narrow, dark shaft on a warm day. So she remonstrated. Jenkins was unappeasable. He argued that it must be very cool away up on the high top, and that the sun's rays never penetrated the stone, though, no doubt the water did, and therefore it must be cool and pleasant inside the shaft from the moisture. Jenkins' arguments were more expedient than scientific, but nevertheless they were sufficient for his purpose.

Rebecca never liked to deprive her children of an innocent pleasure, even though it cost her considerable sacrifice to let them enjoy it. They started up the great shaft, each one with a lantern. Jenkins led the party. His two brothers, Lee and Cassius, followed, and lastly came Rebecca.

It was very dark, not a ray of light shone except what the little lanterns afforded. But Jenkins was not much mistaken about it being cool within the shaft. About half-way from the top was a window, which was most welcome. It let in cool whiffs of fresh air, and the cheerful beams of the bright sunlight.

They arrived at the top, and there, spread out before them, was a splendid view indeed. The bay, the river, the coast-lines beyond, the grain-covered fields in the distance, all these looked very beautiful.

Jenkins enjoyed it much, and was very proud that he had been so instrumental in providing such pleasure for the party. They descended, and were not much fatigued by the climbing.

Time was flying quite fast, while our party were enjoying the view afforded by the great monument, and they found that they had only a few moments in which to reach the depot. They were to take the 4.30 p. m. train. Jenkins had been presented with a watch for his sixteenth birthday. It was an erratic time-keeper, but Jenkins had great faith in its correctness.

Arriving at the depot, Jenkins rushed by one of the officers of the building, whose duty it was to attend to just such matters as Jenkins wanted to know about, and inquired of a traveller who stood near, satchel in hand, if that was the 4.30 train for Philopolis?

"O no, sir," said the man, "I am waiting for that 4.30 train myself."

Jenkins hurried back to reassure his mother who was becoming much distressed.

"Mother, I'm so glad we do not have to take that train. Look how the people are crowding in. Some of them are even jumping in at the windows, others are hanging on to the platforms. I'm glad we don't have to take that train."

While Jenkins was discoursing thus, the officer whom the self-confident Jenkins had so completely ignored in asking for information, stepped up and inquired of Mrs. Castleton if she was to take the 4.30 train. She promptly answered in the affirmative.

"Well, you'd better git on it then, for that's the train yonder which all them people are rushing for."

This amazing news had the effect of stimulating Jenkins to renewed activity. He snatched up the satchels and other light baggage, and led the way for that train he was congratulating himself he would not·have to take.

Mrs. Castleton, with great difficulty, managed to get standing room in the aisle of one of the cars.

Jenkins contented himself with hanging on to the platform as best he could. He does not now boast much of his ability to guide a travelling party.

"Philopolis," sung out the brakeman.

As Rebecca and the boys stepped out of the crowded train upon the great platform, and beheld the innumerable faces that confronted her, she despaired of ever distinguishing Dr. Castleton. He, however, had taken the precaution to stand near the street entrance to the depot, in full view of all who emerged from the building. He spied Rebecca, and was in front of her before she was aware of it. It was an affectionate reunion of husband and wife. They all felt happy at being together once more. They were not long in reaching the "Castleton House."

The family retired early to rest, and delayed reciting their experiences until the morrow, when they would be refreshed by that sweet restorer, sleep.

Rebecca found herself more in the humor for business than sight-seeing or talking, the next day.

She lost no time in seeing that the "Castleton House" was put in proper condition for the reception of guests.

A good many letters were received from friends at home, engaging quarters. So when the great show opened it found the "Castleton House" well crowded with guests.

Rebecca proved herself even a better hostess than she was in other times. The occasion of the "Castleton

House" having been opened, afforded many opportunities for the reunion of old friends.

'Squire Jenkins, now very old, but still hearty, came to look upon "his boy."

The stirring scenes of the intervening years had caused the Castletons to loose sight of their old friend. He, however, had remained all this time quietly gathering his wheat and dispensing justice at his rural home. But it seemed only too plain that the good old 'Squire's race was nearly run.

He hardly knew young Jenkins when he came in, but the boy knew his name-sake and rushed to greet him. The smile that lit up the aged man's rugged face was as kindly as ever, and his good heart was still beating as warmly.

He talked long with Jenkins. He told how he often thought of him, how he had many times spoken of him.

Jenkins was much touched by the presence of his old benefactor, and replied that he had a lively memory of him, and often recalled the past with much pleasure. He also said that he would show him around the city and the great exhibition, and would endeavor to make his stay pleasant and agreeable.

It was almost astonishing how quickly Jenkins became acquainted with the ways of the restless city. Before a week had passed he knew all the principal streets well, and could find his way anywhere in the city.

He was delighted with the wonderful sights he saw.

The crowds, the life, the mighty exhibition, the noble architectural monuments of the great city—all these found a willing and interested admirer in Jenkins Castleton.

Summer spent itself and Autumn came again. It found the "Castleton House" still in a very prosperous condition. Rebecca was well satisfied with her new home. She did not find much reason to depart from the well-settled convictions, so often expressed, that anywhere in the Union she could feel at home.

Dr. Castleton also was much more comfortable than he expected, though he would sometimes get out of patience with the animus of the politics that now ran high, for he found himself in the midst of a great Presidential campaign. He came home one evening from a large political meeting, which he had attended out of courtesy to one of his guests.

"I believe the war is being fought over again," said Dr. Castleton as he and his guest took a seat near each other in the office of the hotel.

"I do not think so, Doctor, this is merely the struggle to reap the full fruits of the victory," replied his friend and guest.

"Well, that may be so," continued Dr. Castleton, "but that must be a terrible war which twelve years after articles of peace have been signed, must be continued still."

"I shall never forget that war," said the guest. "We both have memories of it. Doctor, do you know when this war will end? I can tell you. When your boys and my boys grow up to be men, then and then only will this conflict end."

So spoke James Freeman to the Ex-Chairman of the "Binghampton County Vigilance Committee." So the war between the New and the Old continued to be waged.

CHAPTER XXVIII.

FROM FICTION TO REALITY.

"JENKINS, have you connected yourself with any Sunday School since you came up North?" So spoke an old gentleman who had retired from business and who devoted his time to good works.

"I have not," replied Jenkins. "I have attended service at various churches. Whenever I learned that an eminent divine was to preach at any particular church I would go to hear him. But I have not attended regularly any of the churches."

There seemed to our old gentleman to be here a chance for a little missionary work.

"Well, Mr. Jenkins, I am acquainted with the minister of one of our best city churches—of the same denomination in which your mother has raised you—and I would be pleased to introduce you to him. I think you would find it very agreable to you to meet him and to attend his church."

Jenkins replied that he would mention the matter to his mother and if she found no objections he would be pleased to accept the invitation.

Jenkins excused himself for a moment and mentioned the conversation to Rebecca who was busy in the dining room superintending the preparation for dinner.

She gave her consent and Jenkins returned to the parlor to convey the answer.

The following Friday evening was determined on as the time when Jenkins should be introduced to the Rev. Dr Siddons.

The evening came and Mr. Carrol, for that was the name of the gentleman who was interesting himself in the spiritual welfare of Jenkins—called at the study of the Reverened gentleman in company with the new recruit.

Dr. Siddons seemed much pleased with the young man. It appeared to increase the interest he had in Jenkins when the Reverend gentleman was informed that the young man was a son of the South.

He found Jenkins able to converse with him without tha embarassment usually attending the first interviews of a novice with distinguished men. Jenkins had inherited this quality partly from his mother. He had never suffered that seclusion which is the fate of so many young men. Visitors to the Castleton family often found Jenkins in the parlor. He was introduced to them generally in the conventional formalities that usually accompany such occurences. He was encouraged by Rebecca to join in the conversation, and the presence of his mother, who always knew how to give him some sign of warning only perceptable to himself whenever he was becoming over-forward, reminded him of the modesty that should characterize a youth when in the company of his elders.

Thus the stiffness and awkwardness which the average youth possesses in company was early removed in the case of Jenkins. The experience and exigencies of the parlor had also materially increased his conversational power and quickened his thinking faculties.

So Jenkins made a very favorable impression upon the Reverend Doctor. The following Sunday a new member was added to the Bible Class of the Assistant Minister of the church.

Dr. Siddons' had also a new listener to his sermon that Sunday in the shape of a young man whose erect bearing and intellectual appearance attracted no little attention as he was ushered up the aisle. It might be remarked here that Jenkins was regarded by many as handsome. He had soft looking hazel eyes and a countenance that wore almost constantly a pleasing expression. His cheeks, too, were tinted with a ruddy glow—so much so that fairer ones than he were wont to sometimes coyishly remark that he was a skillful user of toilet paints. "It is only the skill of nature's brush," Jenkins would remark with an air of some satisfaction in reply to these allusions.

The account Jenkins gave at dinner that Sunday of his impressions of the new churrh he was attending showed that he as well as others was very well pleased.

A few months after this Sunday we have just spoken of a Literary Entertainment was given by the young people of Dr. Siddons' church in aid of Foreign Missions. The committee who were arranging the affair requested the teachers of the Sunday School to endeavor to find any of their scholars who would be able to recite or declaim at the entertainment.

It so happened that Jenkins since his earliest years had been a reciter.

He had a good voice, and Rebecca took great pains to see that it was properly cultivated.

Jenkins wore a gold medal on his watch chain which was the trophy of victory in an Oratorical Prize Contest at the Academy Commencement at Burleigh.

It so happened that Jenkins' teacher spied this medal. He, of course, inquired for what it had been awarded. Jenkins told him.

"Just the man our committee have been looking for," said the somewhat astonished assistant. "We intend giving an entertainment in aid of Foreign Missions next Thursday evening week. Now I will report your name, and I hope you will prepare something for us."

Jenkins with the modesty characteristic of a youth who had been under the tutorage of Rebecca Castleton, demurred, saying that he felt scarcely able to recite before such a large and critical audience as no doubt would be present on that evening; and further that there were so many older and better fitted than he that he thought it more appropriate that they should take part.

The assistant observed that there was a degree of technicality about this reply which did not smack much of novicity or incapacity.

"That medal of yours, Mr. Jenkins, speaks very forcibly of your ability.

"I have no scruples about your being able to acquit yourself creditably," said the gentleman.

With this Jenkins consented. He was in reality not much displeased at this opportunity to distinguish himself and it spurred him on to endeavor to do his best.

The night came, and the name of Jenkins Castleton appeared on the elegantly printed programmes. No little curiosity was manifested by some of the audience to know who Jenkins Castleton was. While he had attended services at the Church and Sunday School pretty regularly, he had not become personally acquainted with many of the congregation. More, however, knew Jenkins by sight than knew his name.

The selection Jenkins had made was a touching poem entitled "Our Folks."

It represented two soldiers of the war for the Union in

conversation. One of them had been home on a furlough and was just then returning into camp. The other soldier, anxious to hear the news from home, accosts him and animatedly inquires "How the folks do?" after reciting how in battle—

"When hot saltpetre flames and smokes,
  While whole batallions lie afield,
One's apt to think about his folks!"

he asks about

"The old man, is he hearty yet?
  And mother—does she fade at all?
Or does she seem to pine and fret
  For me; and Sis'—has she grown tall,
And—did—you—see her friend, you know?
  —That Annie Moss; TELL me, Hal,
A lot of news about our folks."

His comrade tells the soldier eager for news, that "all's well," but the last time he saw "Annie Moss" she was *in church*.

"That's likely, for she's always there!"

replied the soldier. "But," said the comrade,

'It was——a——FUNERAL.'
'A funeral! Who, Harry?
  How you shake and stare! Is this a hoax?
Why don't you tell me like a man
  What is the matter with our folks.'"

Is this scene too sacred for profane pen to picture? When honest love rears its noble temple in the human heart and when the structure in a moment's time, with no syllable of warning, is uprooted at its foundations, and tottering, crumbles into nothingness; reader, wouldst thou then wish for some anæsthetic that would speed thee unconsciously past the ruins which bespeak a heart's anguish? Or wouldst thou rather for an instant behold the scene, and then imbibe a copious draught of some Lethian nectar.

"I said *all well*, old comrade true,
    I say *all well*, for He knows best,
Who takes the young ones in his arms,
    Before the sun goes to the west.
The ax-man Death deals right and left,
    And *flowers* fall as well as oaks,—
So fair Annie blooms no more,
    And *that's* the matter with your folks!

See, this curl was kept for yon,
    And this white blossom from her breast;
And here—your sister Bessie wrote;
    A letter telling all the rest.
Bear up, old friend, bear up!'
    Nobody speaks,—the old camp raven croaks,
And soldiers whisper, "Boys, be still, there's
    Some bad news from Granger's folks!'

He turns his back,—the only foe
    That ever saw it,—on this grief,
And, as men will, keeps back the tears
    Kind nature sends to woe's relief.
Then answered he, 'Ah, Hal, I'll try,
    But in my throat there's something chokes,
Because you see, I've thought *so* long
    To count her in among our folks.

> "I s'pose she must be happy now;
>   But still I will keep thinking too,
> I might have kept all trouble off
>   By being tender, kind and true.
> But *maybe not!* She's safe up there;
>   And when His hand deals other strokes,
> She'll stand by Heaven's gate, I know,
>   And wait to welcome in "Our folks."'

As Jenkins, on this evening, recited this noble poem, its pathos filled his soul. He spoke it as nature would have spoken it. He was as oblivious of his surroundings as were the inanimate pillars that supported the edifice.

When he told of the raging battle his eye gleamed with all the fire of the soldier. How he softened when he asked if "Mother fades at all?" When he eagerly leaned forward to learn of "Annie Moss," his countenance glowed with all the burning light of expectant love. Eyes tear-dimmed by natural feeling and the quivering voice of a lover's grief characterized the speaker in the closing part of the poem. As

> "The ear distinctly tells,
>   In the jangling,
>   And the wrangling,
> How the danger sinks and swells,
> By the sinking or the swelling in the anger of the bells,

so did the spirits of Jenkins Castleton's hearers that night sink and swell, as the speaker's emotions guided them.

There was *one* in that audience whose eye followed

Jenkins as he returned with slow and soft step to his seat, as if recognizing the solemnity of the scene, one who was endeavoring by means of her eyes to satisfy herself whether she was in a soldiers' camp or not. Was it fiction or reality?

She believed veritably that the young man must really be the grief-stricken soldier. No, that could not be, for there was no camp around her. "If *this* be fiction, what must be the sublimity of the reality?" So thought she then.

At the close of the exercises of this evening, which was destined to be an eventful one for Jenkins Castleton, the number of the audience who crowded around the young reciter to shake his hand and offer their congratulations was so many that for once he was bewildered.

Dr. Siddons was among the first to congratulate him, and the Reverend Doctor stood beside the young man, on whom many eyes were now turned, and introduced those who came up to offer their congratulations. There was a goodly number of ladies in the audience. These were not the most backward in wishing to congratulate young Jenkins. Some of them were more eager than the rest, and *one* was more eager than all. It was she who had been so impressed by the pathetic story and by its reciter, that, as was observed above, she looked long at Jenkins to satisfy herself as to her real whereabouts.

"Miss Ida Lexter," said Dr. Siddons as he presented to Jenkins the young lady who had been so impressed with the story of love.

"Mr. Castleton," said she, "I do not know when I have enjoyed a literary performance so much as your recital of 'Our Folks.'"

Jenkins, who had stood pretty well the shower of compliments that had preceded this one, was now somewhat confused because of the one who passed it. He knew that the Lexters were among the wealthiest and most prominent families in the congregation, and Miss Ida, though quite young—being a little over fifteen years of age—was the belle of the Sunday School; and in church a stranger's eye was sure to light upon her, and sometimes also to linger there, the beholder being the while beguiled of spiritual thoughts. On the evening in question Miss Ida was attired in a rich costume, and her ornaments, though elegant, were modest—the acme of good taste.

Jenkins recovered from his embarrassment in a moment and replied to the compliment by courteously saying: "I am glad to have been able to afford you some enjoyment, and only regret that I could not make it even more acceptable."

Miss Ida Lexter lingered for quite awhile to converse with Jenkins. She seemed much pleased with his conversation and manners. So the evening's entertainment being over, Miss Ida gave Jenkins a very graceful bow as he raised his hat to bid her good evening at the door.

CHAPTER XXIX.

JENKINS IN A NEW ROLE.

THE time for the closing of the great Exhibition was drawing near. The "Castleton House" was still well patronized. But it could not be judged what would be the state of affairs when the influx of visitors was stopped by reason of the closing of the exhibition. This was a matter which seriously engaged the attention of Dr. Castleton and Rebecca.

Finally the end came. The fears about the effect of the closing of the exhibition upon the business of the "Castleton House" proved to be well founded. It was under a high rent, while not half of its many rooms were filled with guests.

The experience with the "Dickens House" in Burleigh was about to be repeated. Though Dr. Castleton could not complain of the patronage the hotel had received, yet the expenses had been great, as well as the income large. After all it was found that no great amount of money had been made.

It was concluded, therefore, to give up the "Castleton

House," to rent a dwelling on as good a street as their means would afford, and that Dr. Castleton should resume the practice of his profession. So a house was secured on Ash street, a not undesirable location, and after sufficient furniture, then used in the hotel, had been reserved for the new dwelling and the surplus sold, the "Castleton House" was deserted.

Disappointment came again; Dr. Castleton's practice was not what he had expected. Besides it was the middle of winter, a time when domestic expenses in Philopolis are great.

As yet, Jenkins had not started to school. The sights to be seen had been so great and so many, that he doubted if he could give his mind to study. He now, for the first time, perceived the despondency that was beginning to weigh upon Dr. Castleton. Jenkins noticed that fewer dainties appeared on the dining table; that the only servant employed about the house was discharged; and that Rebecca was performing most of the household duties herself. These things Jenkins noticed, and he pondered over them.

One morning after breakfast, he was occupied in reading the morning paper—this he never failed to do—when suddenly he said to Rebecca: "Mother, there is an advertisement here I would like to read to you."

"Well, read it, my son."

F

Jenkins read :

" 'WANTED—A YOUNG MAN OF GOOD ADDRESS and some education, to act as general assistant to the proprietor of a retail dry goods and notion house. Apply, after 3 o'clock p. m., to PHILIP D. ERSKINE, corner of DeHaven and Ludlow streets.'

"Now, mother, I have been thinking for several days whether I could not be of some material assistance to you. I am in good health, and the school year is nearly over. Anyhow, I thought I would endeavor to get some business position, for a while at least. I think I am able to do this, and I am sure I am willing to do it."

Rebecca did not reply to her son's remarks for a long time. Jenkins saw that she was troubled.

"Mother," he said, at length, "I will go up street awhile, and we will talk about this matter again when I return."

So saying, he donned his overcoat and hat, and hastened away. He divined the reason of his mother's silence. He knew that it would go exceedingly hard with her to see her son's education interfered with. When once he entered the business world, would she ever be able to take him out of it and accomplish the long cherished wish of her heart—the education of her eldest son.

These were the thoughts that Jenkins judged were occupying his mother's mind. So he resolved that he would relieve her of the pain of pronouncing the word and would take it voluntarily upon himself.

"Is Mr. Erskine in?" said Jenkins Castleton to one of the salesmen whom he encountered as he entered the establishment of Mr. Philip D. Erskine.

"Yes, sir; step in the counting room," said the man.

Jenkins proceeded to where he was directed, and there found Mr. Erskine. Jenkins' polite address, his conversation, which was much above the ordinary, made their usual impression.

"Mr. Castleton, the position is open to you," at length said Mr. Erskine.

"When shall I begin?" asked Jenkins.

"To-morrow morning, if you wish," replied the proprietor.

Mr. Erskine then invited his new employee to accompany him, that he might show him around the establishment and introduce him to those with whom he would come in daily contact. Jenkins readily consented.

The store was quite on the *qui vive* over the new assistant, especially the many young salesladies who occupied positions behind the counters.

Mr. Erskine introduced Jenkins to some of these. The gentle manner of the young Southerner, his suavity, and his deference—so different from the plain, matter-of-fact way of the average Philopolitan—greatly charmed the young misses.

Jenkins returned home well satisfied with what he had

accomplished. He gave the family a budget of surprises at the tea-table that evening. Jenkins was careful enough to present the matter in the best light possible. He would remain in his new position only until the following Autumn, when he would be able to resume his studies again. His duties were light, and as far as he could judge from first appearances, the people of the establishment were agreeable.

"Well, we will do the best we can, my child," said Rebecca.

"I am entirely opposed to the whole proceeding," declared Dr. Castleton with some warmth. "Who put this idea into your head, Jenkins?"

"I decided upon this course myself. I feel that for the present it is best for me. I do not loose much time, and the experience and knowledge I will gain of men and things may be of some use to me in after life," said the son.

"I prefer that you should do without some extras which your salary will enable you and probably us also to have rather than get them at the cost of drudgery and loss of time from study," answered Dr. Castleton.

"Lawrence, you remember that Shelton family who lived a few doors from us in Burleigh. They owned quite a large place you know; had a garden which extended back for nearly a whole square, and had also a yard full of cedar and magnolia trees in the midst of which stood their house—an attractive place altogether. There were five daughters and three sons in the family.

"They owned a number of slaves before the war. But after it was over they all left them. Mr. Shelton's income as a lawyer was very limited—scarcely sufficient to supply his large family with the necessaries of life. You recollect well how that family lived. They hired five servants—two cooks, two chamber-maids and a negro man. By the time all these were paid, it left hardly enough to clothe them decently and to supply other necessaries. Mr. Shelton wore one single suit, week-days and Sundays, for a whole year. Mrs. Shelton rarely left the house, because she had not proper clothing.

"Their daughter Fannie, eighteen years of age, went half as well dressed as she should have been. Yet how did they occupy themselves? Mrs. Shelton sat all day in a rocking chair in the sitting room. Whenever she wanted a drink of water, or if doing a little fancy work, a spool of thread from the work-box, she called one of the servants to bring it to her—just as she did in slavery times. As to Fannie, she took up her time visiting around and napping—not ever a dust-brush or a broom, or ever the making up of a bed occupied her for a moment.

"The boys, one of them was at school, but the other one would not go, but roamed around the streets or the play grounds. Such a thing as one of those boys taking a business position, or the mother and daughter doing some of the housework, and thus enabling them to use some of the money spent in servant hire to buy themselves proper clothing with, such an idea as this never once entered their heads. Oh, no! It would never do for the sons and daughters of Lawyer Shelton 'to work.'

"Now, Lawrence, do you know that I think those people were extremely foolish. When circumstances change so greatly, it is no dishonor to bow to necessity."

Thus spoke Rebecca. Dr. Castleton merely observed that "Mr. Shelton was right in keeping his family from doing 'nigger work.'" It was still the contest between the Old and the New.

CHAPTER XXX.

A FEW GALLANTRIES.

WHEN Jenkins presented himself the following morning after his first visit to the establishment of Mr. Philip D. Erskine and reported for duty, he received a more detailed account of the requirements of his new position. When not assisting Mr. Erskine in the counting room, he was to be out in the store directing customers to the proper counters and seeing that they were waited upon; in other words, perform the duties of what is called in the parlance of the shop-keepers, a "floor-walker."

Jenkins' courtesy and politeness showed to great advantage on these occasions. The intonation of Jenkins' question, "What do you wish to see, madam?" and the graceful bow that always preceded it gave a pleased expression which it did not often wear, to the countenance of many a customer.

Jenkins also addressed the salesladies as if they were *ladies*. He never, in all the time he remained with Mr. Erskine, addressed them in the gruff style of the floor-walker: "Sallie, show this lady some feathers!" but Jenkins' form would be: "Miss Sallie."

Some of the shelves that held Mr. Erskine's goods were very high. Often the salesladies would have to climb up the step ladder and strain themselves to reach what they wanted; and as often, when they did reach it, the box or other article would be so heavy, that the young lady would have to let it drop with a great thud upon the counter. Jenkins never neglected an opportunity to climb this step-ladder and relieve the salesladies of this labor when he could. For these little acts of kindness and attention Jenkins was highly respected by those with whom he served. As might be expected, among twenty-five young ladies there would be some more pretty or prepossessing than others. It was now and then whispered against Jenkins that he sometimes showed a slight partiality on behalf of one or two. For instance, such small matters as these would be alleged in support of the charge: Three of the salesladies would be unoccupied. A customer comes in to be waited upon. Jenkins has to assign *one* of these ladies to wait upon this customer. He would, according to this charge, invariably call some other than his favorite to perform the duty.

Another circumstance which did not escape the notice of these shrewd observers was that Jenkins, at the tea table (for Mr. Erskine kept the store open in the evening [night], and as many of his employees lived a good distance away, supper was served to them in rooms on the upper floors), it was further alleged, Jenkins would generally contrive to sit by one or else between two of his favorites!

Alas, for the fallen nature of man, there was only too much truth in these charges against the gallant Jenkins. It must be said, however, in palliation of this misdoing, that the favored ones never received an expression from Jenkins that he ever especially exerted himself to make their lot lighter. All they had to judge from was the action of the young man. Neither did Jenkins ever show his preference in such a way that it would be unpleasantly noticeable.

To ward off suspicion he would sometimes call one of his favorites to perform a duty which he might have imposed upon any of the others.

Let us do the young man the further justice of examining his motive for all this.

Jenkins did not employ his spare moments in idleness. He was off from the store two evenings in the week. These he spent in reading and study. Many a time when there was not much business going on, Jenkins would be walking slowly up and down the Erskine establishment (for proprietors do not allow their employees, male or female, to sit down when they are not busy). All have to stand or walk up and down the floor. Jenkins, as he often paced that floor on some unbusy day, found much in what he saw around him to give him food for thought and reflection.

Jenkins would often hear their complaints of weariness and see the haggard look of these young women who stood behind those counters.

One of his so-called "favorites" had been employed in the store since she was fourteen years of age. She was then just twenty. Jenkins detected in this young woman the elements not only of physical, but of intellectual and moral beauty. He heard a conversation on one occasion between several of the salesladies—a conversation which though spoken of the living, reminded Jenkins of those touching lines of the poet on not the physical, but the living, "Death of the young and Fair:"

"She died in beauty, like a rose blown from its parent stem,
She died in beauty, like a pearl dropped from some diadem."

They were talking of the past.

Said one: "Annie, you were not here, were you, when Sallie Thompson first came here?" "No," said the one addressed, "I was not."

"Well," continued the other, "she was just fourteen. I don't think I ever saw a prettier girl. Her cheeks were as round and rosy as they could be. Her blue eyes were always glistening like agates and she was so full of life, too. But I never saw anybody change as she has.

"Look at her how slowly she walks across the floor now. She rarely ever laughs, and she has always a tired look. Her cheeks are quite sunken in, her skin looks as if she were getting toughened in some way, and it has lost its color.

"I am sorry for Sallie. I hope though she will get all right again sometime."

Jenkins heard this conversation. It made a profound impression upon him. He pondered over these things.

He presently saw Sallie Thompson coming across the floor. In spite of the assault upon her constitution of six years of standing from morning till late at night, in the dust and dirt of shelves and boxes, the once ruddy glow of her cheeks struggled very hard to show itself, and it succeeded, though faintly. Still it was sufficient to indicate what *once* was there. Her eyes were yet bright, but looked like a flickering flame.

"She has," thought Jenkins, "had a cruel fate. The youth which God gives to his fair children was, I believe, given them that their bodies might develope fully, that their minds might grow and increase in knowledge, and lastly that their hearts might be light. Womanhood will bring cares enough and more than enough. The oases of their lives are the sweet years of youth which were not given for such labor.

"I am sorry for the necessity which compels such beautiful beings to be imprisoned during the springtime of their lives behind the counters of stores or within the walls of factories. There must be something wrong—fundamentally wrong—in the civilization which nourishes such a state of things as this."

Do you wonder, reader, that Sallie Thompson was one of Jenkins' "favorites?"

Another of his "favorites" was a young woman whose story is shorter, but pathetic enough.

Living in easy circumstances until she was nineteen years of age, educated and refined she looked forward to a happy future. But her father died, and left not enough to support his wife and two daughters. So she found herself, just as she was merging into womanhood, a servant at the counter—for how long she knew not.

Their marriage was the great haven of rest from their labors which these young women looked longingly forward to. This was their beacon star of hope, which shining, sometimes sped their weary hours along more cheerily.

But what is the mature age of such youth as they have had? Their physical frames strained and distorted by unnatural toil, they become imperfect women. The children they bear are degenerate and unhealthy and rarely reach maturity; and a premature death in the midst of what should have been a vigorous womanhood keeps mother and child from long being separated!

So there were some grounds for the sad feelings of

Jenkins, and his conscience was satisfied in regard to the "favoritism."

Taught by Rebecca to look with disgust upon the sloth and idleness which pervaded to too great an extent his native South,—as seen in the case of the Shelton family—his own natural feelings taught him to abhor the excessive labor which holds in bondage so great a number of the fairest young women of the North! "Sloth," he would sometimes say to Rebecca, "is wicked, but I tell you, mother, there is a labor, too, that is also wicked."

Jenkins, no doubt, knew well that all women could not live without laboring in their young days. But what puzzled him was why in a family of six children—three brothers over twenty-one years of age—all strong and healthy; three daughters, and a father drawing a good salary as a mechanic, why it was necessary for those daughters at twelve or fourteen years of age to be sent to a store or shop or mill to remain until they were twenty or twenty-five or for all their lives if they never married? Jenkins could never see why their brothers and their father could not support that family without inflicting such drudgery upon the young girls!

Jenkins looked around him and he found everywhere women doing the work of men. He saw the children of a man busy in the factories and shops and the father himself idle,—unable to get work because the children of other fathers were doing labor that otherwise he could get to do!

Jenkins would get on board a street car. He there saw strong, able-bodied men occupying the seats, and ladies, old and young, standing up clinging to the strap that dangled from the top of the car! No seats were offered to these ladies, and the men were as quiet and unconcerned at the scene as if they were acting perfectly right and proper.

Jenkins passed down the fashionable street of Philopolis. He saw palatial residences owned by men who for the mere sake of money, not for a whit's good to their minds or for the cultivation of the moral faculties—no not for this, no time to devote to such whims as these, but who for money and money only labored day and night, as slaves, from their earliest youth to the latest hour when age would allow them another day's laboring. They early put their sons through the same course.

They did this, when with half the wealth, half the splendor —and they would yet have had much—they might have saved a part of their youth to themselves and to their sons also, saved it for light-heartedness, for joy and for the cultivation of the lofty intellectual faculties with which the Creator has endowed us all, and for the nurturing, expanding and developing of the moral faculties—even more noble than the intellectual. But no time for this. Not ten years out of seventy for these things! Lucre, lucre, give me lucre!

Jenkins pondered over all this.

CHAPTER XXXI.

WAS IT LOVE?

JENKINS was attentive to his church duties. He was found at his post in Sunday School nearly every Sabbath.

The Librarian of the school resigned his position, and the Superintendent in looking around for a successor, decided upon Mr. Jenkins Castleton. The latter accepted and entered upon the discharge of his duties.

This new state of affairs brought Jenkins in more close contact with the members of the Sunday School.

Miss Ida Lexter now found an opportunity to congratulate Jenkins upon his new honor.

We have seen before that our young man was more or less of an admirer of the fairer sex, and he was by no means insensible of the notice he was attracting from the much admired Miss Lexter. But Jenkins bore himself with dignified reserve. He never endeavored to make himself too familiar. Many who received a bow or a smile from the young beauty, thought it was very encouraging for them, and they at once made further advances. But, alas, they had reckoned without their host! Her declination of their attentions was so positive that it left no room for doubt. A courteous bow in the church corridor, or a passing remark in the Sunday School room if they chanced to meet was all the best of them received.

So, when Miss Ida would present herself at the library railing to exchange or take out some volume, a good many noticed that Mr. Jenkins was very attentive, and that the two conversed much *more* over the taking out of a book than was observed in other cases.

The very fact that Jenkins did not attempt to become more intimate, even after unusual attentions from the proud Miss Ida, and that while others took pains to cross her path when Sunday School was over and endeavored to hold her in conversation, Jenkins, on the other hand, always, when he had finished his library duties, walked out the straightest way he could, and gave simply his polite bow if he happened to catch her eye, but did not twist his head all around, or walk in a zig-zag line to the door to do so; this dignified behavior of the young Librarian impressed Miss Ida with the fact that here at least was a spirit as high as hers. This trait in Jenkins was a great attraction in the eyes of the fair charmer. Jenkins was the first one she had found who had withstood the assaults of her attentions. She discovered also that the young Southerner combined no mean intellectuality with his refined manners. His conversation was apt and more finished than that of other young men she knew, to whom wealth of money gave not wealth of mind.

Ida Lexter was one who wanted no riches but those of the heart, and no greatness but that of the soul. She was well worthy of the noble aspiration. Refined, educated, and with it all beautiful ; she had good grounds for her pride. Hers was not a cynical pride. It was simply a high-mindedness which fashioned for itself a noble ideality.

For two years Jenkins had been an attendant at Dr. Siddon's church.

The Good Friday came, on which he was received into the fellswship of God's Annointed. Ida Lexter had knelt at that same altar more than a year before. She seemed happy on this Good Friday evening for some reason. We hope it was because her heart was filled with Christian joy, that it was a holy gladness because of one who had remembered his Creator in the days of his youth.

Easter came and went, and Summer was at hand. It was the time of vacations and country rambles. It was when one loves to loiter by the sea and hear the roar of the wind-shaked surge as it breaks upon the ocean's foaming shore.

Jenkins, after eight months of service was given the usual period for recreation.

F*

His life during these months had been almost unvarying. At his post during the week, at Sunday School and church on the Sabbath. His evenings off were mostly spent at home, or sometimes in making a social visit to a friend. He was not so much dissatisfied with a life of business as he had anticipated. He had good health and, as we have previously observed, he was gaining an experience and knowledge of men and things which would be of value to him in after life.

Jenkins was puzzled in selecting a suitable place for spending his vacation. Philopolis was surrounded with so many and varied Summer Resorts that it would seem a person of whatever taste imaginable might find a congenial place of recreation. Less than a hundred miles away was the sea; the great river that flowed by the city was dotted with beautiful and cool resorts. In easy access by the railroads were the mountains and many points of interest in the interior

Jenkins consulted Dr. Castleton and Rebecca about his choice. They both thought that he would enjoy the mountains better than the seashore.

This much decided, Jenkins himself was left to choose the particular place to which he would go.

He looked over the various accounts he could find of mountain resorts, and finally selected "Tyro's Glen" as the most desirable and interesting. Jenkins left early in the season, before the great band of tourists commenced their summer rounds.

It was the middle of June when he arrived at the famous Glen. It was about three hundred miles distant from Philopolis. The route to it led through some of the most wild and picturesque scenery in America. Jenkins was enchanted with the towering granite crests, and with the railroad stretching for a hundred and fifty miles along the banks of a curling river that forced itself through the mountians.

Arriving at the Glen, he ascended to the high summit and took quarters at the "Tyro Mountain House" which stood "'twixt earth and heaven" to give the traveller a finer view of both. . .

Jenkins arrived just at breakfast time. He partook of this meal as hastily as possible, as he was all eagerness to feast at the banquet of nature which he knew awaited him in the mighty gorge beneath his feet.

Having finished his hasty meal, he purchased a guide-book and started to explore the Glen.

It was, as we have seen, early in the season, and so Jenkins found himself dsecending to the bottom of the gorge with no human being in sight but himself.

As he went down step by step, he would every now and then pause to gaze above him and below at the dizzy precipices that formed the chasm. There the walls stood almost perpendicularly, five hundred feet high! It looked as though the Almighty in a moment of his wrath had smitten the great rock and clove it in twain! High above his head the clouds peered down upon him; the sun's rays strove for admission; the turbid stream which dashed along the bottom, the trembling foliage which skirted the gorge's brink, the weird rythm of the rocks, the rustling winds, the awful depth, the giddy height—all these spoke forth the wild, unlettered, yet harmonious, notes, of nature's eloquence.

He was alone with God and his wondrous works!

His soul unconsciously uttered an apostrophe to heaven. No auditors were there save the laughing waters, the rocks, the winds and the trees. Perchance the birds heard him, for their songs broke in upon the silence caused by the speaker's reverential pauses.

"How infinitely little is man, how infinitely great art Thou," spoke the youth whom the God of Nature had so profoundly moved by His works. "What am I in these presence?" thought he.

It was truly a scene of grandeur, and not more noble were the inanimate immensities around him than was this youth who had the soul to appreciate, and the eye for beauty to admire them. Jenkins had never beheld the equal of the scene. It was no doubt this which caused it to make such an impression upon him.

He descended still lower down until he arrived at the water's edge. Here he viewed how the stream was coursing, clear as dew-drop, down its rocky pathway. He then saw what had caused the great formation he had so admired.

This stream had been flowing for ages over the mountain and had gradually worn the rock away. This process had continued for so long that three miles of pathway had been cut through a mountain of granite. The stream made many windings, and the acute angles of the lofty walls gave ample evidence of its eccentricities.

Innumerable cascades and waterfalls played their melodies over the rock-bound course.

Chameleon pools of water in basins so round that the beholder cannot but believe that they were bored in the rocky bed by some circular drill, give variety to the scene. The water itself is as clear as crystal, and when the sun shines into these pools, each little wavelet on the surface of the water reflects the colors of the rainbow, while the pebbles on the bottom are given the richest hues, looking as if they were a variegated nest of Sapphires, Emeralds and Pearls—the whole forming a scene upon which the eye can dote in ecstacy for hours.

Jenkins continued his explorations of the enchanting scene. Further up the glen the path leads to a rustic bridge which crosses the stream. Here the gorge is wider, and an abrupt turn of the course of the water has formed an angle, beyond which nothing can be seen until the turn is made into that portion of the gorge.

Jenkins was standing in the middle of this bridge and was leaning upon the railing which skirted its sides. He was looking down the long, rocky vista, admiring the ever changing views which every turn of the eye afforded.

The sunlight shimmering down through the foliage struck into the pools, waking their crystal depths into life; —myriad were the phases of magical beauty which held him admirer.

Wrapt up in contemplation of this scene, Jenkins was startled to hear his own name echoing up from beneath him!

He turned slightly around, but seeing no one he concluded it was only his imagination. So he resumed his former position and looked once more at the ever bewitching prospect.

Again, in notes more silvery than before, he heard his name pronounced! "That voice! It sounds strangely familiar!" said the now bewildered youth. There was no mistaking of the word.

He stood still, dwelling upon the memory of the sound which had greeted his ears. If ever he was pale from mysterious awe it was then. He banished the interpretation he had put upon the voice as vain and foolish.

"It could not be hers, yet I'd swear to the sound."

Just then a foot-step on the other end of the bridge roused him from his reverie.

"Miss Ida! It cannot——"

"Jenkins!"

When he recovered his self-possession sufficienty to realize where he was, Jenkins Castleton found that he held in his embrace the unconscious form of the fair Ida Lexter!

CHAPTER XXXII.

TROUBLES.

WHILE Jenkins was away enjoying his vacation, Rebecca was not idle. She was thinking and planning for the future.

She was most anxious that Jenkins should resume his studies in the Autumn.

Dr. Castleton's practice, in conjunction with Jenkins' salary, had been just sufficient for sustaining the family comfortably. Jenkins' two younger brothers, Lee and Cassius, had been attending the public schools of Philopolis, and had made satisfactory progress. While not neglecting attention to her other children, Jenkins was the great object of her solicitude. She was happy to find that each of her boys was one of promise, but of Jenkins she had the greatest hopes. She had watched over his daily life, and had taken every pains to instill into his youthful heart principles of morality and rectitude. As he was naturally studious, she had been gratified to find that her only duty in regard to the suitable education of her eldest son had been to place the means of study within his reach, and the end was accomplished. She gave the tools to the mental mechanic, and immediately the restless machinery of mind would be in motion. A *desire* for knowledge is the mother, and *inborn genius* is the sire, of greatness.

Rebecca saw that Jenkins was unmistakably descended from the mother, and there were also indications that there coursed through his veins the blood of the sire.

So Rebecca visited one afternoon the principal of one of the prominent academies of Philopolis. She made arrangements with him for preparing Jenkins for college. He was to commence the following September. She decided not to write to Jenkins about this. She wanted to prepare a little surprise for him when he returned home.

It is unnecessary to add that the measures taken for finishing Jenkins' education in the North were not approved of by Dr. Castleton. Such a prospect greatly troubled him. "He would rather," he said, "that Jenkins should be taught at home the best he could until they were able to send him South to one of the 'traditional colleges!'" Unwilling to receive the New, he still grasped at the shadow of the Old when its substance was gone.

CHAPTER XXXIII.

A REVELATION.

" Your father's house was noble, though decayed,
And worthy by its birth to match with ours."

TYRO'S Glen wore its wonted aspect. "The regular confusion" of its waters and its granite sentinels gave each other their accustomed counter-sign; not so with the two who had so unexpectedly met on the rustic bridge. Their souls, their emotions, surged more wildly than did the plunging waters of Tyro's Glen.

There had come to Ida Lexter, and to Jenkins Castleton, from whence, they knew not; how, they could not tell—a revelation.

As he looked upon that form, he still clasped in his arms; as her flowing locks waved gracefully over her fair shoulders—as he heard the sobs of joy or grief, he knew not which, our hero stooped to gently kiss the brow that leaned confidingly upon his breast; not a syllable had yet escaped from either of the pair.

"Jenkins," at length said Ida, now recovered, and looking softly up at the countenance which met her glance with that look which only lovers know, "Jenkins," almost unconsciously he clasped her hand in his, "I have cruelly wronged you," and then she wept.

"I do not understand you, Ida—shall I call you Ida? But do not weep this way. I cannot bear to see you thus," said Jenkins with his gentlest accent.

"How I have longed these many months for an opportunity to tell you all," she said.

Jenkins was mystified. He betook himself to thinking what it all could mean. Ida Lexter had changed, it seemed to him, into another being. She never appeared so beautiful as now. Where was that *hauteur* he imagined was hers. Her proud mien, her courtly manner now appeared enveloped in an irresistable mantle of meekness and love.

"If you have wronged me, I know it not," spoke Jenkins. "Even if you had, my fullest forgivness should be yours."

"O Jenkins," said she, "it cannot be that you are so noble as to speak that word to me. Do you not know, have you not felt, my injustice toward you?"

Ida had now become more calm; the magic word "forgiveness" had cast its spell over her.

"Ida—Miss I—"

"No," broke in she laughing gently, "I would rather you—, well, I really think simply Ida is a pretty name, don't you?"

Jenkins was subdued.

"Ida," said he, "I have never until this moment divined what you mean by wrong or injustice toward me."

"And what, may I ask, has dulled your perceptive faculties for so long," said Ida, looking half-smilingly to see what effect this little touch of irony produced.

Jenkins commenced an answer, but suddenly hesitated.

"Now, see," said the charmer, "if you cannot trust me with it."

"You ask what is the cause of my long dullness?" He drew her close to him and looking into the face which beamed upon him, said softly: "The cause may have been my love for you."

The revelation was complete.

The lovers talked long and confidingly together. The wrong which Ida Lexter thought she had inflicted upon Jenkins was that, though she had led him to think by her way of acting that she held him in the highest regard, yet she did not give him an opportunity to return it.

A good many secrets which unspoken love keeps hid came out in the course of their conversation. Their inmost thoughts found utterance. Jenkins declared that though he had breathed the secret to no one, yet he had found himself a lover since the first day he met Ida Lexter!

"The reality of love is sublimer than its fiction!" said Jenkins.

This allusion to the recitation of "Our Folks" awakened a new train of reminiscences.

"I only hope I can make the reality worthy of you. When I entered the Glen this morning I was carried away by thoughts of the wondrous beauty of God's works. Is there a more fitting spot in all the earth for our hearts to beat in unison of love than here, my dear Ida? You are more beautiful to me than all I've beheld to-day" And, full of lover's hope, and happy with a lover's joy, he kissed her ruby lips again!

But presently a look of sadness came over the lover's face.

"Ida, have you thought that my only riches is your love and my only hope, myself?"

Jenkins Castleton thought of the palatial mansion where lived his Ida. He thought of the many wealthy heirs who awaited her, humble suitors for her hand.

"What am I" he would think, "that I should win the hand and heart of such an one?"

"Jenkins, are we not rich in each other's love? What else need we?"—and here she quoted to the scrupulous lover the poet's lines:

> "Your father's house was noble though decayed,
> And worthy by its birth to match with ours,"

CHAPTER XXXIV.

HE CALLED THE PILGRIM HOME.

"Tears fell when thou wert dying, from eyes unused to weep,
And long where thou art lying will tears the cold turf steep."

THE rigors of the Northern climate were sorely felt by the Castletons, reared as they were in the balmy South.

Little Cassius Castleton was the light of Rebecca's household. He was seven years of age, and just then in the happiest period of boyhood. He was a beautiful boy; large blue eyes, fair skin, a wealth of rich golden hair, which fell in dependent curls over his shoulders made him an object upon which a mother's heart loves to dote. He was so tender-hearted that he possessed the qualities of a daughter rather than a son.

It was the pride of Rebecca that in all his life she never found it necessary to give him a single stroke of chastisement. He was the pet of Dr. Castleton. It was his greatest solace to hold his little son upon his knee and talk with him. Little Cassius seemed to comfort much that man of sorrow, and to make his troubles lighter.

When Jenkins returned from his tour of pleasure, he found his home filled with grief. The severe cold of the winter following the spring in which the Castletons arrived in Philopolis was sorely felt. Little Cassius was started to school, but in March he was taken ill. He had great pains in his limbs, and was completely prostrated. It was found that he had acute rheumatism. He recovered somewhat and appeared to be convalescent. But not so. The dread disease attacked his heart, bringing on dropsy. Jenkins had, a few months before this, commenced to keep a diary. In this he noted the principal occurrences of the family. We will transcribe from this diary Jenkins' account of the death of his beloved brother:

"This period is rendered memorable to me by one of the saddest afflictions of my life—the death of my youngest brother, Cassius, the little bright boy who was the light of our household. The dread disease spread on him rapidly, and in a month or so his frame of faultless symmetry became a suffering, bloated mass.

"My father was with him every moment, and seemed to be wasting with his boy. Mother was grief-stricken.

"There was one circumstance which somewhat relieved the sadness of the situation: the sufferer could be propped up in an easy chair. He even could walk with a little assistance. During the long summer days he would sit propped up in his little chair in the front hall-way and enjoy himself looking at the passers-by and at the street incidents.

"Many sympathizing neighbors would endeavor to cheer him by acts of kindness and attention. They sent him also many little presents, for which he always thanked them with a smile.

"He never, for an instant, lost the use of his mental faculties. He would make his usual remarks about nearly everything he saw.

"Amid all his suffering he was patient and cheerful, and many a gladsome smile--born of a spirit which mortality could not reach—lit up his countenance.

"Disease had marred every feature, save his eyes. These were yet as bright as ever were shaded by human brows.

"The dropsy increased. The best medical talent was secured which the great colleges of Philopolis could furnish. They pronounced the case hopeless.

"By September we saw that his end was near. It was on Sunday, September 23d, 187—. In the afternoon of that day, probably with a premonition that death was near, my mother sent me for some friends of the family who resided on ——— street. They came.

"As it was inconvenient to assist the sufferer up and down stairs, a couch was prepared for him in one of the back parlors, on the ground floor. Little Cassius was reclining his head upon a centre-table which was placed between two windows which opened into the street from the front parlor, thus affording him a view of what was going on outside.

"Mrs. H———, the friend I had gone for, came in and endeavored to cheer the sufferer by her words of kindness.

"About 9.30 o'clock, my father, assisted by Mrs. H———, proceeded to put little Cassius to his bed. They rolled his chair toward the back parlor, which is connected with the front one by folding-doors. I sat in my seat watching them. As they rolled him on towards the door, little Cassius had his face turned toward me. Just as they had passed the door-facing and were getting out of sight by moving behind one of the folding-doors,—just as his chair was making the turn, Cassius looked at me. *I caught that look.* It was the last he ever gave me, and it is before me now, as vivid as it was when his dying eyes cast it on me. When they bent to lift him tenderly, lo, his spark of life had fled! How calmly and peacefully had his spirit flown! His battles were o'er; his struggles ended. On Tuesday, the 25th, we left our threshold to see him to his last resting place.

"Dr. Siddons performed the funeral ceremony, and with the beautiful and impressive services of the church, his body was lowered into the vault where it reposes to-day.

"Thus passed away a creature of earth. Death seems like a storm to strike down the most beautiful and noble structures. We seem born but to pass quickly away. Strange that it should be so. Strange that some are permitted to linger long on the shores of time, while others, in the zenith of their hope and beauty are gathered early into the sheaf.

"But

> 'The ax-man Death deals right and left
> And flowers fall as well as oaks.'"

A few days after the funeral, Jenkins composed with his own hand this poem, which makes up in devotion and love for what it lacks of rhythm.

"CASSIUS.

"His march from cradle to grave
So short a one the Maker gave,—
A bud blossomed but to fade,
To bloom and die only made.

"Vacant now is his wonted place,
Absent 'ere his beaming face:
Yet on memory's lasting page
Are they, undim'd by age.

"His gentle voice is silent now;
Nevermore to his cheek to bow
And implant the envied kiss,
Till met in the realms of bliss.

"The Autumn leaves were falling;
The angels gently calling,
Bade the innumerable throng
Rejoice, and unite for a song.

"One more spirit was ascending
To taste of the joys unending.
A gentle commotion did arise
Among the host in those sacred skies.

"'See, he cometh to the Throne of Grace
With a sweet Angelical pace"
He receiveth the blessing of the King;
Then in chorus a new song they sing.

" Opened here wide the book of life!
' Here's the name, which is no more strife ;
Wherein it is found on these pages
Partake thou of the wake of ages!'

" He taketh now the blissful rounds ;
Heaven is filled with joyful sounds !
Joy over the pure and guiltless one
That needed no repentance to be done.

" Cassius! Let thy spirit active be,
And fly o'er thy kindred below thee!
Let their end unceasing be at last
With thee to join when all else is past.

" Then throughout Eternity's endless years,
Reunited, no more parting, no more tears,
Forever, subject with thee and those
Of the realms of sweet repose!"

CHAPTER XXXV.

A GREAT ERA.

WE must now pass over two years in as many moments. We must follow Jenkins to the Academy. Having gone through the usual experience of a preparatory course for a year, we must find him robed in all the majesty of a college Freshman.

At college he was a conspicuous figure. He was farmed among his associates as "Orator Castleton." Class-meetings, "Philo," and all occasions of college festivity resounded with his extemporaneous oratory. His classmates were often enthusiastic on these occasions, and seemed to look upon the youth whose warm Southern blood, united with the broad idea of Northern solidity which were rapidly permeating his mind, as a kind of prodigy.

We would wish that we had the space to spare for relating in detail the adventures and experiences of Jenkins at the college of Philopolis. They would be exciting and interesting. But these we cannot give. Our book, like the age in which it is written, matures speedily.

Jenkins Castleton was a vorocious reader of the newspapers. He was as familiar with every fluctuation in the world of politics as were men who were politicians by profession.

We have said that Jenkins kept a diary of all things he did, said or heard worth recording.

We shall copy from this diary the impressions and feelings of the young man during this eventful period. We do not desire to picture a faultless hero, but the hero as he was. For this reason we shall transcribe *verbatim* what he wrote. Some of what the reader will here peruse, he will see would never have been written by a wiser or more prudent thinker than was Jenkins at this time. He was unhinged by the unbridled bent of youthful enthusiasm. But with it all he was earnest. He felt in his very soul every word he uttered. This will excuse many faults.

We give his opinions as showing the effect of an ancestry of *tradition*, an infancy of *war*, and a boyhood of *strife* upon the youthful mind of an American. If these effects have been evil, let their cause be removed completely and forever, that future generations may be saved from a like fate.

"Well, a year at college; a year at a Northern college; I might fill a volume with what I think. But I forbear. Suffice it for me to say that the college of Philopolis will exercise an important influence on my life. Its memories, its teachings will be long felt and retained.

"But outside of college; in the stir and bustle of Philopolis—here is where my triumphs and my defeats have been accomplished; and here I first set sail my fragile bark upon the sea of politics.

"I will jot down the most important of my doings outside of college. These are many.

"I must, in all candor, say that I have somewhat neglected my college studies for other matters, such as literary societies (I belong to three), lectures, social entertainments and the like. As I have acquired somewhat a reputation as an elocutionist, I am called upon by a good many churches to assist them at literary entertainments.

"This takes up my time; I attend them and have to get up early the next morning, and learn my college lessons. But most of my spare moments were taken up in reading political history.

"In June of this year, there assembled in the city Riago, the Rupublican National Convention to nominate a candidate for President of the United States. *   *   *   *   *

"This convention had more to settle than to name the candidate. A great American principle was either to be rejected by it, or be more firmly established in the hearts of the people than ever before.

"General Uriah S. Gover was a most prominent name before the convention, and he represented in his person the 'Third Term,' or as I take it, the *Indefinite* Term.

"General Gover had the most powerful support that ever appeared before a convention for its nomination. He had on his side in his supporters gigantic intellect numbers, money without stint and the greatest executive ability on the American Continent. But what were all these against patriotism, love of time-honored institutions sanctified by the wisdom of our fathers? It is the glory of America that here patriotism and the spirit of the great founders of our government have, in the end, conquered.

"The fathers of American Liberty put forth union as the tie that binds together the durability and glory of the Republic. Union has triumphed over its every foe.

"Our fathers, by example and precept, have declared to their children that it was not safe for one man to be President of these United States more than for two terms. And, thanks to the brave men who accomplished it, the only time this principle was ever given battle to it, triumphed. It has been forever vindicated in the defeat of Gen. Uriah S. Gover for a renomination for the Presidency.

"The convention, being unable to agree upon any of the more prominent candidates, the anti-Gover factions united and nominated Gen. James A. Gaveson for President. The Gover faction was placated in being given the Vice Presidency in the person of Gen. Chuvius A. Anson.

"The nomination of Gen. Gaveson struck me very favorably. I knew him to be a man of liberal opinions, of vigorous intellect and of commanding presence as an orator.

"I read some words he had uttered from his seat in Congress, and they had made my heart glad. 'The man who attempts to get up a political agitation in this country upon the dead issues of the war, will find himself without a party and without support.'

"'Veritably' I said, 'the period of advancement Abraham Lincoln had already reached James A. Gaveson had finally reached fifteen years later: 'With malice toward none and chairty for all.'

"I hailed the nomination of James A. Gaveson as the harbinger of a new and glorious era.

"A few weeks later the National Democratic Convention assembled in the city of Ornati. A host of great names were before it. The sage of four years before was there, that his wrongs might be redressed. Eminent statesmen and soldiers of the war for the Union were named as worthy of the high honor of nomination.

"The choice of the convention finally fell upon Gen. Winfred S. Highery.

"I was electrified. Gen. Highery had shed his blood for his country on many battle fields. He was one of the heroes of the Republic.

"I saw maimed ex-confederates flocking to his standard. I saw veterans of the war for the Union enthusiastic over his nomination.

"I observed these things and watched the current of affairs.

"A while after this there was a conference of the great leaders of the Republican party. I saw that at this conference it was resolved, that only one section of my country should be canvassed in the interest of Gen. Gaveson. I regarded this as placing the unvarnished seal of sectionalism upon the canvass of the Republican party.

"I did not want to see the American eagle flying from the Atlantic to the Pacific with his Southern wing drooping. I wanted to view the majestic bird soaring with every pinion in full play, wafting him triumphantly from sea to sea and lake to gulf.

"I hated sectionalism. A party animated by it I did not believe to possess those great and inspiring principles of brotherly justice which would tend to restore the almost broken bonds of union between the sections of our country.

"I read over many times and carefully the letters of acceptance of the two illustrious candidates for the Presidency.

"Gen. Gaveson with a long experience in public affairs gave this, taken from his letter of acceptance, as a summary of his views on the nature and structure of our institutions:

"'It should be said that, while Republicans fully recognize and will strenuously defend all the rights obtained by the people and all the rights reserved to the States, they reject the pernicious doctrine of State supremacy, which so long crippled the functions of the National Government, and at one time brought the Union very near to destruction.

"They insist that the United States is a nation, with ample power of self-preservation, that the constitution and laws made in pursuance thereof are the supreme laws of the land; that the right of the nation to determine the method by which its own legislation shall be created cannot be surrendered without abdicating one of the fundamental powers of the government.'

"I often pondered over these words. I could not understand them. Republicans will strenuously defend all the rights obtained by the people.' From what power higher than they, thought I, did the people obtain rights? I believed that all rights of government existed inherently in the people, and were obtained from them. The people, I thought, 'delegated,' and what they did not delegate was reserved to them. I was unable to come to any conclusion as to what was that high and sovereign power above the people, from whence they could 'obtain' rights.

"I often pondered over the words of Gen. Gaveson. They were past my wisdom.

"'They reject the pernicious doctrine of State Supremacy.' I had heard of 'State Rights;' I had heard of 'Nullification.' I had suffered much on account of 'Secession,' but of 'State Supremacy,' I knew nothing. If it meant that one State was supreme over another State, I could not see how that could be. If it meant that any State or number of States were supreme over the General Government, I could not understand that either, for the constitution gave the General Government unconditional and absolute supremacy in the exercise of certain powers with which it had been expressly intrusted by the people of the States.

"I could not comprehend the words of Gen. Gaveson.

"'They insist that the United States is a nation.' One of the most familiar of words is the word nation. Men have given it various meanings, however. But I was under the impression that they all agreed upon one point, namely, that 'a nation is composed of individuals.'

"No mean authority defines the word as 'a *people* living under one government, a *race*, a *stock*.' Never could I find an axample of a nation composed of States.

"I pondered over the sayings of Gen. Gaveson, but they were past my understanding.

"I read also the letter of Gen. Highery, accepting the nomination of the Presidency. In it he said:

"'If called to the Presidency, I should deem it my duty to resist with all my power any attempt to impair or evade the full force of the constitution, which in every article, section and amendment is the supreme law of the land.

"'The constitution forms the basis of the Government of the United States.

"'The power granted by it to the legislative, executive and judicial departments define and limit the authority of the General Government.

"'Powers not delegated to the United States by the constitution, nor prohibited by it to the States belong to the States repectively or to the people.

"'The General and State Governments, each acting in its own sphere, without trenching upon the lawful jurisdiction of the other, constitute the union. This union, comprising a general government with general powers, and State government with State powers for purposes local to the States, is a policy, the foundations of which were laid in the profoundest wisdom. * * * * *

"'The war of the union was successfully closed more than fifteen years ago. All classes of our citizens must share alike in the blessings of the union, are equally concerned in its perpetuity and the proper administration of its public affairs. We are in a state of profound peace. Henceforth let it be a purpose to cultivate sentiments of friendship and not of animosity among our fellow-citizens.

"These views of our government I understood better. The full and fair enforcement of the 13th, 14th and 15th amendments to the constitution of United States; the supremacy of the law; the preservation of the general and the State governments under a perpetual union, and above all the reign of peace and good-will; these I believe were the true sentiments for a true American.

"The platforms of the two great parties reflected the sentiments of the candidates.

"I determined to take my stand.

"For the reasons above given, and on account of the centralization tendencies of the Republican party, which I believe to be contrary to the spirit of the constitution, and which ultimately, unless checked, will prove the weapons in the hands of Tyranny for the overthrow of Liberty, I opposed the election of Gen. Gaveson to the Presidency of the United States.

"The first political speech of my life, (and I note the fact with great interest,) was made before the 'Gen. Highery Club' of my own ward.

"Though not a voter, I nevertheless joined the club.

"It was on a night early in September, that I made my first political speech. I must say that when the evening came, I felt much agitated. I had prepared a few notes of general observation.

"I was to speak before men who had heard some of the most distinguished and gifted political orators in the country.

" I was therefore considerably apprehensive as to my ability to interest them, and not to appear entirely an amateur.

" I had been careful to draw upon my stock of wit and to bring out a few of the comical stories I knew, thus getting my auditors into a good humor.

" About the time I found them becoming a little grave from following my arguments, I would throw out another joke; into the field thus enlivened and recuperated by laughter, I would launch again with my argument.

" I spoke for about a half an hour and was no little encouraged by the generous applause I received at the close o my speech.

" Two weeks afterwards I spoke again before the same club and acquited myself at least satisfactorily.

" I next spoke before the ' Young Men's Democratic Club.'

" A somewhat novel and amusing incident occurred at this meeting, which I think is worth relating.

" My friend, James R. Sloan, a rising young lawyer of Philopolis, was to speak also.

" Another young gentleman, a friend of us both, exhibited no little curiosity to see Mr. Sloan and myself on the huskings. But our friend was a strong Republican. Nevertheless he accompanied us to this meeting of the young men's club, at which we were to speak. He requested us not to mention his politics, as he was about to attend a Democratic meeting and he cared a little for his life. We promised him safety from detection.

" I made a fiery speech, denouncing in the severest terms the party to which my friend belonged He, in order to keep up the mask, cheered and clapped the strongest points I made against his party, just as enthusiastically as did the 'Democratic unterrified.' Finally my friend Sloan and myself finished our speeches.

" Before we knew what was going on, the President of the club hallowed out: ' We will now be addressed by Mr. ———' (my Republican friend). I realized the terrible situation at once. But my Republican friend was equal to the emergency. He immediately arose and said: ' Mr. President, for me to say anything in addition to what you have already heard, would simply be adding *perfume* to *beauty*. I therefore propose three cheers for the whole ticket (but I don't say which ticket).'

"This last sentence was uttered with his hand to his mouth, and in such a low tone as not to be heard by anybody except myself and Mr. Sloan, who sat near. Mr. ———'s sally was greeted with great applause.

"The laughter of the gods, as described by Homer, could not have been more hearty and more vigorous than that we three 'politicians' indulged in over this little incident 'after the performance.'

"I made a number of speeches after this, but I regard one I made at a large meeting in an adjoining ward as my most worthy effort.

"When I say worthy, I speak relatively. No doubt the efforts were modest in themselves, but derived their credit from the fact that one so young spoke them.

"It was before a large audience, on the same platform from which the distinguished Col. —— had spoken. Col. ——, before the war was a Democrat, but since he had been but a Democrat in Republican garb; but the garments having become thread-bare, he now had donned a new outfit of the old pattern, and with powerful pen and eloquent voice was supporting Gen. Highery for the Presidency. But the Colonel will speak no more. He has since been gathered to his fathers.

"My friend Sloan was also a speaker there on this evening.

"Having put the usual arguments of the campaign in as new and fresh a form as possible, I offered to the audience as the particular and, if I may so speak, *original* part of my speech, the following:

"Coming down ——— street on my way from college, on the afternoon of that day, a man who was distributing business cards handed me one of them. I noticed that on one side of the card was an advertisement and on the other a well-colored map of the United States.

"My eyes glanced quickly over the States of Massachusetts, Pennsylvania, Virginia, the Carolinas and all the galaxy. I thought I had never seen a more symetrical and imposing map of any country under heaven than that which bore the magnificent appellation: 'The *United States of America.*'

"But again I looked.

"I glanced over the bays of New England, the rivers of New York, the lakes of the North West, and the out-spreading plains.

"What, thought I, is not this the '*Solid North?*'

"Again I looked.

"The slopes of the Blue Ridge glided southward. There was the 'Father of waters rushing impatiently to the gulf.' Broad fields of snowy cotton loomed up before my imagination. What, thought I, is not this the '*Solid South?*'

"With sad heart I placed this map in my pocket.

"I came home, and once in my room, I took a little camel's hair brush, and dipping it in ink, I drew a broad, black line across the map along the famous course marked out years before by the surveyors, Mason and Dixon. '*This*,' said I 'shall be my speech.'

"So, when evening came and I found myself standing before a large audience, after a few remarks of a general nature, I drew from my pocket the map I had placed there a few hours before, and pointing at the bold line across it, with all the intensity of aroused feeling and with my voice at its full compass, 'There,' I cried, 'is the *black* line of *sectionalism* drawn by the Republican party through the map of our country—a line which we had thought had been wiped out years ago by bayonets—by victorious bayonets, that pierced the hearts of brothers in making invisible that which marked the dividing line between North and South.' I then tore in tatters the unholy map, and amid the great enthusiasm of the crowd I took my seat.

"I made another speech a short while after this, of which I must make brief mention.

"The posters which dotted the fences of the ward gave the names of some of our noted men as the speakers.

"In the presence of such distinguished lights I did not expect to shine. I went, however, to the meeting expecting to be only a listener.

"I arrived a little early and occupied the time greeting such of the voters and politicians present that I knew. Hon. Samuel S——, with whom I was acquainted, spying me, invited me to a seat upon the platform. I accepted.

"The meeting was called to order and the chairman introduced, after pronouncing a fitting eulogy, the Hon. Samuel S—— as the first speaker.

"Mr. S—— spoke for about three-quarters of an hour confining himself chiefly to the question of the Tariff. Mr. S—— is a graduate of one of our American Colleges and a gentleman of learning and culture. He is very argumentative, but somewhat cold in style—unsuited to interest and arouse popular assemblies. In all his speech the countenances of his hearers were not enlivened by a single smile, nor the steady tread of argument relieved by a single joke.

"The other eminent speakers who were advertised were not present.

"The eyes of the large audience somehow or other turned upon me (there were many there who had heard me speak at other meetings).

"The chairman came over and asked me if I could not say a word. I told him I had not prepared a speech and felt hardly equal to the task. He said he would risk that. Finally I consented.

"Mr. S—— as he was leaving to address another meeting, whispered into my ears as I was about to rise to speak. 'Give them something on *reconciliation*.' I nodded assent.

"Presently the chairman said: 'We will now be addressed by Mr. Jenkins Castleton— a young representative of the Solid South.'

"There was a deal of appaluse as I stepped forward—applause which would have disconcerted older heads than mine, because it made you feel that the audience expected much while you could give but little. But I chose to regard it more as a brotherly tribute to my native South than to myself personally. So my first words were that: 'These sounds of welcome from loyal Philopolis to a son of the South assured me that the cords which bind this Union together are still unbroken.

"'I am proud to be the representative of a South solid for a Union General!'

"This aroused great enthusiasm, and soon I forgot my inexperience as a stump-speaker, forgot that I had nothing prepared to speak and plunged regardlessly into the sea of improvised thought, caring little what I said, providing it conformed to the thought that filled my whole soul —*reconciliation*.

"I spoke of the power of this country united morally as well as physically. I mentioned what a crime it was for a great party to deceive the people by falsities and heresies.

"'The Republican party,' I said, 'just after the close of the war nominated Gen. Uriah S. Gover for the Presidency. Why? He was the leader of the victorious Union armies. He passed through the North. Flowers were strewn in his path, ' Hail to the *conqueror* of the South.' Upon this plea Gen. Gover was elected to the Presidency.

"'*Now*, twelve years later, they have nominated for the same high honor, Gen. James A. Gaveson.

"'What is the potent plea of the Republican party? With what cry do they fire the Northern heart?' '*Elect Gen. Gaveson because the South is not conquered.*'

'"Twelve years before: '*Elect Gen. Gover because the South is conquered.*'

"'Was ever such inconsistency shown by men? In short, in electing Gen. Gover by declaring that he *had conquered* the South, had suppressed rebellion, had humbled rebels, they simply *lied*, or else in now saying that the South is NOT conquered, that rebellion still rears its head, and that rebels are yet dangerous, they more grievously LIE. The principles of their two campaigns are irreconcilable. There is a glaring, sinful *lie* somewhere, and *truthful* people cannot afford to support a lie.'

"'The campaign cry of the Republican party that the South is not yet conquered, that rebellion still has a chance to accomplish its ends, is a slander upon the martyred heroes of the Republic. It is but declaring that the three hundred thousand patriots who fell that the union might live fell in vain.

"'Is it possible, that after having had all but intterrupted power for twenty years, unlimited supplies of money, millions of men, far in excess of your enemy—is it possible, that having had all this you have not yet *conquered the South ?*

"'If this be so, unfaithful servants begone! Incompetent rulers, make way for abler men. Your statesmanship is *vain*. You know how to *achieve* victories, but not how to *reap their fruit*. I repeat, that if you tell the truth in saying that you have not after such an expenditure of blood, treasure and power yet conquered the South, you are unfit to rule a free people. If you do not tell the truth in saying so, you are infinitely more unfit, being guilty of the greatest crime against liberty—the deceiving of the people.

"So in the name of worth and truth, I banish you. Neither incompetency nor untruth should obtain in the greatest Christian Republic of all time."

So the battle raged. But the people did not think with the fiery Jenkins. The great Republican party bravely followed its leader, and the people bestowed the crown of victory upon their chieftain's head.

So the war went on—the war between the Old and the New.

CHAPTER XXXVI.

MODERN EDUCATION.

JENKINS Castleton was free from the bonds of traditional custom.

The Old was shattered and the New was unformed. So Jenkins was left, like all young men of his age, to gather up for himself the scattered fragments for a career.

Will the reader have the patience to hear something more from Jenkins' diary?

It is upon a more pleasant but not more patriotic topic than the last extract. It shall not be over long.

"During all this campaign I never lost a day from college. I would be out at college attending to my duties there during the day and haranguing some crowd at night on politics. So I was in almost continued mental activity.

"Through it all I had a rosy cheek and rarely felt fatigued.

"I try to sleep all I can and I generally walk out to college and back each day. It is three miles distant.

"This six miles of daily walking no doubt does me much good.

"My food is plain and substantial—few dainties.

"My only beverage is nature's crystal water. I suffer no headaches occasioned by the previous evening's wine. This is no doubt greatly in my favor.

"I have neither time nor space to give a full account of my life at college for the past year. I will say in a general way that it did not differ materially from the previous year.

"I joined 'Philo' some time since. It was not long before I had gained here, deserved or undeserved, quite a reputation as a speaker. One of the most discouraging sights to the intelligent observer is to see the average Philomathean attempt to make a speech. Taught by a narrow and semi-barbarous system of education to despise and neglect the cultivation of the human voice, one of the most mighty weapons God has given to man; and taught to look upon the use of the arts of speech as tricky and unmanly—inspired by such teachings as these it is no wonder that college men, three-fourths of whom intend to follow professions where their success depends entirely upon their ability to *think* and to *talk*, no wonder that in so many cases these prove utter failures.

"'You must think' so goes established college maxims, 'but in your youth, when the mind is pliant and elastic and can easily be trained in the direction desired, is no time for developing the spontaneous thinking faculties of the mind (I speak of spontaneous thinking powers as those which act by reason of the individual's own personal effort, their operations not being prompted by text-books or tutors). In youth pore day and night over your text-books, get high average marks at college, and when you have been graduated and have your minds crammed and jammed with text-book knowledge—when you have exercised exclusively the taking in faculties of your mind, and have neglected entirely the letting-out faculties (your hours at home having been taken up in trying to get all *out* of the text-books and *into* your head that you could, and then the professors at college having used their time in driving said knowledge home far into the deep recesses of the mind, having made all efforts to get the knowledge into the mind, but none at all to instruct you how to get it out when wanted), yes, when you are a vast reservoir of knowledge, without an outlet main, when you are a big hogshead of book-wisdom without spiggot or bung—then is the time to develope your powers of original thought, of speech and of expression!'

"Believing such a system of education to be fundamentally wrong, I have not followed it.

F*

" I have not, however, too much neglected the text-books.

" I generally pass the examinations. I have tried to cultivate all the faculties of my mind.

" I have studied the text-books enough to give me all the routineness and mechanism of thought I needed.

"The reasonable and proper study of the college text-books and a right attention to the instruction of the professors will quicken the powers of the mind, will, above all, discipline it and prepare it for being educated. The student who graduates with the highest honors, performs every college duty to text-books and teachers and gets from those books and those teachers everything they have to give, ought to have a well disciplined mind, ought to have in his head every thought contained and implied in the classic lines he has studied, and have also a well grounded knowledge of the sciences. What then can such a student say he really possesses? He has on the mental armor for the battle of life—but only the *armor*. He's the Iron Horse, but the steam is not in it yet. It stands motionless upon the track of humanity. He's a loaded cannon, but it has as yet no spark with which to send forth its thunders into the world.

He has the armor, but he cannot yet wear it. Armor is useless without a man to buckel it on. This steam for the Iron Horse, this spark for the silent thunderer; this man for the mailed armor—these come, perchance, from on high, and cannot be created by man, but they can be found, can be brought to light by man if they exist in him. The student so equipped as to have the acquisitions enumerated above, which he received from his college, knows not, as yet, whether he has the motive power, the fire and the manhood for giving life and motion to his machinery. How can he find out this vital knowledge?—Alas, he may not be able to do so at all. His machinery is so large, so complicated and so weighty that his life, like the waxen image on the hearth, melts away ere he can finish the search. The coveted treasure may be there, but it is so covered up and hidden that it would be a life's labor to find it. Even if found it may prove too weak to move the ponderous machinery. Some such faithful young men never reach the buried treasure, others never try. No one can do this work for the searcher. It all lies in him. It's a power that no college can give, no tutor. It lies in the man himself if it be anywhere and none but he can bring it forth. 'Well, what of all this?' you say. Why just this: 'You had better search for the power, for the spark, for the man before you build the machinery! The machinery must be built to suit it and not it the machinery.

"'Well,' you say, 'I don't understand what you mean by all this. Give me an example of a case in which the 'spark' and the 'armor and the man' was first found and then the 'machinery,' as you call it, built to suit.'

"Your request is a pertinent and natural one, and I will comply with it with pleasure.

"Just what consciousness is to the mind, is what this 'spark' is to education. The mind cannot operate unless the thinking subject is conscious. So in education it accomplishes nothing without this 'steam.' This much premised let us take a case in point. Here's a boy five or six years of age. You talk with him on the various subjects that he may have become familiar with in his limited experience. You ask his opinion of this and that; you arouse his interest in this direction and in that.

"You stimulate his *curiosity* about some subject. The chances are that he will think about it to some extent at least; certainly he will think more about it than if his interest had not been awakened at all. What thinking upon that subject the child does after he leaves your presence, what ideas concerning the subject different from the ideas you suggested to him this child may have, will be spontaneous thinking in the sense in which I have defined it. One afternoon you are sitting at the front window and this boy is sitting near you studying his school lessons for the next day. You interrupt him by saying, "Come here a moment, Horace, and look at this street car. The driver is now turning that wheel which is fastened to that iron rod and this runs into the bottom of the car."

"O yes," says Horace " that's the 'brakes!'

"You say no more. The child resumes his studying.

"'A few days afterward Horace sees a street car standing on the track.

"'O,' says Horace to himself, 'this is what Uncle James was talking to me about the other day. Look there! That iron rod running into the bottom of the car has a chain fastened to the end of it, and look, when he turns the wheel, the chain coils around the rod and that pulls the brakes against the car wheels.'

"Here's some more spontaneous thought. Horace is just beginning to see where the 'spark' is, just beginning to hear the puffs of the ' steam.'

"Horace's mind is ofttimes diverted from his text-books in order to think a little spontaneously. He is just the age when the mind developes most quickly, and the direction it now takes will practically settle his mental constitution for life. If he were now to exercise to an inordinate degree his 'taking-in faculties' to the almost total neglect of his 'letting-out faculties'—as is often the case with young boys—he will be for life a 'taking-in man.' But if he in his younger days set *both* the 'letting-out' and the 'taking-in' faculties to work side by side, he will become the man capable of performing the greatest things.

"Horace keeps up this general course of mental life till he becomes a college Freshman. Here he meets some grave obstacles to the mental courses he has hitherto pursued. He finds that if he performs to the letter the work laid out for him by his college curriculum it leaves him no time for any *other mental work* whatever. He finds *no* room for exercising any but the 'taking-in' faculties. For self-protection he determines to exercise his 'letting-out' faculties as he used to do.

"He writes a good deal, he talks still more, keeps himself posted about current events, and reads some in history and general literature. He finds then that his average marks at college have fallen in exact proportion to the amount of exercise he has given to his 'letting-out' faculties. The college authorities begin to regard him as an indifferent student.

"Horace loved to hear eloquent pulpit orators. He meets Professor ———— on one Sunday evening at church. The next morning Horace fails in reciting to the Professor. The Professor looks at Horace frowningly and makes a remark about over-religious youths, and says that when *he* went to college he made *everything* subordinate to his college studies.

"Horace silently takes his seat and gets a mark not far removed from a cipher. He was still obstinate enough to think that there were some concerns more vital to him than college studies.

"Another Professor informs Horace that there are some things that people have to risk in this world, and one of those things is that the college curriculum is the best possible for the student, and that he is the best educated who gets the highest averages—that is, who studies the text-books most faithfully, and who most accurately reproduces their contents in examination papers.

"Horace was wicked enough to think that a kind God had given an unfettered mind to him as well as to the Professor. Horace risked nothing. He took his free mind and soared with it to wherever spontaneous thought prompted. In other words his opinion of the average college was expressed by the following words of a great journal:

"'The theory of the public schools is that the child whose tenacious memory best stands the strain of successful cramming is the best scholar. Such a child gets a better average than his competitors, and carries away the prize. Such children are probably the least troublesome to teachers. But youthful prodigies rarely attain to healthy maturity. Their hot-house luxuriance cannot be maintained. On the other hand, there has been no end of eminent dunces. Sir Isaac Newton, Sheridan, Goldsmith, Sir Walter Scott, Dean Swift, Gibbon, Dryden, Shakspeare, Milton, Napoleon and our own Dan Webster, were all uncrammable boys. Can a list of crammers be made to match them?'

"It will be observed that Horace kept up his manly course. He was rewarded. He made his mark in life.

"It must not be thought from this that I think the young man who does not go to college is better off than the one who does.

"This is far from my opinion. But what I do think is, that the minds of many young men are destroyed by the text-book tyranny of our colleges, and that if a student will continually guard himself, if he will *think* more than he *studies*, and if he will be careful to take only the *kernel* of college fruit and leave the *hull*, he will be incalculably benefitted by his college course. But if, instead of this, he becomes a text-book slave, I shall look for his epitaph and find it reads about thus:

"'Slain by mental tyranny, here lies one who sleeps in the bosom of obscurity.'

"I have also read volumes on various subjects. This has given me general information. I have read the daily papers. Thus I have kept a pace with the living world. I have participated in the meetings of the several literary societies to which I belong. This has exercised my 'letting-out' faculties. I have mingled more or less in society—some of it gay and vivacious. At times I found myself in parlors where wit—another mighty weapon of the human mind—was the presiding genius, where the presence of ladies—often young and fair—tended to the cultivation of those gentle and enchanting qualities which so ennoble the sterner nature of man.

"I once heard the human mind compared, very aptly I thought, to *wax*. Early in life the wax of the mind is soft and pliant—easily shaped into the forms desired. As you grow older the wax becomes harder and, as a consequence, more difficult to mould.

"I have wished to start *all* the faculties of my mind on the road to development. I did not want to make rabbits of all my faculties, nor tortoises, nor lambs, nor lions, nor foxes, nor yet dumb swine. I wanted to make a happy family of them all. I wanted each to have full show. I wanted none of them outstripped and left behind, and others worked to death, but a happy medium of labor for each.

"I wanted them also well *disciplined*. In times of din and strife when I needed the lion's roar and the lion's might, I wanted the tortoise, the rabbit and the fox to be sufficiently well trained so as not to intrude themselves. Likewise the lion must know how to control himself, and not interfere or hinder the lamb, the fox and the rabbit in the performance of their proper duties.

"This is my idea of education. I may be wrong in this idea. I may not. I was ingenious enough to devise, and bold enough to follow it. I may be ingenious enough to *give it up*, if I find increasing experience proves it unwise."

CHAPTER XXXVII.

TIME DULLS HATE, BUT QUICKENS LOVE.

"That love was no passion that waketh by day;
A fancy, a fashion that flitteth away.
'Twas life's whole emotion, a storm in its might.
'Twas deep as the ocean and silent as the night."

WE have followed Jenkins to college; we have seen him on the hustings, and we have unfolded to the reader, to some extent, the secrets of his heart. A great writer has said that "The heart counts for something even in negotiating the great interests of empires." While the heart goes for something in shaping the destiny of nations, it goes for even more in deciding the fate of an individual. So completely are we under the dominion of the heart that every day adds another to its already many triumphs. To one its dominion gives death; to another, life. Joy and misery it metes out to each in proportion to the yearnings of the heart that are satisfied in this life, or that are unsatisfied—joy for the former, misery for the latter.

So Jenkins Castleton was no exception to the common rule. The human heart had over him its wonted dominion.

We left Jenkins and Ida Lexter in the great Glen—alone with each other in the deep converse of love. It seems that Mr. Lexter and family were in the habit of spending part of the Summer of each year at the Glen. Jenkins was not aware of this fact, and so his meeting with Miss Ida was a genuine surprise.

It was not long before Mr. Lexter and wife came up with Jenkins and Ida. The family had started to explore the Glen together, but Miss Ida, as was often her wont, wandered on ahead. They, too, were no little surprised at seeing Jenkins, and greeted him courteously. But they could not judge from the demeanor of the two young lovers that anything unusual had happened to them—much less could they tell that pledges of love had passed between them.

At length the party returned to the hotel.

Jenkins remained at the Glen for two weeks. During this time he met Miss Ida on several occasions, in the parlor of the hotel. He saw her also at an evening reception given to the guests, but at each of these meetings he passed only a few words with her, and even these were of a general nature. The most experienced eye could not discover any extraordinary relations between the young couple. It had been mutually agreed upon by Jenkins and Ida that the "revelations" which each had made to the other should, for the present at least, be kept a profound secret.

The time when Jenkins was to depart came. He found the Lexter family in the parlor and bade them good-bye. He shook hands with them all, Miss Ida receiving a grasp of the hand just enough stronger than that given to the others to be taken as a final pledge of fidelity. Autumn came and Dr. Siddons' church was reopened, when Jenkins resumed his duties as Librarian of the Sunday School.

Miss Ida Lexter, in common with the other members of the Sunday School, came to the Librarian's railing to get out books. She and Jenkins conversed a little, of course. But that was all. Such a thing as Jenkins seeing Miss Lexter home from church, or of calling at the Lexter residence, never once entered the otherwise restless brain of the young Librarian. It would have been but little trouble for him to have been invited to call at the Lexter residence. He did receive invitations, and he did call as a welcome visitor to some of the first families in the congregation—families which stood quite as high in the social scale as the Lexters. Jenkins' address and the refinement of his manners easily gained him entrance into the higher social circles, and his wit and conversational powers made him a conspicuous figure in whatever company he appeared.

Indeed, he sometimes met the Lexters at dinner-parties to which he had been invited. He paid, on these occasions, no unusual attention to Miss Lexter. Indeed, if he had paid half the attention to the Lexter family that he did to others, he would have received many an invitation to dinner at the Lexter mansion.

Miss Ida one day was unusually merry. There was a very quiet company seated around the dinner-table. Mr. Lexter made a remark, which certainly seemed a very casual one, but it nevertheless was of great interest to one who sat at the table that day.

Mr. Lexter said that "he had enjoyed very much the dinner given by Mr.—— a few days ago. Mr. Castleton, the Librarian of the Sunday School was there, and was very entertaining. He had often wished to invite him to dine at his house, but the action of the young man toward the Lexters was so *formal* that he had felt a delicacy about inviting him!"

This was a victorious moment for Ida Lexter. Never before had she realized what nobleness there must be in Jenkins Castleton. She felt prouder of him at that moment than at any previous time. With nothing but himself, but his own worth and grace and ability, he had conquered the social prejudices of wealth and position. She could afford to await her time.

Jenkins Castleton had resolved that whenever he called at the Lexter mansion he would call there as one for whom no apology, on any ground, need be offered for his coming. Until that day arrived he would hold himself aloof.

He knew he possessed the richest treasure the Lexter mansion held—the love of Ida Lexter. He was content.

The following year Miss Ida Lexter made her *debut* in society. Jenkins often read her name in the papers as having been among the notables at great society events, at fashionable marriages and receptions.

He sometimes met Ida upon the streets. He would raise his hat in the accustomed way, but he gave and also received a look from her he loved and trusted, which spoke more of fidelity than ten thousand words could ever speak.

The language of love is as varied as the flowers and as changeable. It speaks sometimes through a simple shake of the hand. It loiters oft between the syllables of "Good morning." It inspires life to a hasty glance, and rides on the ripples of a smile. It gives a tongue to silence and light to darkness. It defies distance and gives the lie to time. "It rides on the billows and laughs at the storm."

Ida Lexter smiled upon many a handsome suitor, but Jenkins knew full well the song that oft echoed from her lips.

> "I hear from others gentle words;
> I scarcely heed the while;
> Listened to but with weariness,
> Forgotten with a smile."

CHAPTER XXXVIII.

THE SECOND MARTYR OF THE REPUBLIC.

"Freedom shrieked when Kosciusko fell."

NAPOLEON declared that he "found the crown of France upon the ground and took it up on the point of his sword."

Gen. James A. Gaveson found the crown of state upon the ground and took it up by command of the people. They bestowed it upon him.

Cincinnatus of old was summoned from the ploughshare to save a people in their *distress*, but Gen. Gaveson was called from the tow-path to rule a nation rejoicing in prosperity.

Never did a President enter upon the duties of his high office with grander prospects than did President Gaveson. His worst enemy wished him well.

The defeated South asked only for *justice*, and the North for *security*. He was schooled in the practice as well as the theory of government. He knew the wants of his people. He was undoubtedly able, and there was no reason to think that he was unwilling, to satisfy them. In one hand he wielded power, in the other statesmanship; while his heart, from whence sprang the life-blood of both, throbbed with a tireless patriotism.

Jenkins was standing one Summer's morning on the doorstep of the Castleton residence, having just finished reading his inveterate newspaper. Rebecca had, a few moments before, gone out shopping. Presently Jenkins observed her returning in great haste, and apparently very much excited about something.

"Come, Jenkins, quick, put on your hat. Great crowds are up street. *The President has been shot!*"

Jenkins was utterly horror-stricken. He asked his mother what she meant. He received the same information again. Almost mechanically, in a kind of mental maze, he rushed up street to the newspaper bulletin-boards, around which crowds in the wildest state of excitement were gathered.

"It must be a hoax," declared some. But additional telegrams confirmed the dreadful news. It was true. The President of the United States had been shot down beneath the shadow of the nation's capitol—stricken by the assassin's bullet! The President was about to take the train to join his beloved wife who, just recovered from a recent illness, awaited him in a distant city.

The circumstances attending the terrible event are telegraphed to wherever the wires stretch, and news is eagerly received by the horrified multitudes.

Mrs. Gaveson is speeding on to reach the bedside of the stricken Chief Magistrate. The multitudes follow by telegraph the progress of the monster locomotive with its single car along a track cleared of every other train.

The thoughts of millions are upon that one woman. Mothers weep. Ten thousand wives are in anguish.

The train nears the city! She is there! She approaches his bedside! The surgeons bow their heads! No attendent looks upon the sacred scene! They retire. She's alone with him!

A nation holds its breath.

> "Morn came and went,
> * * * And men forgot their passions
> In the dread of this their desolation."

'Twas a mighty suspense.

The people prayed that he might live.

Hope at last begun to shine. He was on the road to recovery. There was no North, nor South, nor East, nor West. The voice of the people was one. Enemies became weeping friends. Faction found not where to show his head.

Jenkins had a dream. Methinks he saw a stranger first landing on our shores.

"What mean," said the stranger, "what mean these words of strife that come to my ears?"

He learned it was the quadrennial battle of polls. The people were choosing their national rulers.

The stranger watched the combat. "How fierce!" said he. The one side were fighting with strength of banqueters, and the other with the desperation of famishers.

The stranger fled in terror from the scene. Ere long he returned. A combat yet more terrible was going on.

"What means," said the stranger, "what means this mighty commotion of the people?"

He was told that it was a wondrous war—a war in which the people were all upon one side.

"What! Are not these the same whom I saw in terrible combat with each other a short while ago?" They were the same.

"O mighty Republic!" said the stranger, "love lulls the passions of thy sons to sleep. When the battle's over conquerors and conquered become joint victors, and when your common chief falls, together you weep."

Jenkins awoke. The dream was fulfilled.

The people continued to pray and to hope. Death seemed to be retreating. Life was again appearing—but only for a season.

He sinks. No, he is rallying. Hope is again revivified. Human skill exhausts its ingenuity. Tenderest care administers to him. Loved ones devotedly watch o'er his bed. Mother, wife, children—all are breathing as he breathes, and sink as he sinks. The world sits watcher at his bedside.

"Doctor, what are the indications?" said the stricken man, as if he were a careful general wishing to learn the true position of the enemy.

"There is a chance of recovery," replied the surgeon.

"Then, we'll take that *chance*," said the valiant, though fallen man.

Grim death had no craven spirit to battle with. 'Twas conqueror meeting conqueror, and the contest was as to who should be *more* than conqueror.

One by one the citadels of life are stormed. The attack is fierce and the resistance most obstinate, but the citadel is taken by the enemy.

Sorrow again bows down the people.

"Doctor, where is *mother?* Can I not speak with her for just a moment?"

Exhaustion having loosed his mind from its moorings, it drifts out unguided and unpiloted. Whither does it drift? *To Mother!*

"Doctor, will you get me pen, ink, and paper?" requests the restless sufferer.

"Mr. President, you must not have any cares of state on your mind. You must be perfectly quiet."

"Why, Doctor, I am not thinking about affairs of state; I only *wanted to write a line to mother!*"

He was strong, indeed. He does write to "mother."

As the attenuated muscles of this loving son who thought not of the sceptre of power so lately fallen from his hand; who brooded not over the blasted hopes of a noble ambition, but whose thoughts were of mother—as the attenuated muscles of his right arm grasped as best they could the pen and wrote those lines so full of hope, so brave, that he might remove from her who so grieved for him a pang of sorrow,—we felt indeed that there beat beneath that breast a heart "soft as sinews of new-born babe."

"I am so weary, Doctor, of this sultry air. Take me to my country home, or else let me go to some cottage by the sea, where the air is sweet and pure."

The consultation of surgeons was held to consider the sick man's request. "It cannot be done," said they, "it will kill him."

He wanted to *leave*. He longed for *home*. He was *restless*.

"Doctor, I *can* stand the *journey*. I am *prepared* for it. Let me go."

Science, art and human wisdom could not resist such an appeal.

Railroad tracks, in a few hours, stretch themselves along streets where the steam monster's deep breathing was never heard before. The springs, balances, and nice adjustments of the train hold gravity to its centre and motion seems to move not.

The curious train starts on its course. The stricken man waves a *farewell* to the sea of uncovered heads assembled at the station. Such a journey the world never saw before. It was a journey not through the heart of a country, but through the heart of a people.

"Doctor, how many more stations are there to stop at?"

"*Not many*," said the surgeon.

Ere long the welcome roar of the waves as they broke upon the sand was heard by the passengers on this curious train.

Again had the railroad stretched over unaccustomed land. It touched the very door of the cottage that was to receive the sufferer.

He is placed upon his couch. The window of his room overlooks the sea. A cornice of the cottage protrudes out so far as to obstruct the view of the ocean from the window. The cornice is removed. The cool, invigorating air which probably had been wafted over many miles of pure sea, comes in copious whiffs—a sweet balm to the stately sufferer. He revives.

He wishes to be even nearer the sea. His reclining chair is placed almost in the window. The devoted wife sits by him lovingly holding his emaciated hand in hers.

The white sails of the ships look so majestic as they go speeding by. The ceaseless movement of the sea—the emblem of life; the foaming billows rolling upon the sands—very like the sands of time; while beyond stretched the boundless waste of waters—the embodiment of Eternity itself. Look on, thou noble sufferer! Thou beholdest the similitude of thine own great soul.

O, how patient he is, and how gentle. He bids wife a sweet good-night; the surgeons make their last examination for the evening and retire. All have left save the faithful watchers.

The patient is apparently sleeping—endeavoring to reform the scattered forces of life for to-morrow's battle with death. Stillness envelopes all around, and is unbroken save by the waves dashing upon the shore. The stars are twinkling merrily in the clear sky, but all else rests.

"Oh this pain, this pain!" is the cry that breaks upon the stillness of the night. The startled watchers spring to their feet. The cry came from the sufferer. "Call Dr. Blair, quick, quick!" said the vigilant watchers. The Doctor came.

His practiced eye instantly saw that life was only lingering that it might say good-bye to earth.

"My God, he is dying. Call Mrs. Gaveson!" cried the surgeon. She entered. She grasped his hand. His lips moved not, but a last glance of his eye told that he knew whose palm lay in his. She reclined her head upon his breast. She pressed his hand once more and he was dead!

The widowed heart could restrain its anguish no longer.

She knelt by the couch for some minutes. The silence of sanctity reigned. So deep were the emotions of every one present that it seemed a moment when earth held only mortal bodies, while the thoughts and the immortal spirits of the living appeared to have left their confines for the time and mounted to the infinite!

No such death scene has ever been witnessed like unto that of James A. Gaveson.

"Oh, this pain, this pain." Better this last word than "*Et tu, Bruté!*"

Where shall we look for last words that so touch us as the last ejaculation of the dying Gaveson?

Shall we find it in "*teté d' armé?*"

"Angels might well draw aside the curtains of the skies to look down on such a scene."

"This," said the expiring statesman of a former generation, "This is the end of earth. I am content." Here was one who had run his course, and fulfilled the full measure of his time."

"Oh, this pain, this pain!"

He began life under the cold pressure of poverty; and he ended it with "Oh, this pain." But between that beginning and that end there was a period of happiness, of triumph and of glory.

Over the corse of bleeding Cæsar, Antony might well ask: "Are all thy conquests glories, triumphs, *spoils* shrunk to this little measure?"

Conquests James A. Gaveson made, but they were for his country.

Glory was his, but it was that glory which is the shadow of virtue; triumphs were decreed him not by the Senate, but by the people. *Spoils* had he none; but the demon spirit of spoils pursued him unto death! The close of such a wonderful career could not but attract the notice and arouse the sympathies of the civilized world. Not for a day only, but for many weeks did the world ponder intently over his fate and more intently over his life.

Over the same railroad track which he traversed in coming to the sea, he now returns—dead!

"Go slowly when you pass us," telegraphed the young students, who had forgotten all thoughts of study, "Go slowly and we'll strew the track with flowers."

The heavily-draped Funeral Train on its way passed over many a rose and many a lily, the sweet tributes of love. Everywhere the people gathered around the stations to uncover their heads in tribute to the illustrious dead.

At length he is laid in state beneath the dome of the Capitol—the scene of his many triumphs in life.

Night and day the people marched in solemn procession to take a last and longing look at the martyred hero. Royalty places its wreath of affection upon his casket and from all the governments and peoples of the earth come words of condolence.

The last sad journey is begun. He goes to be laid a' rest hard by the beauteous lake in his native West.

No such funeral was ever solemnized before.

It was a cosmopolitan funeral in the fullest sense of that term.

Gen. Gaveson, having been more of a Christian than a sectarian, and more of a patriot than a partizan, his obsequies afforded the world a happy opportunity of showing that the human heart is at last the master of prejudice and partizanship. So around his tomb men forgot all but their veneration for the fallen chieftain.

It were well that we sing over his memory the consoling stranzas which were sung over his tomb.

> "Thou art gone to thy grave, but we will not deplore thee;
> Though sorrow and darkness encompass the tomb,
> The Saviour has passed through its portals before thee,
> And the lamp of His Love is thy guide through the gloom."

"Mother" was listening most devoutly to these sacred notes, and they seemed to dry the tears in her eyes already bedimmed by the gathered mists of fourscore years. She felt that she would not be long deprived of her 'boy.'

But the tenderest chords of feeling were touched when wife and children heard the sweet strains of their loved one's favorite hymn :

> " Ho, reapers of life's harvest,
>   Why stand with rusted blade
> Until the night draws around thee
>   And day begins to fade?
> *   *   *   *   *
>
> Mount up the heights of wisdom,
>   And crush each error low;
> Keep back no words of knowledge
>   That human hearts should know.
>
> Be faithful to thy mission
>   In service of thy Lord,
> And a Golden Chariot
>   Shall be thy reward."

So they laid him away, where no pains or cares now disturb his gentle sleep.

It would be needless for us to enter upon an analysis of the character of the noble dead, or to review his brilliant achievements. The simple recital of his death is our eulogium. The tears the reader has shed over the preceding pages of this chapter, and the emotions their perusal has brought forth are the grandest panegyric our humble effort can pronounce.

Reader, we know not who thou art, whether Jew or Gentile, Northerner or Southerner, Republican or Democrat. We know not whether your native hills are in

Europe or Asia, or whether you hail from the "Dark Continent." But we do know this; that you, in common with all mankind, have shed a tear over the grave of James A. Gaveson.

When you have finished this, reader, and are more composed, we would have you at some time of leisure peruse a volume of American history. You will there find recorded the deeds of James A. Gaveson.

Future generations will study his great character. They will know him as one of the few well-balanced, great men. He was not supremely great in any one sphere of human action, but he was great in many spheres. Napoleon or Cæsar, and possibly a few of his own countrymen, outstripped him in the race for military glory, but where were they when peace came and the fruits of war were to be gathered?

James A. Gaveson was not unmeritorious in war, and he was a master in peace. He was not uninteresting to the child upon his knee, and he was a Hercules in the throes of debate. He was not unfrequently a visitor at the firesides of his horny-handed farmer neighbors, and he was often the central figure in a company of the rank and intellect of the National Capitol.

It was not with an ill grace that he presided at the bi-monthly meetings of a literary society, and he was a grand and imposing figure presiding over the destinies of fifty millions of people. He was a well-balanced man. He was an American; as son, father, General, Congressman, Senator-elect, President, Christian, he fulfilled his duty fully. Ennobled by his life, he is sanctified by his death.

Broad as was the compass of his great mind, and deep and encircling as was the love of his kindly heart, they were not so broad, so deep as his open grave.

Who can comprehend what lies buried in that grave? What deeds of future patriotism are encoffined there? What notes of eloquence yet unborn were lost to the world forever when those lips kissed their mother earth? What hopes are sepulchred there? How many weeping statesmen beheld the fond ambitions of years entombed with him? What hates, what loves had men laid down in that big grave?

The sacrificial death of James A. Gaveson has done more in one supreme moment to unite the hearts of the American people in one fraternal band of union than the mighty thunderings, conquests and results of four long years of war.

This is not strange. It is not inconsistent with the nature of man.

Hear how in his lifetime he would restore peace to his country! O, that his immortal shade could be given the boon of knowing how gloriously his death has completed his life's work!

In his inaugural address, his first and last formal declaration to his people as their President, the second martyr says :

"In our beneficent work, sections and races should be forgotten and partizanship should be unknown. Let our people find a new meaning in the Divine Oracle which declares that 'a little child shall lead them,' for our little children will soon control the destinies of the Republic.

"My countrymen, *we* do not *differ* in our judgment concerning the controversies of past generations, and fifty years hence *our children* will not be divided in their opinions concerning *our* controversies.

* * * * * *

"*We may hasten or retard, but we cannot prevent, the final reconciliation.* IS IT NOT POSSIBLE FOR US NOW TO MAKE A TRUCE WITH TIME BY ANTICIPATING AND ACCEPTING ITS INEVITABLE VERDICT ?

* * * * * *

"Let all our people, *leaving behind* them the battle fields of dead issues, move forward, and in the strength of liberty and the restored Union WIN THE GRANDER VICTORIES OF PEACE."

Education, Reconciliation, Forgiveness, Liberty, Union, Peace. These, all these James A. Gaveson *offered* at the moment of his accession to the Presidency. What American citizens could ask more? These, all these James A. Gaveson *gave*, and *gave abundantly* on that starry night when he yielded up his life. What American citizen is there so base as not to cherish and preserve faithfully the sacred gift?

James A. Gaveson has gone from the limited bonds of this life to the illimitable future. The least of all he had is buried with him. The richest gems of his crown are still ours—no not ours, but the world's. His virtue, his

wisdom, his heroism are of the undying. His was a fame which might well lend sweetness to the poet's fancy:
"It walks upon earth, but lifts its head in heaven."

He sleeps.

"Give him place, O ye prairies! In the midst of this great Continent his dust shall rest, a sacred treasure to myriads who shall pilgrim to that shrine to kindle anew their virtue and patriotism. Ye winds that move over the mighty places of the West, chant his requiem! Ye people, behold a martyr, whose blood, as so many articulate words, pleads for fidelity, for law, for liberty!"

CHAPTER XXXIX.

IMPRISONED LOVE.

IT was a hard struggle for Ida Lexter. To smile with her lips and at the same moment sigh with her heart; to appear contented, and be really wretched; to talk to one and think of another; to wear an enforced and perpetual mask—this was now her lot.

With Jenkins, the situation was somewhat better. He had his studies with which to occupy his mind; he had no suitors for his hand to whom he had to make a show of favor, as Ida was compelled by circumstances to do; he did not find it necessary to pay any homage to *this* or *that* fair lady. His heart's desires were already satisfied. He sometimes went out into company to rest his mind from serious studies, and to gratify his desire for conversation, in which he always delighted.

Jenkins one day received the following note from a young gentleman friend of his, who resided on one of the fashionable streets of Philopolis. The note was also signed by the sister of the young man, and as she was a young lady of no little literary taste and culture, Jenkins enjoyed a visit to this house very much. The note ran thus:

"PHILOPOLIS, Oct., 188–.

"ESTEEMED FRIEND:—We extend a cordial invitation to you to call Thursday evening, the 29th inst. We expect a few friends, and would be pleased to see you present.

"Hoping you are well, we remain   Very Truly,
"JAMES T. FARMAN,
"EVA FARMAN."

Jenkins accepted the invitation. He found a brilliant company of ladies and gentlemen present. Some were strangers to him, and so he had to be put through the usual formalities of introduction. He noticed that some person in the front part of the parlor was receiving unusual attention. A number were gathered around the person, whoever he or she was, and all seemed to be conversing freely and laughing heartily.

In a few moments Miss Eva Farman addressed Jenkins, saying: "Mr. Castleton, I wish to introduce you to a valued friend of ours ;" and with this she escorted Jenkins to that part of the parlor where the above mentioned interested group were gathered.

"Professor Dayton, Mr. Jenkins Castleton," said Miss Eva, leading the young man forward.

"Happy to meet you, sir," said the Professor.

"How do—" Jenkins' sentence was cut short by his perceiving that the Professor was about as fine a specimen of the educated and cultured *negro* he had ever seen. For once Jenkins was embarrassed and confused. The natural impulse of Jenkins was to call for his hat and coat and leave the house at once. He felt insulted at being invited into a parlor where a *negro* was received as one of the company. But upon reflection he concluded, that as the Farmans did not know that Jenkins was a Southerner, and therefore could not be expected to entertain such liberal views as they did on the negro question; and as he knew they would not for the world have intentionally offended him upon such a delicate point, Jenkins, with a self-sacrifice that was commendable to him, concluded to make the best of the situation, and observe the phenomenon for his instruction. So he extricated himself from his unpleasant position by hastily taking a seat which happened to be then vacant. It was just next to the Professor's.

"Mr. Castleton," began the colored guest, "I have often seen you."

"Ah," said Jenkins, " may I ask where?"

"On the platform and on the 'stump,'" promptly answered the Professor. "I have listened with great interest to some of your speeches. You seem to believe in the saying from Lacon, 'if you can't put *fire* into your works, put your works into the *fire*.'"

"I am glad to find that I was able to interest you," responded Jenkins. But I fear I put too much 'fire' as you term it into my speeches."

"Well, I don't know about that," broke in the Professor, "there is such dryness and slovenliness of style about most of our speakers that I think it would be a great blessing to have them pay more attention to the study of style and eloquence."

Before continuing further, it might be well to give the reader some account of who Professor Dayton was.

He was a master of one of the fine arts, and considered one of its best expounders and teachers. Besides other attainments Professor Dayton was a linguist. He spoke fluently French and Spanish, and his English was faultless. His accent was peculiarly mellow and fascinating. His knowledge of general literature and the poets was so considerable that he could illustrate almost any ordinary incident or remark with an apt quotation.

Jenkins and the Professor were soon so earnestly engaged in conversing on various literary topics that Jenkins forgot the gay surroundings, the music that rang out from the piano, and even heeded not the songs that filled the room with their "concord of sweet sounds." He even forgot that *he himself was playing his part in a scene which he never would have thought possible in real life!*

The conversation of the Professor and Jenkins was interrupted by a request that Mr. Castleton favor the company with a recitation. He complied and accomplished the task in a very creditable manner. Ere long the company dispersed and Jenkins returned to his home that evening, thinking of the wonderful contrast between the "Old and the New."

Let not the reader suppose for a moment from reading the above that the negro is received, as a general thing, into the social circles of the whites in the North.

Professor Dayton was an extraordinary exception.

He himself did not associate with negroes, and his business was almost entirely with the whites.

He was perfectly polite and unobtrusive. In company he gave himself abundant opportunity to be ignored; any lady or gentleman could easily be oblivious of his presence without the least inconvenience. There were, however, usually very few who did not enjoy the wit and conversation of this cultered negro. As a general thing there is between the negroes and the whites a great gulf fixed.

In Philopolis there are separate Public Schools for the colored population. Whenever a colored parent chooses to use the undoubted right which the law gives him of sending his children to whatever Public School he desires, it is considered such a wonderful thing that the daily papers of Philopolis mention the incident as an item of news. Every now and then a Theatre Manager is up before a Magistrate, charged with telling a negro who applied at the Box-office for a seat, "that the price of tickets was raised to ten dollars each."

One rarely sees a negro in any part of the Theatre in Philopolis, except up in the Amphitheatre, and even then the gallery " Gods " often make a suppressed demonstration of uneasiness at the sight of the poor negro.

For fifteen years after the close of the war for the Union Philopolis never enjoyed the satisfaction of seeing a single one of its 30,000 colored population appointed on the Police force of the great city or elected to a single important office, and when at last a Democratic Mayor appointed *four* colored men on the Police force of Philopolis he was roundly denounced by his own party, and the Republicans felt themselves rebuked. A van driver rather than ride beside a *negro* policeman resigned his position.

This nearly total exclusion of the negro from the social circle, and his being practically deprived of many public rights and privileges is not regarded by the people of Philopolis as inconsistent with a thorough-going Republican city.

If there be one thing which is settled beyond a doubt by the testimony of all history it is the fact that no people can have institutions in advance of the progress of the people themselves.

The people attain a higher state of advancement and then their institutions mould themselves to suit the new order of progress. So the fiction of the equality of the negro which obtains in the United States at the present time is but another proof of the universal law—that people mould the institutions, and not the institutions the people.

· In some of our most enlightened States—those of New England for instance—States which are considered as representatives of the highest type of American civilization, there live many whites who have never been slaves, who have always dwelt in the midst of industry and thrift, where law and order prevailed, and who are yet considered by their state as unworthy of the elective franchise and are by constitutional provisions deprived of the right to vote.

Yet the people of these same states who did not think free whites capable of the franchise because they could not read or had not property were most eager to guarantee the the Elective Franchise to negroes, who, in addition to having been all their lives abject slaves, could neither read nor write and hardly knew what property was!

To come down to the bottom of things, a sentimentality, the advocacy of which would attain certain ulterior results, and political necessity had more to do with the guaranteeing of the franchise to the negro than any great feeling of its propriety or its justice. Many thought that patriotism and the security of the country required the election for a second term of President U. S. Gover. A full negro vote would secure this end, so the vigilant patriots took good care to have the proper amendmets proposed and adopted before the then impending Presidential Election.

There is no more powerful weapon of appeal to the masses than to tell them of Poetic Liberty. The brilliant apostrophes to Liberty made by anti-Slavery orators some years before this time were always peculiarly fascinating to the minds of the masses and could be repeated now with good effect. It would be a stinging rebuke to the wicked past to return at once that freedom which had been so unjustly taken from the negro!

"Reason insists that every man shall have his own without postponement." Under this logic Poetic Liberty carried the day, and, whatever may now be the opinion as to the wisdom of the guaranteeing of the elective franchise to the colored race, there can be no doubt about the fact. The *guarantee has been given.* It stands as the fundamental law of the land, and that man or party which strikes a blow at, or attempts to evade the full force of, that amendment strikes an equal blow at other muniments of the constitution which guarantee our most sacred rights.

"Equality before the law," then, is a privilege as dear to every *white* citizen as it ever could be to a colored one, but let no man confound "Equality before the law," with "Equality in my *house.*"

Civil Rights are as precious to the "Confederate Brigadier" as they can possibly be to the struggling negro. But make no misconception. "Civil Rights" and "Social Rights" do not flow the one from the other.

The very essence of the social right is found in the marriage right. It is folly to say that those who cannot intermarry should move on the same social plane. When most States have laws against miscegenation, it seems strange that there should be found so many philanthropists weeping over the social exclusion of the colored race!

"O'erstep not the modesty of nature."

Neither justice nor patriotism demand that the modesty of nature be overstepped.

Every public and civil right guaranteed by the laws should be given the colored race.

Give the colored man the right, and accord him the privilege of riding in the street cars of the great cities, but do not deny me the privilege of changing my seat to the other side of the car, if I so desire. Or if it be a warm day and the car is crowded with colored dames, do not prevent me from going out and standing on the platform for "fresh air." If I stop at a hotel and go into the washroom to prepare for dinner, and see a colored brother just relinquishing the towel, do not keep me from going up to my room and performing my ablutions there during the rest of my stay at the said hotel.

If it becomes "inconvenient" for the colored parent to send his children to a public school *erected especially for his folk*, and he sends the little ones to the public school where my children go, do not imprison or fine me if I withdraw my children from said place of instruction and send them to a private academy or school.

If I happen to remove to some State where there is no law against miscegenation, do not count me cruel if I forbid the colored gallant (as I do some white ones) from calling upon my daughter with matrimonial intent.

All these political and social problems will solve themselves; and as the years go by we shall surely see that those two races which lived together in harmony when one was enslaved by the other, can assuredly dwell together now in peace when both are *free*, and when both have, under the law, equal political rights!

More good can be done for the colored race by building a log school-house in some of the regions of the South than by reciting apostrophes to *Liberty* to them or entertaining them with extravagant praises of their capabilities and their hopes. A few hints as to how to make better terms with the farmer who owns the land he lives on for getting "bigger shares of the next crop," or how to get his necessary "meal and bacon" without paying three prices in the form of "orders"—a few such hints as these will do the negro a vast deal more good than to tell him about his glorious descent from the "gentle Ethiopians" with whom Homer tell us Zeus and the other gods were wont to banquet every year!

The rains and the winds are not more necessary to the

welfare of this country than are the negroes. They have a work here which none others can do. Just as the *negro himself* was the wealth of the South before the war, so *now* is his *labor* indispensable to its prosperity. Therefore, let the negro respect *himself*, and not be the slave of this or that political party. If the Republicans tell him of " forty acres and a mule," the delivery of which however is always to be delayed until *after* the *next* election ; or if the Democrats will give him no vote at all or else permit him to vote only their ticket—if one party has for him only ingratitude and the other party nothing at all except it be a surrender of his right to vote for whom he pleases, then he had better vote for neither party but cast his vote for himself. Let him start the " Colored People's Party."

Let every colored citizen cast his vote solidly for a candidate of his own race and party. Ere long in districts where the balance of power rests with the colored vote, we shall begin to hear of "compromises." The ticket on which appears a colored candidate, be it Democratic or Republican, carries the day. A few lessons like this will have a most salutary effect.

We end as we began. Do not try to make a negro a white man or a white man a negro, but let each respect himself; and then both will get their several rights and fulfill the destiny which is marked out for each in this Republic !

It may be well to close this chapter with a quotation from a recent writer on the subject in hand:

"If it were not for the colored voters in the four great States of the North, the Democrats would have the four Governors and all the State officers, eight Senators and a large majority of the Representatives from those States. The Democrats would now have the President, both Houses of Congress and the Supreme Court were it not for the negro vote at the North. Yet, in the face of this fact, the Northern Republicans have never elected a negro Governor or other State officer, or sent a negro Senator or Representative to Congress. We do not believe they have ever even elected a negro to a State Legislature or a county office. The Republicans of the North are far more intolerant toward the negroes than are the Democrats of the South. Republican boys at the North will not tolerate a negro cadet at either the Military or the Naval academy. Yet in the face of these facts the negroes at the North vote constantly and solidly with the Republicans. They are so servile in their devotion to the Republican party that they have not the resolution or independence to compel it to do them justice, which they are fully able, as far as numbers are concerned, to force them to do at any election. This is one of the worst traits in the negro character. He lacks independence, resolution and self-respect. Just so long as these features of his character predominate, so long will he be the 'hewer of wood and the drawer of water' to the white man."

So much for the position of the colored race in the North. In the South his wrongs have sometimes been more terrible. This all reminds the writer of a story he once heard: Two dogs were fighting over a bone. A Negro, a Democrat and a Republican were standing by. The trio were observing the contest with lively interest.

At length the Republican said: "Jake, I understand you are not going to vote at all at this election. I hope that is not so. You should never forget what our party has done for you. So come and vote with us." The Democrat also said, " Now, Jake, you try a new plan. The old one doesn't seem to work well. You come and vote with us, I think you'll like it." Then the sable brother said, " Gemmen, what you both says is all bery true. But look at dem two dogs. Dey's both fighting over dat *bone*, but de *bone* don't *fight*. So is I simply de *bone* dat you two is arter."

Son of the colored race, whither shalt thou fly for refuge!

CHAPTER XL.

THE NEW PRESIDENT.

THE accession of Vice President C. A. Anson to the Presidency of the United States was not simply a change of rulers. It was a change of *dynasty*. The recalling to the throne of England of the son of Charles the I., after twenty years of rule by Cromwell; the House of Hanover succeeding the House of Stuart was not a more distinct change in the character of rulers than was that which occurred in the Government of the United States when Gen. Gaveson died.

Gen. Anson was the staunchest of "Stalwarts." Gen. Gaveson was a liberal statesman. The one believed firmly in the wisdom of a "Third Term," the other regarded this as a dangerous innovation.

Rarely in the history of the world have a people accepted a ruler not of their choice with such good grace. And it may be likewise said that never did a new ruler use his unexpected power with more modesty. There was no indecent haste to flaunt the flag of vengeance in the face of the men who a few short weeks before had rejoiced that the Stalwart Vice President and his friends had been humbled.

In his inaugural address the new President declared that the memory and policy of his predecessor should be respected. The cabinet, containing the near and trusted friends of the late President, were treated with great courtesy and requested to retain their Portfolios until their successors entered upon their duties. The first annual message of the President to Congress gave almost universal satisfaction; and the message had one commendable characteristic in the similar documents of all his predecessors since the close of the great civil war. He did not allude to the "unhappy differences" existing between North and South. He presumed the country to be *united*. He felt himself the President of *one* people. His very silence on this subject of Sectionalism spoke more peace than the many melifluous periods and harmonious cadences of "brotherly love" which have so often been spoken.

President Anson possessed two qualities which have come to be recognized as the surest means of making an administration *successful*. He was a *gentleman* and *he never forgot a friend*. These two qualities may be summed up in the single phrase, a *thorough-going politician*. A *successful* administration in the early days of the Republic meant an administration which was most faithful to the constitution of the United States and the laws made in pursuant thereof, and that promoted measures for the welfare and advancement of the people.

THE NEW ADMINISTRATION. 251

A *successful* administration at the *present* day is one that is most faithful to the *men* and the party which elected it. That President who had the courage to say, "He who serves his country best serves his party best," and who dared to put his own precept into practice—that President who really acted as though the civil war were closed was heartily repudiated by both the great political parties—by the Republicans because he had no "backbone;" by the Democrats because he would not surrender out and out to them and their policy. This President who was not the first to advocate non-partizanship, but who was the first since the close of the war to put it into practice went out of his high office, and his administration was considered by both the political parties, and by a great majority of the people, as a splendid failure. He had advocated and practiced the precepts of civil service reform just far enough to be considered by his own party an irregular Republican, and used just enough of non-partizanship to make the lovers of peace hungry, but not satisfied. To sum up he had just enough of "civil service" reform and non-partizanship to make his administration "unsuccessful." President Anson saw these political danger-signals, and he was determined to profit by them, and promoted measures which would gain the *favor* of the people at the succeeding election.

Once faithfulness to the *Republic* was the grand test of

success; *now* it is faithfulness to *party*. Once the *welfare* of the people was the watchword of politics; now it is the *favor* of the people. It must be said that the *favor* of the people and the *welfare* of the people are not always the same. Some very dangerous principles of government have gained wide favor among the people of the United States at various periods of their history, because a *few* great men advocated and labored zealously for those principles. A few great and ambitious men led the South to secession, and it was three or four leading spirits that roused the North to action and fed the fire of its persistence. It was a keen disappointment to nearly one-half of the delegates to a great national convention that the "Third Term" was not successful. Yet who will say that had not a few men of surpassing intellect and ceaseless activity advocated that principle that it would ever have attained such favor? This dominion of *great men* flourished to a wider extent in the earlier days of the Republic than it does now, but it is still a powerful factor in our government. In addition to this still enormous power of *great* men we have the shackles of party; and between the dominion of these two potentates—great men and party—there is little room for the vast body of the people to have their proper influence. And this tendency to destroy the "happy mean" which should exist between political parties is, unfortunately, growing rather than diminishing. Capital is concentrating and labor is organizing. The contest for office is not now between the candidate and the *people*, but between the candidate and the *nominating* convention.

Get the nomination and the votes of the people can be counted on with reasonable certainty. The "happy medium"—the election—is no longer of any force. Election day is often the least anxious day of all. But on the day of the *nominating* convention the soul is aroused to its nether depths, and the mind is all afire. Thus insensibly a foreign and unrecognized body has usurped the power which belongs rightly to the people themselves. Probably the deadest letter in our laws is the Twelfth Amendment to the Constitution of the United States which declares that "the person having the largest number of votes for President shall be the President, if such number be a majority of the electors appointed,"—in other words, that the President shall be *elected* by electors appointed by the people of the several States. But of all days that are looked upon with little concern is the day upon which the President is *elected* according to the *constitution*. But that day, long preceding the day set for the election, when the people of the various states choose their *electors* is the momentous day, and the next morning the telegraph has informed us that the choice for President is settled.

In the first place two National *conventions* (bodies foreign and not recognized by the Constitution of the United

States) limit the choice for President to *two* men. How many citizens of the United States consider this suggestive state of affairs?

How many live in the midst of great political changes and yet perceive them not! History shows us that nations grow gradually and institutions decay gradually.

And just as one article of the Constitution of the United States has decayed or become practically inoperative, so unless the great body of the people exercise keener vigilance, will other more vital portions of that constitution become a dead letter.

President Anson constructed his cabinet on a consistent Stalwart basis. The House of Representatives was organized in accord with the ruling powers.

The political weather-cocks all over the country made haste to point in the favorable direction.

The President could satisfy all "claims of friendship" and still have offices left for placating the other factions of his party. He had a full hand and he played his cards well.

No distinguished Senators resigned because the President could not suit them with Federal appointments. No deadly feuds within his party grew out of his management of it.

Men who were wont to slur at the ability of the new President and talk, during the gloomy days that his predecessor was languishing, of "*what* a President we will have " should the revered Gaveson die—these complainers now hid their heads.

There was a certain political angel from "Fairy Land" or some other ethereal region known as "Civil Service Reform." It was worshiped as a Goddess by many good people. It was a being so pure and undefiled that it was difficult for it to find a spot on this mundane sphere holy enough for its habitation. Be this as it may, one thing is certain, that before a stern man of affairs like President Anson the fairy fled. "Appoint only fit men to offices," was the motto; but there was a parenthesis; (*you can always find fit men among your own friends.*)

> "He new created the creatures,
> That were not his, I say, or changed 'em,
> Or else new formed them, having both the key
> Of officer and office, he set all hearts i' the state
> To what tune pleased his ear."

The makers of discord within the party never had such trouble to accomplish their ends as now. Men began to see that there was no hope for the opponent of the methods and principles of the ruling powers within the party ranks. That Republican who wished to strike down his party and its chief soon found that to accomplish that end he must become an open enemy.

CHAPTER XLI.

IN THE TOILS.

THESE stirring scenes that were being enacted in the world of politics were *not* unobserved by the ardent Jenkins. His opinions began to become more settled. It was some disappointment to his now fast ageing father that his son was not that Southerner which the old man hoped him to be. Young Jenkins could not be aroused to enthusiasm by those ideas and those "traditions" which gave a glow to the pallid cheek of Dr. Lawrence Castleton. The Doctor could not understand it. He could not see why different circumstances should cause men to be animated by such different ideas. It was the same contest of other times between the *Old* and the *New*, and the *Old* was retreating.

But there were some other matters which engaged the attention of Jenkins Castleton—matters of the *heart*.

Jenkins felt that the time had come when he must lay some definite plans concerning the future of himself and his betrothed. He determined at the first opportunity to consult Ida Lexter about their mutual cares. The opportunity came ere long. Christmas was approaching—the gay and festive season. It was time for the Sunday School of Dr. Siddons' Church to hold its Christmas Festival. It was customary on these occasions for the Sunday School room to be tastefully decorated with ivy and *immortelles* and other appropriate emblems.

Jenkins, being somewhat tall, was usually a valuable assistant on these occasions.

The Tuesday evening came, on which the young ladies and gentlemen of the Sunday School were to put up the decorations. Jenkins was on hand early, moving around busily and chatting gaily with those about him. A keen observer would have noticed that the eyes of the young Librarian turned to the entrance-door more often than necessity would require; and if he handled the streamers of *immortelles* he was endeavoring to hang, a little nervously as Miss Ida Lexter entered, it was probably unobserved.

Having finished hanging the *immortelles*, Jenkins proceeded to furnish the ladies who were seated in various parts of the room with ivy leaves with which to fill up the wire frames of crosses, stars and other designs for adorning the walls. Miss Lexter was quite far removed from the rest of the ladies, as she was busy filling two large crosses. They were to be placed in the rear of the room in a conspicuous position, facing the entrance doors; and so

Miss Lexter was selected to employ her taste in arranging them.

Of course Jenkins must keep *her* supplied with ivy leaves !

Our gallant Jenkins no sooner perceives the needs of Miss Ida than he hastens over to her laden with leaves.

"Oh, Mr. Castleton, you are very kind and attentive to the ladies this evening. *You seem not* to neglect *any of them*," was the somewhat expressive greeting of Ida.

Jenkins smiled pleasantly at this allusion to his anxiety for the fair workers, and said, as he proffered some choice leaves to Ida, "Yes, Miss Ida, I have now furnished the other ladies with more leaves than they can use in an hour, and so I am ready to serve you for a long time."

The eye of the fair worker looked up wistfully at Jenkins, and he caught a glance which told that some thought other than of the ivy cross she held in her hand was in her mind.

"*So*," she said, shyly, "you *are ready* to serve me a long time. For—for—*how long ?*"

"*For life*," answered the young lover in accents which conveyed more meaning than his words.

"But Ida, you look so pale. Are you ill?"

"No Jenkins, no. Those last words of yours brought me a sad reflection."

"What do you mean. I—I—I—hope !"——

"For the best," said she.

Jenkins now held the cross while Ida continued placing the leaves in order. "Jenkins," she at length said, after a silence of several minutes, "I am now about as wretched as it is possible for a young heart to be."

Jenkins' cheeks blanched under this unexpected blow. The thoughts that ran through his mind in those few seconds were terrible. "What, just after an expression of life-long fidelity from me she is wretched. Is she not sacrificing all her pleasure for my sake and for the sake of our vow, and is she not yielding to the burden? I fear I am asking too great a sacrifice."

Such were the thoughts that went flashing through the brain of the young lover.

He could not speak.

"Here, Ida, is a '*mistletoe*,'" at length he said. She took it and meekly placed it on her breast.

The cross was finished and Jenkins hung it in its place.

"Now," said Ida, "we will finish the other one. Don't look so sad Jenkins, because I do. Come, I want to tell you something. Hand me some more leaves." The cheerful manner in which Ida now spoke quite reassured Jenkins and his cheek assumed its wonted hue.

"I must tell you, Jenkins, what my trouble is. You know that Mr. Jerome Lenardine. *Well I am engaged—*"

"Is it possible?" exclaimed the wretched Jenkins who

dropped his wreath and had not the self-possession to pick it up again.

"I am," said Ida coolly, picking up the fallen wreath, "I *am* engaged—to *you*." And unlike one so wretched she laughed as merrily as the sky-lark when he greets the first beams of the rising sun.

And Jenkins—well he felt like a coward.

It might be well to state here that Mr. Jerome Lenardine was a young and handsome millionaire—such as only our great cities produce. He was the inheritor of his father's wealth and the head of a firm which had many and extensive dealings with Mr. Lexter, father of Ida. In many financial straits Mr. Lexter had obtained relief through the generosity and kindness of Mr. Lenardine. He was, therefore, an especially welcome visitor at the Lexter mansion, and rumor was fast coupling the names of Miss Ida Lexter and Mr. Jerome Lenardine together. Some were sure that they were engaged.

At a late fashionable reception, Mr. Lenardine had paid almost exclusive attention to Miss Lexter.

This much known, the reader can be able to appreciate fully the import of Miss Ida's words to Jenkins.

"Well, if you will just hand me that large, fine leaf over there, I will try and finish what I had to say," commenced Ida, "and now *please don't make any more demonstrations.*" Jenkins blushed: and the knowing smile that played over the countenance of this loving tormentor did not tend to lessen the embarassment of the young man.

"As I was saying, Mr. Jerome Lenardine is a man that I abhor. My father and in fact all the family, wish me to look with favor upon his attentions. This I cannot do. I feel that there is coming for me a hard trial in the not very distant future. Meanwhile, *I shall trust to you, Jenkins.* No more now. I will either see you soon again or write if it is necessary.

"Now, the wreath and cross are done and so let us hang them in their places."

Jenkins, without saying more, took the cross and proceeded to place it in position. But he stealthily drew out the last leaf of ivy which the hand of Ida had put there and hastily placed it in his pocket. He then hung up the cross and entwined the wreath of *Immortelles* around it.

"That is very tasty indeed, Miss Lexter," said the Superintendent of the Sunday School as he was approaching. "I suppose you have had a hand in this work too, Mr. Castleton," said the Superintendent addressing Jenkins. "Yes sir," said the latter, "I gave some little assistance to Miss Lexter."

CHAPTER XLII.

THE GREAT IDEA OF THE NORTH: "LIVE TO LABOR."

"THERE is a perennial nobleness, even sacredness in work. * * Work, never so Mammonish, mean, is in communication with Nature; the real desire to get work done will of itself lead one more and more to truth, to nature's appointments and regulations which are truth. * * Labor is life. * * All true work is sacred; in all true work, were it but hand-labor, there is something of divineness. Labor, wide as the earth, has its summit in heaven."

So spoke one of the profoundest thinkers of all time.

In yet sweeter accents have the poets sung cheerful strains to the toilers of the world. Their sacrifices; their hardships; their losses and their fates have been enwrapped in a mantle of enchanting colors, and their often hard pillows have been made less cruel by the folds of an imaginary down.

In every people there is some ruling idea, some social pivot around which their character and institutions turn. What is the great idea of the North? Its millions of spindles with their ceaseless hum; its roaring wheels; its furnaces with their eternal fires; its marts; its cities; its palaces and temples; its wealth; its power—from these can be known the general idea of it all: "*Live to labor.*"

There is not a spot in the whole North that shows the marks of laziness. All is motion, activity, work, life. The country roads might almost with justice be elevated to the dignity of streets. The farmer's wagons travel swiftly along. In the towns and cities, everybody walks at a quick pace; funeral processions trot to the grave yard. The signs hung up in various places of business inform you that "Time is money." Many foundries, factories and machine shops run continuously day and night.

Here is a little street in a large Northern city. The houses in it are small, but neat, evidently the homes of workingmen and their families. The reader walks along this street about three o'clock in the afternoon of a week-day. You ring the door bell, and there appears a mother with a little child in her arms. "Good afternoon" you kindly say, "I came to see how you have been." "Come in" is your greeting from the housewife. You are ushered into a room that is plainly but tastefully furnished—everything is clean and by no means uninviting. "Well, how is your husband?" you begin with, having availed yourself of the proffered seat. "He is at work, but as to health he cannot complain," says the wife.

"And Lizzie (a daughter twelve years of age)?"

"Oh," replies the mother. "she is at the *factory*."

"And your oldest son Sam?"

"Why he's at work at the *shop*."

"And little Jimmie."

"Oh, he's coming down stairs now. He's a telegraph messenger boy, and as he's on the night force and has to be up all night he sleeps what he can in the day time."

And just then Jimmie came into the room, dressed up in his uniform, with his gossamer overcoat and rubber boots and leggings, for protection if it chanced to storm, ready for the night's work. Jimmie was cheerful and smiling, but he looked pale from his unnatural lot.

After Jimmie has left, you talk long with his mother, until the whistles and the bells and the unusual passing to and fro on the pavement outside tell you it is six o'clock, and the close of a worksome day.

Lizzie comes in looking weary and sallow, with eyes that shed no childlike lustre. She that was created to be "a fair young girl, with light and delicate limbs and wavy tresses" was aught else but the reality of the poet's dream. Emaciated body, litheless limbs, bloomless cheek—she had nothing but her own innocent and beauteous spirit which "Divine labor" was unable to destroy.

Then the father, his tin bucket on his arm, appeared. He was a man as he was a boy. Good nature and health seemed his treasures.

Tom came rushing in. He was robust, but there played across his face the smiles of ignorance.

It soon comes time for the housewife to spread the evening meal, and you would not keep the hungry longer from their joy. So you take your departure.

A short while after this visit, you have accepted a fashionable invitation. Mingling in the brilliant company, the spacious drawing rooms, the rich tapestry, the *display* of diamonds and magnificent costumes suggest what to your mind? What is the genius of the occasion? You engage in conversation and you find the topic is the fashions, the *news* of the day, and personal gossip. But everyone wears an air of freedom, conscious that he can speak his mind freely on any subject without incurring anybody's social displeasure. You are conscious of being in the presence of magnificence and luxury. The ladies are as fair as the flowers they wear; their eyes, bright and sparkling. Their cheeks of roseate hue, and they are full of vivacity.

The *menu* would satisfy the palate of the most exacting *connoisseur* of the culinary art. You must be extremely hard to be moved indeed if you are not charmed with the scene. Your pleasure will only be marred somewhat if you begin to reflect upon the terrible sacrifices of time, labor and life it has cost to attain much of this wealth and magnificence.

The most prominent feature is *wealth*, not intellect. In the preceding call you saw *labor*. In this one you see the fruits of labor—of *manual* labor.

For where one guest present will have gained his wealth

from intellectual work, ninety and nine will owe their fortune solely to manual labor, either personal or hired.

Intellect is not essential to enter and maintain yourself among the *élite* of the North, but wealth is indispensable.

A princely merchant usually regards four years in the counting-house more useful to his son, than as many years at college.

The Literati are the chosen few hundreds who have *mind* for their household god; millions have *gold*. All strive to pile up *wealth*, to make fortunes—the making of men and women is a small matter. "Things, *things, wealth, wealth*" is the cry.

Here stands a noble pile—the hospital. It cares for the stricken sons of toil. Excessive labor furnishes patients. Philanthropy takes them in and ministers to their wants and thus labor and philanthrophy, those potent factors in civilization, flourish side by side. The great North teems with charity and with labor. Its factories are full of young girls and its houses of correction full of strong men!

This iron rule of money produces also many moral evils.

It sharpens the ingenuity of thieves and produces crimes unheard of in less wealthy and less powerful countries. It imprisons the mind, narrows the soul and leaves man little time to think of aught but wealth, still less to think of himself and less yet to contemplate his God!

The great moral ideas which have originated and been

agitated in the North were started by the few. The many at first condemned and persecuted and slew.

The bulwarks of *money* withstood long and vigorous attacks and its power is not yet spent.

But wherefore all this?

Do you want to destroy society? No, far from it, my reader. "What will you then?" Why this: More *men* fewer *things*. Instead of wealth for the social pivot, we would have *man*.

In him is all that is worth striving for in this world, Action, Love, Freedom, Mind, Soul—these are in him. That pyramid of wealth built upon the furrowed cheeks of children, the drudgery of fair young women, the lives of men, shackled minds and smothered human souls will one day fall of its own fearful weight and "great will be the fall thereof."

CHAPTER XLIII.

THE LEADING IDEA OF THE SOUTH—"LABOR TO LIVE."

THE state of things narrated in the preceding chapter made a deep impression upon the youthful, but observing mind of Jenkins Castleton. He compared these things with what he had seen in his native South.

When he first landed in Philopolis it seemed to him that nature wore a strange aspect. Mother earth was hidden under a mass of stones and bricks.

The wagons rattled over the streets that for miles and miles were nothing but stones. Huge walls of stone and brick stretched far on every hand.

He thought then of the muddy highways of Burleigh, and of its wooden buildings.

He contrasted the active and eager gait of the pedestrians with the calculating, easy step of the Southerner.

In the South every man takes his time, except in a fight, and then he "takes time by the forelock."

Business is rarely so pressing as to deprive him of his "afternoon nap."

He likes money, but he does not particularly love to

labor for it. He had rather inherit it from rich ancestors. He will labor to *live*, but as to laboring for pure labor's sake, he declines it always. It may be doubted if a man could be found in all the South who voluntarily would expose himself on a stormy day and run the risk of laying the foundations of a fatal disease for five dollars, or even less money, and an able-bodied father, who would allow his daughter to bear the bleak blasts of winter in going to and from manual toil, in order to increase the family coffers, would be considered almost without the pale of civilization.

Enter a retail dry goods establishment in a Southern city. You will find every clerk to be *male*. These salesmen have to be paid a respectable salary, and so take off a great deal from the profits. The merchant is consequently *poor*. He might be rich could he hire young girls to do this work at a salary of three or four dollars per week.

The factories are few. There are fewer millionaires. Everything is slow. Nature wears her pristine aspect, and has been disturbed as little as possible. A railroad *here* and *there* breaks somewhat the face of the land. But there are yet many regions of the South not penetrated by the iron belts, fertile spots where rich products perish for want of transportation.

The "poor white trash" work when they must and do the least they can in the most time. One of them will sit on a dry goods box and whittle sticks all day, rather than clean the streets or carry the hod.

The former work is done only by the chain gang, and the latter by negroes. The Southerner, be he of the poor white trash or of the aristocrats, thinks more of *himself* than of money; and he will engage in no occupation for money's sake, which he considers menial.

Let the reader now, on some balmy afternoon, visit a Southern home. First, you call at the domicile of the "poor white trash." It is either an unpainted frame house in the suburbs of a town, or it is a hut upon some country hill-side.

You knock (the door-bell is never seen in such a place) and a young girl opens the door; you enter. The furniture is meagre. A short bench or a three-legged stool is offered you, of which you avail yourself. As you are somewhat thirsty you wish a drink of water, which is handed you by the little girl. She got it from the "pail" on the "shelf," and you drink it out of a "gourd." Presently the mother comes in and addresses you politely. Her appearance is not very attractive. Her "home-spun" dress is not immaculate, but there is no haggard look about her face. She is healthy and not ill-formed. The little girl is about the same age as the one the reader met on a similar occasion in a Northern city. There is bloom on her cheek and lustre in her eye. She moves with unwearied step—

the simple, unfettered child of nature. As the sun begins to sink behind the Western hills and the dews of night come on, the father of this family with his son "Sam" arrive from their work. Their coats are probably hanging on their arms and one suspender doing duty for two.

You are struck at once by their contented countenance and their humble manners. Over the whole scene is cast the glamour of pastoral life. An indifference to and ignorance of the affairs of the surging world of activity characterizes their conversation.

The evening meal of "corn bread," "pork," "sorgum," coffee and "hoe cake," they relish exceedingly. A gentle current of humor flows through them all, because the father and son, though having worked all day, have not strained every muscle to its fullest tension, or rushed at break-neck speed. They have taken "their time." So a few minutes rest just previous to eating makes them feel almost as fresh as in the morning. They, therefore, do not hang under the dull pall of exhaustion, lifting the cup to their lips with weary hand and in silence, because to talk is laborious in such a condition; but they eat with relish, and their native love for a joke is sure to bring out the recital of one, if anything humorous has occurred during the day. They speak, too, in a dialect unlike any other on the globe.

"They'll come in the doh (door),
 And tell you of 'Mister Moh' (Mr. More),
 How he missed the 'Quars' (cars),
 And mixed up all his and others 'affars' (affairs).

"He had just come from the 'stoh' (store);
 But the 'steem injine' had gone 'befoh' (before).
 On the 'phlatform' he laid his 'poke' (pork);
 And his 'taters,' too, he did 'tote' (carry).

"And so came 'arter' (after) time.
 We 'lofed' and 'loafed,' but 'Byme'
 "By" I said, "'Old Hoss-fly;'
 You'd better give dem 'taters' to the mule,"
 And den I went off to 'scule' (school)."

Great ignorance rises up before you as you listen to all this. But you also observe that there is a naturalness about the whole that is pleasing. You cannot but think that what these people want to do is merely to live; year by year they tread the same pathway, neither degenerating nor progressing. There never comes a crisis in their lives. Their souls never weather a storm, and they think but of themselves and of nature. Of money they have little and know little. They are not unhappy; a majority of them fill out the full measure of years, and at last their rude, but simple life "is rounded with a sleep." A little wooden slab at the head of a mound on some sloping hill-side tells the last of the story.

From this home you at length depart, having learned more of the wonders of your country than you ever knew before. You have been at the "negative pole" of the southern battery, and it now behooves you to visit the "positive pole."

It is difficult to describe the scenes at the post-bellum mansions of the *élite* of Southern society. A half-dozen printed blanks with the same words upon each will, if only the several names be inserted, pretty accurately describe the scenes of a society event in as many different Northern cities. Society there has come to be a great machine; all is formality. Not so in a Southern mansion. You miss the display of wealth, gorgeous costumes, and perhaps the diamonds. Hospitality and a personal interest of each guest in the other seem prominent features of the occasion. The personal beauty of the ladies is even made more prominent by contrast with the simple elegance of their dress. The Duke of Aranza, addressing Juliana, voices the feelings of most Southerners:—

> "* * * She's adorned
> Amply that in her husbands eye looks lovely—
> The truest mirror that an honest wife
> Can see her beauty in,
> Thus modestly attired, a half-blown rose stuck in thy hair,
> With no more diamonds than those eyes are made of,
> No deeper rubies than compose thy lips,
> Nor pearls more precious than inhabit them,—
> With the pure red and white, which that same hand
> Which blends the rainbow, mingles in thy cheeks,
> This well proportioned form (think not I flatter)
> In graceful motion to harmonious sounds
> And thy free tresses dancing in the wind."

There is no rushing, no hurried movements of carriages. All *take* their time.

The conversation, into which the ladies enter, may be about the latest congressional speech, for politics is a home thing with the Southerner, and a person who cannot speak intelligently of current affairs, of the general principles of government and also more or less of poetry and literature finds his entrance to the charmed circle barred. Wealth is not requisite; intelligence is indispensable. As a people they wish for just so much wealth as will enable them to make the most of *themselves*, as will ennoble and develope the best qualities of social life.

A recent writer in a Northern Magazine says of them: "In studying the Bourbons I have been forced to conclude that nothing has yet been attained anywhere much better than the domestic life of this class of the Southern people, in its intelligence, refinement, beauty and general elevation and wholesomeness."

Between these two extremes "the poor white trash" and the Bourbons or *élite*, there is the middle class, great in numbers but feeble in influence and power. It contributes nothing toward forming the institutions and character of the Southern social fabric. It complacently follows the higher element in peace and war, not, however, from a sense of servility, but from conviction. It thinks that the direction of affairs falls naturally into the hands of those who from education, culture and experience can be the better judges. But whenever there is found a man of merit, of intellect and conspicuous worth among the great middle class, he is recognized and he rises. From thence have come many of the brightest intellects and the noblest men the South has ever produced.

What then is the *genius* of the South?—*Men*, not *things*. If the choice be between a busy humming factory and a *noble* man or woman, the South would be *strongly inclined* to choose the latter.

Next to his God a Southerner worships *honor*, and next this, *woman*. He regards her as the noblest work of creation—a being too beautiful to be marred one iota for the sake of any earthly riches, one whose burdens should be lightened to the greatest possible degree. "Men," say they "may *labor* to live, but woman only to be *more a woman*."

There follows, as a natural consequence of this great devotion to *persons*, some evils. It takes away a feeling of natural freedom which everyone desires to possess. It mingles a man's *opinions* with the man himself. One of the most glorious features of the North is, that there a man holds his position in society for what he is worth *socially*, whatever those social requirments may be, and not for what he's worth as a *business* man. He retains his reputation as a lawyer for what he is worth *legally*, and not financially. He has an influence in politics for what he is worth *politically* and not *socially*.

As an example, take the experience of Jenkins Castleton in the social circles of Philopolis. In all his experience he never found his politics or his nativity to interfere with his prospects *socially* or financially. Some of his warmest friends were those strong on the other side politically. There is an air of freedom and justice in such a constitution of society that makes it eminently powerful and inviting.

Not so at the South. The politics, and the institutions there are so wrapped up in the individual, that his position on such questions affects his standing socially and financially. There is sometimes a collateral reason for this state of affairs. For instance, a man cannot as a general thing enter the *élite* of Southern society, if he be a *Republican*. That is the fact as it appears.

But why, we ask, is it so?—Because a man cannot be a Republican there without associating more or less with *negroes* and carpet-baggers (most of whom are of unworthy character). The Bourbons therefore regard a man who associates with negroes and white men of indifferent characters as unfit to enter the best society. If the higher classes of the whites were divided politically as they are in some Northern localities, there is no doubt that this social exclusion would be greatly diminished, but still it would probably exist to some extent. In this as in other things, the great personal life of the people comes to the front. It is not so much on account of *Republicanism* as on account of *Republicans* that this social exclusion exists.

But this principle does not obtain in the North at all.

Young Jenkins was compelled to associate *politically* with men in his city who were anything else but *élite*, but this did not effect his *social* standing in the least. The genius of the South then is personality—*Man*. "What," you say, "do you wish to do about it?"—"Tear down the Southern social fabric?"—No, my reader, we would not. We would have less *personality*, more *materiality*.

> "They soon grow old who grope for gold
> In marts where all is bought and sold;
> Who live for self and on some shelf
> In darkened vaults hoard up their pelf,
> Cankered and crusted o'er with mold;
> For them their youth itself is old.
>
> "They ne'er grow old who gather gold
> Where spring awakes and flowers unfold;
> Where suns arise in joyous skies,
> And fill the soul within their eyes;
> For them the immortal bards have sung,
> For them old age itself is young."

CHAPTER XLIV.

A CRISIS.

A TIME had now come when the courage and the fidelity of Ida Lexter were to be tried to the utmost. Jenkins had for some time noticed the growing pallor on her cheek. She did not appear at the Librarian's desk in the Sunday School of Dr. Siddons' church with that cheerful spirit that usually characterized her. Jenkins recalled the gloomy and mysterious words she had spoken to him a few months before on the occasion of the decorating of the Sunday School room for the Christmas festival. He recollected that she then told him that she was wretched, and that *she trusted to him.* These things began to trouble the mind of Jenkins. He tried to fathom the inwardness of it all, but he could not come to any conclusion, so many different interpretations could be put upon the matter.

One evening about this time Mr. Jerome Leonardine called at the Lexter mansion, and sent his card to Miss Ida Lexter. As Ida was about to enter the drawing room her mother whispered into her ear that she hoped Ida would receive Mr. Lenardine with the kindness and respect due a valuable friend of the Lexter family.

A PROPOSAL.

Jerome Lenardine was in appearance at least the model ladies' man—tall, graceful, handsome and wealthy. But his soul was as incapable of a genuine and unselfish love as were the stones of the street; so in contrast with the noble and generous nature of Jenkins Castleton, Lenardine coveted the beauty of Ida Lexter; his pride would be pampered could he defeat his rivals for her hand.

Castleton, on the other hand, coveted her love; he longed for the life-long union of their mutual hearts. None knew better the difference between the characters of these two men than Ida Lexter.

So on this evening Jerome Lenardine had come to accomplish his long-cherished object—the winning of the hand of Ida Lexter.

Miss Ida received him pleasantly. She seemed to be unusually merry. Lenardine took this as a propitious omen.

At length, assuming a more serious air, Mr. Lenardine, looking earnestly at Ida, told her in studied accents that probably she had already divined something of the meaning of his attentions and devotion to her; that he had felt himself much encouraged; that he now looked forward to the fruition of his hopes, and would ask her hand in marriage.

During this recital Ida bore an interested look, neither appearing embarrassed nor showing any evidence that what was said to her was being unfavorably received.

"Mr. Lenardine," she presently said, "I am impressed with the importance of your request; and I need scarcely tell you that you are favored by all the family. So you can, I know, give me three days in which to give you my final answer."

"Certainly, Miss Ida," said the suitor, who was satisfied from Ida's demeanor that he had gained a conquest, "I will do so with pleasure."

Then the conversation turned upon general society matters, both talking freely and pleasantly together. The hour of ten o'clock having arrived, Mr. Lenardine took his departure, after having received an invitation to call again in three days for his answer.

On the morning of the second day after the above related interview, Ida received a letter. The superscription indicated plainly the hand-writing of Mr. Jerome Lenardine. It was from him; and the contents of the letter must have been extremely interesting to Ida, for she read it over a number of times. A few hours after the receipt of this letter Ida informed her mother that she would not be at home for dinner, as she had been invited to spend the day with a lady friend. Ida then started on her intended visit.

Evening came and she had not yet returned. Mr. Lexter was seriously troubled. He inquired where she was. Mrs. Lexter said that she had gone to spend the day with a lady friend, but had not told her whom.

Messengers were then dispatched to the most intimate friends of Ida, but these latter all said that they had not seen her that day. There was great commotion at the Lexter mansion the next morning. Inquiries were privately sent to every place where it was likely she might have been, but no word of her was heard.

Mr. Lexter did not wish to report the matter to the police authorities, as he desired to avoid the publicity connected with such a procedure.

The third day came, the day on which Mr. Lenardine was to receive his answer. No traces of Ida Lexter had yet been found. Mrs. Lexter was so overcome by the fearful shock that she was prostrated and confined to her bed.

Dreadful thoughts came over the minds of the Lexters on this third day. They anxiously looked over the daily newspapers for an account of the finding of the "*body of an unknown young woman.*"

It was now evening, the time when Mr. Jerome Lenardine was to receive the answer of Ida Lexter to his momentous question.

Mr. Lenardine had probably heard that Miss Lexter was not at home; anyhow he did not call on the appointed evening.

A week passed by and yet no word from Ida Lexter! On the following Sunday her friends, and especially Jenkins, noticed her absence from church. Mr. Lexter informed those who inquired about her that she was visiting a friend.

A short while after these events the society notes in the newspapers announced that "Mr. Jerome Lenardine, the young millionaire, had sailed for Europe."

CHAPTER XLV.

A MYSTERY.

> "O, how this spring of love resembleth
> The uncertain glory of an April day;
> Which now shows all the beauty of the sun,
> And by-and-bye a cloud takes all away."

THE weeks passed by and still there came no tidings of Ida Lexter. The Lexter family were unable to explain her absence satisfactorily to the many friends of Ida who inquired after her. She had among these some near and dear friends of her girlhood, and they could not understand why Ida never once wrote them a word. It began to be known among the immediate friends of the Lexters that there was something mysterious about the continued absence of Ida. It became at last a matter of conversation at Dr. Siddons' church, and of course it was not long in reaching the ears of Jenkins Castleton. He was deeply grieved. But, like the Lexter family, he could not fancy where she might be. The awful thought of her death fell like a pall over his soul. He pondered as his sleepless nights rolled away over every word Ida had uttered to him, in order to find, if possible, some explanation of the mystery, some clue to its solution.

"*You know that Mr. Jerome Lenardine!*" These words Ida had uttered on one impressive occasion. They yet rung in his ear.

"Jerome Lenardine!"

The burning brain of young Jenkins was racked with the sound of that name.

As if he had suddenly caught upon some new thought that he feared he might lose, Jenkins sprang from his bed, hastily lit the gas, and throwing a cloak about his shoulders seated himself at his writing table.

"*Jerome Lenardine sailed for Europe about the time that Ida Lexter disappeared!!*" hastily wrote the almost frenzied lover. He looked at the sentence. It seemed to tell a terrible tale. He read it and re-read it. He could not, he would not believe that such unfaithfulness, such falsehood had a habitation in the breast of Ida Lexter.

Seizing the paper upon which was written this stinging sentence, he muttered deeply: "It's false, it's false. There's *foul play*, the blackest foul play somewhere!!"

And he covered his face with his hands already moistened by copious tears, and bent over the desk—the picture of despair.

Aurora, the rosy-fingered Goddess of the morn, appeared in the eastern sky; she sent her soft rays forth and they fell upon that head still unraised, still bowed down in desolation. At length he slowly looked up and gazed out upon the morning. It seemed to calm him somewhat. The time had come for action. After thinking intently for some minutes Jenkins took pen and paper and wrote the following letter :

"PHILOPOLIS, May 13th 188—.
"MR. ALFRED S. LEXTER.

"DEAR SIR :—Owing to the present crisis in my affairs and also in yours, I deem it my duty to write to you upon a subject of the deepest interest to us both.

"It is now more than three years since I first met your daughter, Miss Ida Lexter, at Dr. Siddons' church. Almost unconsciously, we were from our very first meeting deeply impressed with each other. Deep down in the hidden chambers of my heart was a love which for months I dared not breathe even to myself. As I would sometimes see her the centre of a group of admiring friends; as I looked upon her heavenly face, and caught the glances of her beaming eye, reflecting only the nobleness of an angel's soul; as her voice, which to me had a sweeter cadence than all other earthly sounds, fell on my ear, I felt myself enchanted by a reality which I supposed existed only in the fancy of the poets. Surely this is enough to describe the scene! No, it is still undescribed. Just as the sun from its exhaustless bosom feeds light to a thousand planets, so did the voice, the eye, the form, the grace and virtue of Ida receive an additional lustre from a guileless beauty.

"I still looked upon her. 'She is not for me—vain the thought. Oh is there any toil that I could undergo, is there any possession that I could ever have, which would make me worthy of her?—worthy of a smile or a look of hers?'

"You may think that I am wandering in some dreamland and am now describing to you an imaginary scene. But alas, it is a terrible reality!

"I must hasten on with my story.

"The months flew by. Wrapped up in my studies, I kept down as best I could the feelings of what I regarded as a vain and hopeless love.

"Summer came. I went to spend my vacation among the mountains. Among the places I visited was Tyro's Glen. I started early one morning to explore the great formation of nature. I was alone. I lost myself in contemplating the mighty wonders that on every hand surrounded me. I felt myself so near to God that I uncovered my head for fear that I stood in the very presence of the Deity.

"I paused upon a rustic bridge which connected the rocky banks of the turbid stream that makes its weird music in coursing over the bottom of the gorge. I was looking down the long granite vista, enjoying its multifarious grandeur, when I was startled at hearing my own name sounded by a voice coming from below—a voice whose sound strangely touched a hidden chord of my heart.

"I need say but little more. You well know whose accents those were. I could command my heart no longer, and there in the presence of God's mighty works it unbosomed itself; its inmost secrets burst forth. And, oh, when I found that a love as deep, as true and as secret had for many weary months filled the heart of Ida herself, I felt that my cup of earthly joy was indeed full. For me the winds did not then sigh in vain, nor the limpid waters roll along to a listless beholder. I then renewed my faith. I veritably believed that

> ' The harp at nature's advent strung
> Had never ceased to play;
> Nor that the song the stars of morning sung
> Had ever died away.'

"We pledged a life-long fidelity to our sacred vows, but none save He above was ever to know of what had passed, till a more propitious time should come.

"Autumn came. I returned to my duties. The behests of love fell hard upon one so little used to struggling. It was so hard for Ida Lexter to wear a mask. Society laid its claims upon her. Parental duty and trust ever and anon said: 'My child, confide in those who hold you so dear. Tell them all.' Then came another strain. A wealthy suitor for her hand, favored by family and friends, appeared upon the scene.

The too tender chords could no longer withstand the shock. Finally she disappeared, and for all we know may now be with God. But wherever she is, if living, I believe her true to the vows she made; or if she sought relief in the cold hospitality of death, still I shall believe that even in the presence of the King of Terrors her latest breath re-echoed but the words, 'I am yet true.' If this be so, may the angels nobly guard her place of rest!

"I have to remind you, in closing, of a little coincidence which may or may not have escaped your notice, namely, that *Mr. Jerome Lenardine sailed for Europe about the time of Ida's disappearance!*

"I have every reason to believe that Jerome Lenardine is a bad and unscrupulous man; and as he is still abroad, I am haunted by the thought that he is in some way connected with this mystery. I have taken the liberty to give this hint because of an anxiety and sorrow which is second only to that of loving parents who have lost their dearest treasure. I have thus frankly spoken because I deemed it but my simple duty. I have told you all. If I have loved not wisely but too well, may I find forgiveness in the abundance of your generosity, and for the sake of her who is gone.

"With that profound sympathy which can only come from a fellowship of sorrow, and asking that the blessings of heaven may fall upon you and yours to soothe you in this great affliction, I remain

"Very truly,
"JENKINS CASTLETON."

This letter was mailed and duly delivered to Mr. Lexter. It was a great surprise. But it was very welcome. Any ray of hope was welcome then.

Mr. and Mrs. Lexter were both very much satisfied with the honest statements and frank confessions of young Castleton. Mr. Lexter wrote a kindly letter in reply, thanking Jenkins for his sympathy and requesting that he should call at the Lexter mansion at the earliest possible moment, when all matters could be fully discussed and plans laid out for solving the mystery of Ida's fate.

Jenkins called the very day that he received this letter. His meeting with the Lexter family was very affecting. Mr. Lexter warmly grasped his hand and bade him welcome.

When Jenkins left the Lexter mansion late that evening (for he remained to dinner) plans had been laid for an exhaustive search and investigation into the doings and whereabouts of Jerome Lenardine.

CHAPTER XLVI.

THE DEAD WOOD FALLING OFF.

* * * * * * * *

We must now pass over two years and view the changes that have taken place.

The world of politics was never so astir as now. Another presidential election was near at hand, and as a matter of course the "politicians" were all agog.

But a few years had produced a mighty revolution in the spirit of the people. President Anson had not succeeded in all his plans. In spite of the liberal garb he at first wore, his walk was quietly but steadily along the "Stalwart" path. The body of the people had not been indifferent to the drift of affairs. So we need not be surprised to find that the contest had now come to be between the "machine," wielded by a master hand, and the disorganized people. The following extract from a well-known political writer expresses the situation and the feeling that prevailed about this time:

" We must look elsewhere than to the man on horseback, for the form of despotism which is likely, if any, to triumph over our republican institutions; it must be something which not only carries on the traditions of the Republic, but is built directly upon the principles of authority, which has prevailed under the Republic. This authority, all will admit, is *Party*.

"According to our unwritten constitution, party is the highest authority in the land. Neither are the expressed provisions of organic law, nor the honor and welfare of the country, nor the fundamental principles of free government ever allowed to stand in the way of the interests of party. Nor is it ever admitted in practice, hardly even in theory, that the government has any duties towards any but the members of the party which it represents.

" A party under our system is an association of persons who combine together for the purpose of conducting the government. Some common political principles or points of policy are convenient for the purpose of keeping a party together, and especially of attracting voters; but these are no way *essential*. Nothing is more common than for persons, even those occupying high and influential positions, to subordinate entirely their private opinions, whether as to men or doctrines, and to give their assent to measures to which they had before been entirely opposed.

*   *   *   *   *   *   *

" From these two well-established facts, that party is the highest authority in the land, and that the sole object of party is the possession and management of the machinery of government, it necessarily follows that the only part of governmental action which is of any importance or value is *administration*. A further consequence is that Congress, which *was primarily a legislative body*, and which still attends *occasionally* to the business of law-making, finds it expedient to devote most of its energies to the details of administration, in this way relieving the executive of a considerable share of his burdens, and making sure that the interests of party shall not be sacrificed, even in the most trifling matters. Under the system of government thus developed, the men of mark and influence will, of course, be men of administrative ability, whether it is a strong masculine power to control other men, or skill in finesse and intrigue. What used to be called statesmanlike qualities, knowledge of the principles of government and of the needs of the country, and of the capacity to adapt measures to the desired end—qualities that are useful in legislation—are no longer *in demand;* legislation beyond what is called for by the needs of the *party* is an impertinence.

* * * * * * * *

" Our party system already possesses a method for the transmission and retention of power, perfected or nearly so, by a long series of experiments, which have been applied on the largest scale and with the happiest results. In this method, *popular suffrage* plays an essential, but by no means *controlling* part. With a few improvements in detail it will be wholly in the power of a *group* of statesmen, when once in the possesson of the government, to secure themselves against being deprived of their authority by any change in popular sentiment, however great. The boldness and thoroughness with which this method has already been carried into execution on one occasion, and the warm approval with which the best citizens greeted its success on the ground that a change of party in power, *even by the popular will*, would be disastrous to the best interests of the country, are facts of the best augury for its success in the future.

* * * * * * * *

" Meanwhile the American people are tired and discouraged. Twice they have been cheated by the politicians out of what seemed a hopeful promise of reform.

* * * * * * * *

" They thoroughly despise the present order of things as shown by the contempt with which the politicians as a class are regarded, yet they follow these very politicians like a flock of sheep. What wonder that the leaders are shameless and defiant when they feel sure that all talk and criticism will cease on election day? Little do they care for indignation and contempt if the *offices* are secure. ' *Oderint dum probent*' is their motto; 'disapprove as much as you like, only give us *your votes*.' So long as this is the spirit in which men vote, the rule of the oligarchy is secure, for the highest allegiance is to party, and *they* are the party."

To such a lamentable state had politics come that the people, who are always slow to anger, at last rose in their might. They gave the two great political parties a chance to catch the spirit of the hour. But the politicians had learned nothing. When the platforms of the two great parties came out they showed the same old composition of knots and rotten timber.

Below, in one column will be found the "official" platform; in the other the "real" platform of the several parties as they now appeared.

DEMOCRATIC PARTY PLATFORM.

OFFICIAL.	REAL.
THE DEMOCRATS OF THE UNITED STATES IN CONVENTION ASSEMBLED DECLARE:	THE DEMOCRATS OF THE UNITED STATES IN CONVENTION ASSEMBLED DECLARE:
First. We renew our allegiance to the Constitution of the United States as interpreted by the founders of Democracy, expounded by a long line of statesmen, and preserved through the fidelity and patriotism of a free people; and we reassert the doctrines embodied in the last National Convention of the party.	*First.* We consider it best for *policy's* sake to support the *whole* of the Constitution of the United States; but we have never officially declared our belief in the justice of those new Constitutional Amendments (the XIII, XIV and XV); nor have we ever admitted the constitutionality of the Reconstruction measures. They are a hard pill for us to swallow, for by their aid our brethren of the South were held down in Republican bondage for ten years, and the Federal Government kept out of our hands for twenty years. But if we can only get the Government into our hands *this* time, we'll certainly return the compliment to the Republicans, and hold the Government by *the aid of those same amendments* for the succeeding twenty years. Oh, no! We don't want the amendments repealed! Not we! P. S.—Fidelity and patriotism are only found within the ranks of the Democratic Party.
Second. Opposition to centralization—the gradual absorption by the Federal Government of power not rightfully belonging to it, thus breaking down the	*Second.* The plank in official platform on centralization expresses about what is our honest opinion upon the subject. But it must be remarked, that when we

barriers which the States could oppose to a central despotism. With *divided* powers, it would be impossible, with *consolidated* powers, easy for liberty, though preserved in form, to be destroyed in *substance*.

had possession of the Federal Government before the war, the "founders of Democracy" some times, on occasions of great party danger, used unauthorized Federal powers, and we found their use pretty convenient for party purposes. But we never brag about this like the Republicans do about the many unauthorized powers they have used. We prefer to manipulate the *States*, and then put these several manipulations together to make an entirety. The Republicans, on the other hand, want first to get the *entirety*, and then manipulate *this*. Thus, when they sin, it permeates the *whole* country, as for instance, the law creating the Federal Supervisors of Election. But when *we* sin, it is confined to the particular locality in which the sin is committed, as for instance, a little bull-dozing in the Southern States.

Third. No sumptuary laws; separation of religion from Government, that there may be no political church or sectarian state. Common schools, efficient in character and adequate in number for the needs of the whole people.

Third. We believe in free-dom, free-whiskey, and many of us in free-trade. So we honestly wish for no sumptuary laws. They'd cause us to lose votes, so we could not afford to pass such laws, no matter how just or how needful they might be. Free schools would not damage some of our voters—nor any other kind of schools.

Fourth. Home rule; honest money, consisting of gold and silver and paper currency convertible into coin on demand, and the strict maintenance of the public faith, State and National.

Fourth. Our financial plank is meant to be pretty flexible. We have plenty of room for all kinds of principles, if only the holders of them vote *one* way (our way). Greenbackers, Inflationists, and Hard-Money men are alike welcome to come under our ample fold, if only they bring their *votes* with them. It is *votes* that we want. We do not particularly need either men in principles, if we can get *votes*.

Fifth. A tariff so regulated that it will not destroy American manufactures or oppress the people, giving revenue to the Government, *life* to the manufactures and *protection* to all.

Fifth.—The Tariff! Now you have struck us in a tender spot. In our last National Platform we called for a "Tariff for Revenue *only;*" and High Protectionists and Free Traders were alike enthusiastic in their support of the ticket nominated on that platform. Just previous to an election, we must appear to the people to be solid for the principles of the platform (and we always construct a platform that we think will take with the people); and then *after* the election, when measures come up in Congress, we vote as we *please*, and if

Sixth. Republics of the past having perished by the supremacy of military power, and as the nations of Europe are still suffering from the same oppressive evil, we demand the subordination of the military to the civil law, that our people be not made familiar with the chosen weapon of tyranny.

Seventh. We demand a civil service, the entrance to which shall be through honesty and capability only; and we demand further, that existing abuses shall cease and thorough reform begin.

Ninth. The existing administration is but the prize drawn in the "lottery of assassination;" it does not, and has not, represented the sentiments of the people of the United States; it has been the tool of faction; it has vetoed measures meant for the people's good, and has used every possible means the ingenuity of politicians could devise to perpetuate its own despotic power.

Tenth. The right to a free ballot is a right preservative of all rights, and must and shall be maintained in every part of the United States.

Eleventh. The great Presidential fraud of eight years ago is not yet for-

we are reminded that we are voting *differently* from the way we talked during the previous campaign, we reply: "You know there was an *election* pending then."

"When I was single, Oh then!
When I was married, Oh *then!*"

Sixth. These are about our honest opinions concerning military power. We prefer an easier, quieter and more effective weapon than the bayonet. A *ballot* is worth more to us at any time than a bayonet.

Seventh. Civil Service! Another tender spot. This Civil Service is a hard thing to manage satisfactorily. In the early years of the Government's existence offices, except Cabinet and other important positions, which affect the policy of the administration, were held for life or during good behavior; and it so continued until the "spoils" system was instituted by that good old Democrat, Andrew Jackson. The sentiment that "To the victor belong the spoils" is deeply grounded in human nature, and cannot be eradicated. We might, however, be induced to adopt the life-tenure or during good-behavior system, but this can be done by us only after *we get in power.* Then we would be profoundly persuaded that the system is practicable and just (Selah!).

Ninth. To these expressions concerning the present administration we heartily say, amen! One remark only is needed in regard to vetoed bills supported by us. Our advocacy of anti-Chinese bills was only for political claptrap. We wanted to get the votes of the Pacific States, and these we had to have, and to obtain these votes we renounced some of the cherished traditions and time-honored principles of our party. The party's interest must always be served, even if our principles go.

Tenth. Of this plank we have only to say, that we will ———, until we have thoroughly ——— (Selah!). These are our honest sentiments about the *ballot.*

Eleventh. There are some honest sentiments in this plank also. But it is to

gotten by the people of the United States, and they still have condign punishment in store for the perpetrators of that shameless crime against popular liberty; and as the power then fraudulently achieved has since been used to perpetuate Republican rule, it is the bounden duty of the people to now vindicate their outraged liberties at the polls.

Twelfth. Free ships and a living chance for American commerce on the sea and on the land; no discrimination in favor of transportation lines, corporations or monopolies.

Thirteenth. The Democratic Party is the friend to labor and the laboring man, and will protect alike from the oppression of monopoly and the license of the commune.

Fourteenth. No more Chinese coolies to be allowed to come to our shores to degrade and injure honest labor.

Fifteenth. We congratulate the country upon the work done by the Democracy during the past eight years in guarding the liberties of the people, in bringing about retrenchment and reform in many departments of the Government, and above all, in its zealous efforts to re-establish the reign of peace and good will, thus securing prosperity at home and national honor abroad.

be noted that we never renominated the defrauded Democratic candidate for the Presidency, that the people might render him poetic justice. We knew he had a righteous cause. But he wasn't at that time an "available" candidate. He couldn't serve the ends of the party, so we had to toss him overboard. Justice must always give way to party necessity. So we didn't renominate him.

Twelfth. There is a deal of honesty in this plank also, but it is mainly a bid for the support of working men. Powerful corporations control so many votes that it would never be expedient for the party to be openly hostile to them. Our policy toward both monopolies and labor will be governed by the probable support our party can get from each.

Thirteenth. This plank is very general, because in these days of "progress" it cannot be stated definitely what a party's principles really are, as these are determined, not by standards of *right*, but entirely by questions of *expediency*.

Fourteenth. We only want the vote of the Pacific States. *Accordingly* an anti-Chinese plank is inserted.

Fifteenth. This is said always by every political party, and, of course, we follow the custom of the times.

REPUBLICAN PARTY PLATFORM.

OFFICIAL.

THE REPUBLICAN PARTY in National Convention assembled, after having served the Nation for twenty-four years in peace and war, submits the following summary of its achievements, which it takes pride in recounting: Its efforts in behalf of Freedom have been ceaseless and successful; it took the Nation's flag, torn down and insulted by rebellion, and

REAL.

THE REPUBLICAN PARTY in National Convention assembled, submits the following summary of its achievements: We have *had possession* of the Government for twenty-four years, and have had in all six Presidents, only three of whom were elected by the people. Two of our Presidents came in by reason of their predecessors having been assassi-

re-unfurled it to wave triumphantly in its pristine glory; it reconstructed the Union of the States; it banished slavery from our soil, now made forever sacred to Liberty; it transformed abject slaves into sovereign citizens; it has demanded justice first, and peace afterwards; it has given equality to the laws; it has raised the value of our paper currency from thirty-eight per cent. to the par of gold; it has restored upon a solid basis payment in coin for all the National obligations, and has given us a currency absolutely good and equal in every part of our extended country; it has raised the credit of the nation from the point where six per cent. bonds sold at eighty-six cents to where three and four per cent. bonds were eagerly sought for at a premium; under its administration railways have increased from 31,000 miles in 1860 to more than 90,000 miles to-day. Our foreign trade has enormously increased; our exports far exceed our imports; without resorting to loans it has, since the war closed, defrayed the ordinary expenses of the Government, besides the accruing interest on the public debt, and has annually disbursed more than $30,000,000 for soldiers' pensions; it has paid more than $888,000,000 of the public debt, and by refunding the balance at lower rates, has reduced the annual interest charge from $151,000,000 to less than $89,000,000; all the industries of the country have revived, labor is in demand, wages have increased and throughout the entire country there is evidence of a coming prosperity greater than any we have ever enjoyed. Upon this record the Republican Party asks for the continued confidence of the people, and this Convention submits for their approval the following statement of the principles and purposes, which will continue to inspire its efforts.

nated, and one was put in by force and fraud. Our fraudulent President was not really a Republican, and he didn't stand by the party; there have been also several Democratic Congresses, but nevertheless we claim that there has been substantially Republican rule since the war. By "Freedom," we mean freedom to vote for the candidates of the Republican Party, and wherever our candidates are successful, freedom must be regarded as existing and *vice versa*.

We say in our official platform that "it" took the nation's flag, which had been torn down, etc. Of course this "it" refers to the Republican Party. But we know it was not our "Party" that suppressed rebellion, but that it was the Government and the people of the United States, among which people were many Democrats, who bled and died for the Union. Nor was it our "Party" that abolished slavery. It was the people of the several States, who legally abolished slavery by adopting the amendments to the Constitution of the United States, and as the required number of States could not have been obtained without the aid of the Democratic votes in those States, it is plain that our "party" did not abolish slavery. But our party must never cease to claim the credit of abolishing slavery. We needn't be too exact with the people, and as voters rarely investigate carefully into political matters, they can be blinded on many points.

The people must be taught the habit of implicitly obeying the "leaders" and all questioning must be staved off. Nothing would injure the party's prospects more than absolute peace and good feeling between the two great sections of our country. Therefore, if a few outrages be committed down South just before election times, and if we can make the people believe these outrages were committed in the interest of Democracy, why then we are sure of a large Northern vote. If there were perfectly free speech and free thought, and a free action in every part of the United States, the mission of our par)y would be ended.

For on this point only are we all united, and on all economic questions the members of our party differ widely. Peace would ruin us. Give us justice first, for under this head we can take a wide latitude.

About equality to the laws we need not be too explicit. In times of great party danger we have found it necessary to pass certain class legislation, in order to secure the support of the money power. The same is true of the amendment making it impossible to prevent any person from voting on account of race, color or previous condition of servitude, as was true of the other amendments. The people of the States, not our " Party," adopted it. We know that suffrage emanates from the *States*, and that the Constitution of the United States confers upon no one the right to vote.

In some States Negroes cannot vote for Congressmen, Presidential electors or even for State officers, because they fail to comply with the election laws of the *State*. Now the Constitution of the United States is the Supreme law of the land, and therefore above all State laws in conflict with it, hence *if* the Constitution of the United States conferred the right to vote upon the negro, no State law could deprive him of it in any instance. In some States we know that men *who are not* citizens of the United States at all can vote for Congressmen, etc., showing that suffrage emanates from the States. But this must not be explained to the negroes. They must be taught that they get all their rights from the Federal Government, and that the States are comparatively unimportant.

We did not pass those amendments, because we wanted the negro, but because we wanted his *vote*. As the vote of the negro is to the Republican Party, *so* must the Republican Party be to the negro.

We say, in almost the exact words of our last National platform, that "it" (meaning our *party*) raised the value of our paper currency, restored credit, &c., and that "it" (our *party* again) paid the expenses of the government and the interest on the public debt! Now we well know that our party *did not do* this, but that it was the Government of the United States which did it. We will have to regard all the Government's revenue as belonging to the party, if we admit that the *party* paid all these Government expenses. We want the people to see no difference between our party and the Government. They are to be regarded as one and the same.

We say in our official platform that

railways have increased under our administration, and that the industries of the country have revived, that labor is in demand at good wages, and altogether that general prosperity has reigned. We might, with equal credit to ourselves, say that under our administration occurred the greatest financial panic and distress that ever befel America; that the fiercest labor strikes known in history occurred under our benign administration; that laboring men all over the country have organized in order to free themselves from intolerable oppression. That under our administration happened a terrible Yellow Fever epidemic, and also that a few years after the epidemic came great floods, destroying many lives and millions of dollars in property; that during our administration the sun has shined every day; that the refreshing rains have come so that the earth might bring forth her increase and thus give prosperity to the land; that also many miles of railroads have been built by private corporations with which the Republican Party had nothing to do; that, finally, all great good fortunes and calamities alike, which have no relation whatever to politics shall be put to the credit of the party in power! ! !

The "leaders," of course, know that all this is mere gammon. But as the people are too busy to bother with politics, we party managers have to do the work for them.

First. We affirm that the work of the last twenty-four years has been such as to commend itself to the favor of the nation, and that the fruits of the costly victories we have achieved through tremendous difficulties should be preserved; that the peace regained should be cherished; that the dissevered Union, now happily restored, should be perpetuated, and that the liberties secured to this generation should be transmitted undiminished to future generations; that the party which saved the nation in peril will serve it well in its security; that the order established, and the credit acquired should never be impaired; that the pensions promised should be extinguished by the full payment of every dollar thereof; that the reviving industries should be still further promoted, and that our commerce already great should be steadily encouraged.

First. Some of our work during the last twenty-four years we, of course, think commends itself to the favor of the nation; but we have performed some political labors, which need not be referred to any oftener than possible. Such as what is vulgarly termed "8 to 7," "Star Routes," "Visiting Statesmen," "Carpet Bag" Governments in the South, electing no negroes to office in the North, "Whiskey Rings," etc., etc. "The costly victories 'we' (our party again) have achieved." We, of course, know that the Government and armies of the United States had a little something to do with the achieving of the costly victories referred to; but our leaders must recollect that the people must be taught that the party is everything, and the Government itself little or nothing. With our party in power the Government will live, and *vice versa*.

We have been somewhat unfortunate in *preserving* the victories we say *we* have achieved; for though we never cease to boast that we freed the negro, yet in the same breath we say he is now in practical bondage in the South! We let the "Rebel Brigadiers," outwit us in capturing the negro (for we thought we had him), and then we turn to the people and ask for sympathy. So the leaders must tell the people that our party is necessary to "keep down" the South. We ask that "the peace regained should be cherished." But in every campaign we have found it necessary to preach the gospel of hate. We didn't want to do it. Our souls longed for rest, but then the party required otherwise. No matter what our honest feelings are we must suppress them and obey the party behests.

The leaders must continually tell the people about certain "results" of the war which are yet to be secured, which can only be secured by the Republican Party. The leaders know that if there were really any such "results," which have not *already* been secured, new amendments embodying them would be at once proposed by us. If there are any "results" which have not been properly secured, it is *our* fault. But we know there are no legitimate results which can be yet secured. We want something to agitate upon. Nothing is better for this purpose than imaginary "results" of the war.

The liberties secured to the people of this generation are complete submission and obedience to the will of the "bosses." These liberties should certainly be transmitted undiminished to future generations.

A strong general Government, with centralized power having its minions at work in all the States, is surely a great advantage to the ruling party, and these powers of Government always used to the party advantage, will tend to perpetuate indefinitely the party's rule. The rights of the several States can be trampled on one by one, almost imperceptibly. Thus the principles of a "strong" National Government, which "saved the nation in its peril "can, providing *our* party is in power, "serve the nation in its security." "Reviving industries," means the rich manufacturers. That is the laws and the policy of the Government are to be such that a certain class of our people receive benefits accorded to no others. This is the essence of aristocratic government, but we can't help it. Our party wants the money of the rich manufacturers. So we are compelled to favor them.

Second. The Constitution of the United States is a supreme law and not a mere contract; out of confederated states it made a sovereign nation; some powers are denied to the nation, while others are denied to the States; but the boundary between the powers reserved and those delegated is to be determined by the national, and not by the State tribunals.

Second. This plank is one of our most important dogmas. About the historical and political truth of it we are not concerned. It is one of the most potent means of perpetuating our power that our keen invention ever devised. Of course, as long as we have the General Government in our possession, we want it to be as *strong* as possible.

Our Official plank declares that "the Constitution of the United States is a supreme law, not a mere contract." *This* is what it suits our purpose to declare. But we know the Constitution itself says something different from that which our plank does. But as not one voter in ten thousand ever reads the Constitution of the United States, the boomerangs of our stump speakers pass very well for true constitutional doctrines. The Constitution itself (Art. VI) says: "This Constitution and the laws of the United States which shall be made in *pursuance thereof*, and all treaties made, or which shall be made, under the authority of the United States, *shall be the supreme law* of the land." It will thus be observed that the phrase, "and not a mere contract" is put in by us, and is simply our campaign opinion. For we know that our statement, that "out of confederated States it *made* a sovereign nation," is absolutely without foundation. Nations are *born*, they *grow* and *then* the *Nation* makes *the Constitution*, and not the Constitution *the Nation*. And what's more, the Constitution did not make anything. It received powers from another source. "We, the people of the United States do *ordain* and *establish* this Constitution for the United States of America." Hence, we see that the very preamble of the Constitution contradicts our platform. Yet we inserted this very plank in our last National Platform, and we have taught the same doctrine to the people for a quarter of a century. Party necessity required it, and historic truth must always give way to party necessity.

We know well that the last article of

the Constitution reads: "The Ratification of the Conventions of nine *States* shall be sufficient for the establishment of this *Constitution between* (not *over*) the States so *ratifying* the same."

And the fact is, that the people of the States ratified the Constitution *one by one*, and not as one solid nation. This settles what is meant by the phrase, "We, the people of the United States." If this meant the whole aggregated body of the people inhabiting the territory covered by the United States, then the framers of the Constitution carried their idea into effect in a very queer manner. Instead of submitting this Constitution to this whole and solid nation, they cut the nation up into little fragments, called the "Conventions of Nine States," and made the establishment of the Constitution contingent upon *all* and each of these nine fragments adopting the instrument. They did worse. They even fixed matters so that nine of the *smallest States*, containing less than *half* the population of the whole country, to establish the Constitution "between the States" so ratifying the same, thus leaving the greater portion of the people without the pale of the great charter of liberty! This proves that *numbers*, mere population, had nothing to do with establishing the Constitution, but that *States* did.

We often speak of the Constitution as if it was something over and above the States; when, in fact, we know that the *States* are as much, or if not more, a part of the Constitution as anything else. The word *State*, either in its singular or plural form, occurs in the Constitution of the United States about *one hundred and twenty seven times!* While the word *nation* does not occur at all! Hence we see that the framers of the Constitution did not think it worth while to even mention what we say the Constitution made, namely, *a sovereign nation*.

Third. The work of popular education is one left to the care of the several States; but it is the duty of the National Government to aid that work to the extent of its constitutional power. The intelligence of the nation is but the aggregate intelligence of the several States, and the destiny of the nation is

Third. This plank refers to the common school, and not to *political* education. This latter we will take into our *own* hands. Our political education means no political education. The more we can arouse the passions and the prejudices, and the *less* we *instruct* the minds of the people on political subjects,

not to be guided by the genius of any one State, but by the average genius of all.

Fourth. We affirm the belief, often avowed by us, that the duties levied for the purpose of revenue should so discriminate as to favor American labor; that no further grant of the public domain should be made to any railway, or other corporation; that slavery having perished in the States, its twin barbarity, polygamy, must die in the territories; that the protection everywhere accorded to citizens of American birth must be secured to citizens by American adoption; that we esteem it our duty to improve our water courses and harbors; but insist that further subsidies to persons or private corporations must cease; that the obligations of the Republic to the men who preserved its integrity in the hour of battle are undiminished by the lapse of twenty years since their final victory. To do them perpetual honor is, and forever shall be, the grateful privilege and sacred duty of the American people.

the better it will be for our party. A little true political knowledge on the part of the people would knock some of our party teachings to the wind. "Knowledge is power" was written by Lord Bacon, an old fogy. With a rank and file politically listless and ignorant and with a brilliant and able leadership, our party's rule is secure. Political ignorance is a mighty power.

Fourth. The word "labor" used in our official plank really means the *rich manufacturers.* We are continually talking about our love for American "labor." But as it is the great moneyed kings and rich manufacturers who furnish the "sinews of war" for our campaigns, we must shape the policy of the Government so as to "protect" them. Nearly all the rich men of the country belong to our Party. We are emphatically the rich man's party. Our party leaders are mostly worth millions. We always talk about our advocacy of the equality of all men, of the high and low, of the rich and poor. But it must be borne in mind that the votes of the poor and the lowly go to the support of our party, whose policy is always directed by the *rich,*

About the grants of the public domain which our party voted to make, something need be remembered. For constructing railroads the North has received directly from the Government 32,488,806 acres, while for a similar purpose the South received 12,365,351 acres. Railroad corporations in the North have received for building railroads 139,341,000 acres, while a single Southern railroad (run chiefly by Northern capital) has received 9,520,000 acres. For constructing canals the North received 4,405,986 acres, while the Southern States have received *not one acre!* These are the official figures. Yet we continually taunt the South for its poverty! We say, how terrible it is for such a *poor* section of the country to attempt to dictate the policy of the Government! Oh, if the people did know the inner workings of our party, what would they do! For the establishment and support of schools the North has received from the Government 70,213,574 acres of the public lands. The South has received 6,434,446 acres. Yet how have we taunted the South for its ignor-

Fifth. As the unrestricted immigration of Chinese to our country produces great evils and seriously menaces our institutions, it is the duty of Congress to restrain and limit that immigration by the enactment of just and adequate laws.

Sixth. We affirm that the patriotic life and martyred death of James A. Gaveson, late President of the United States are among the most glorious heritages of this nation To cherish his memory and profit by his example of noble deeds well done will be the grateful duty of this and succeeding generations.

Seventh. We charge upon the Democratic Party the habitual sacrifice of patriotism and justice to a supreme and insatiable lust for office and patronage; that to obtain possession of the National and State Governments, the control of place and position they have obstructed all efforts to promote the purity and conserve the freedom of suffrage and have devised fraudulent certifications and returns ; that they have, by methods vicious in principle and tyrannical in practice, attached partizan legislation to bills upon whose passage the very movements of government depend ; have crushed the rights of individuals; have

---

ance and illiteracy! Verily we are the party of justice and equality!

There is a big difference between a Democratic and a Republican grave in a battle field. The marble headstones don't designate any difference between them, but our party principles and practices do.

Fifth. This plank is contrary to the genius of our party, contradicts our pet theory of the brotherhood of man, under the inspiration of which we made the ignorant African an American citizen. The need of votes induced us to advocate the common brotherhood of man in the case of the negro, and the need of the votes of the Pacific slope induces us now to deny that common brotherhood in the case of the Chinese. In other words, we deny in the beginning of the second century of the Republic, what we gloried to acknowledge at the dawn of the first —that all men are created with equal rights. Thus the principles of our party must change with the requirements of the times ; but the requirments of the times are what *we* require.

We require that our party shall continue to rule, and that, like the nine hundred families of Sparta, the spoils of office shall remain in our hands.

Sixth. We affirm that the patriotic life and martyred death of James A. Gaveson, late President of the United States, are among the most glorious heritages of this nation. To cherish his memory and profit by his example of noble deeds well done will be the grateful duty of this and succeeding generations.

Seventh. This plank was substantially inserted in our last National platform, but as it fits as well now as it did then, we insert it again.

It may sound a little curious to thinking people to hear us talk about the "insatiable lust for office and patronage" of another party, when we ourselves have, for twenty-four years, used every means known to human ingenuity to satisfy our "supreme and insatiable lust for office and patronage." But to such a state of serenity have the people come that a party can declare or do anything, and they will vote for that party.

If there are any methods more "vi-

advocated the principles and sought the favor of rebellion against the nation; have endeavored to obliterate the sacred memories of the war, and to overcome its inestimable and valuable results of nationality, personal freedom and individual equality; and we submit it to the practicable, sensible people of the United States to say whether it would not be dangerous to the dearest interests of our country to surrender the National Government to a party which seeks to overthrow the existing policy, under which we are so prosperous, and thus bring distress and confusion where there is now order, confidence and hope.

cious in principle or tyrannical in practice than our party shackles and the dictum of our "bosses," we would certainly like to find them, for our present methods of rule are losing their novelty. "The rights of *individuals*" are indeed not crushed in the Republican Party, for their individual power is seen in its full vigor, for our party is ruled by *three or four individuals!*

It is certainly monstrous at this late day for the Democratic Party to seek the aid of "rebellion against the nation." Behold the "rebellious" aid the Democratic Party has invoked. It nominated a *Union* General as its candidate for President, and it has received the votes in Congress of "Rebel Brigadiers," whose disabilities were removed by Republican Congresses, and whose political power is due solely to the weapons put into their hands by the *Republican Policy!* We admitted these "Traitors" and "Rebels to Congress, and then we turned our indignant faces to the nation and said: "Behold Treason has installed itself on the floor of Congress!" May the people never wake from their slumbers! At every Presidential election for twenty years, we have said that the National Government was not safe in any hands but our own. We now repeat the declaration. There is nothing to show that we will not continue to declare the same thing; thus we clearly outline the practical establishment of our Spartan political aristocracy—namely, that only a certain class of the citizens of the United States should hold office under the National Government.

Eighth. We declare that the able administration and just policy of President Chuvius A. Anson shows to the American people that the chaplet of the martyr has not fallen to an unworthy brow, and that the confidence and gratitude of the nation are due to such a faithful and patriotic public servant.

Eighth. This plank is to express the opinions and feelings of those of our party who are known as "Stalwarts." The opinions and feelings of the rest of the Republican Party in regard to the President are so various and so many, that it would be vain to attempt a classification of them.

Upon this record the Republican Party asks the people to again support it, as its worthy sons, who have been famishing upon the fatness of office for a quarter of a century, should not be abandoned now in the hour of their need.

PLATFORM OF THE COUNTRY'S PARTY.

OFFICIAL.

THE PEOPLE OF THE UNITED STATES in origin and destiny are a *nation*, but are not so politically. Politically they are citizens of the several States and of the United States, which operate under a Constitution ordained and established by the people. This Constitution declares that certain powers were delegated to the United States, and certain other powers prohibited to the States; that the powers not so delegated nor so prohibited are reserved to the States respectively, or to the people; but the boundary between the powers delegated and the powers reserved is never to be decided so as to unduly consolidate powers in the Government of the United States, or give to the States inordinate rights, and it is the indispensable right of the United States, and of the several States to preserve their respective existences under a perpetual Union.

Second. We declare that the political parties of the country are, in their present state, unworthy the support of a free people.

Third. The war for the Union was a triumphant success and has closed. Peace now reigns. Let hate and sectionalism therefore be banished from the shores of a united country.

Fourth. Justice and equal privileges to all men.

Fifth. A Tariff which shall be established, modified or abolished as the needs and welfare of the whole country demand. The questions of Protection and Free Trade are not absolute principles, but are questions of expediency to be determined by the peculiar situation and needs of each particular nation, but either should be abolished or established by any country, according as the one or the other would become oppressive, or promote its general welfare.

Sixth. The people of the United States having suffered for years from party tyranny, insolent bossism, and a system of political spoils more monstrous

REAL.

THE PEOPLE OF THE UNITED STATES in origin and destiny are a *nation*, but are not so politically. Politically they are citizens of the several States and of the United States, which operate under a Constitution ordained and established by the people. This Constitution declares that certain powers were delegated to the United States, and certain other powers prohibited to the States; that the powers not so delegated nor so prohibited are reserved to the States respectively, or to the people; but the boundary between the powers delegated and the powers reserved is never to be decided so as to unduly consolidate powers in the Government of the United States, or give to the States inordinate rights, and it is the indispensable right of the United States, and of the several States to preserve their respective existences under a perpetual Union.

Second. We declare that the political parties of the country are, in their present state, unworthy the support of a free people.

Third. The war for the Union was a triumphant success and has closed. Peace now reigns. Let hate and sectionalism therefore be banished from the shores of a united country.

Fourth. Justice and equal privileges to all men.

Fifth. A Tariff which shall be established, modified or abolished as the needs and welfare of the whole country demand. The questions of Protection and Free Trade are not absolute principles, but are questions of expediency to be determined by the peculiar situation and needs of each particular nation, but either should be abolished or established by any country, according as the one or the other would become oppressive, or promote its general welfare.

Sixth. The people of the United States having suffered for years from party tyranny, insolent bossism, and a system of political spoils more monstrous than the history of the world ever before furnished, demand that these evils be wiped out, and that liberty and justice be restored.

Seventh. The evils of the spoils system can only be removed by electing men to the high offices of Government, who do not believe in the spoils system and who will not make appointments chiefly for factional or partizan services, but will appoint only honest and worthy men. It is useless to enact laws breathing Civil Service Reform, while the execution and enforcement of laws, which is their life, is accomplished by those elected under the influence of the spoils system.

Eighth. The people of the United States are not insensible of the great benefits and conveniences derived from adequate transportation lines, but the interference of great corporations with the governmental action, state and national, is no longer to be tolerated. The people demand protection against the growing power of gigantic monopolies which, unless checked, will subvert the dearest rights of the people.

Ninth. The history of free States shows that parties that have long continued in power became finally corrupt, and as both the great political parties of the United States are governed by essentially the same methods, we, the representatives of the people in National Convention assembled, declare that the time is ripe for a new political combination, in which the interests of country shall supercede those of party, in which there shall be no iron-clad rules subversive of free thought and individual opinions; that the caucus which has come to be the dictator of principles, as well as men, shall be confined to the selecting of *persons*, but not principles and the dictates of conscience, and, finally, that when our party shall have been corrupted by long rule, and shall have ceased to subserve the ends for which it was founded, it will be the duty of all good citizens then to abolish it, and institute new safe guards for liberty.

Thus the positions of political parties were distinctly defined. It was a clearly-drawn battle between the combined "bosses" of one party and the "fossils" of the other, pitted against the people. The same old campaign cries which had long surfeited the ears of the people were heard again. The New South, composed mostly of the younger men, and the New North, composed of all men of goodwill and true patriotism—men who believed that the war had been successfully closed; that the Union had been restored; that it was time to bring country to the front and send party to the rear, and, finally, men who sincerely wished to educate a generation of *Americans*. It was not doubtful as to what would be the stand taken by Jenkins Castleton in this great fight. Jenkins was born and had been reared during his youth in the South, and had received his early education there, while it was finished in the North. Thus he had imbibed strong prejudices neither way. So circumstanced, Jenkins was especially happy at finding the opportunity to join the new party of power and progress. So the last great struggle between the New and the Old was at hand.

CHAPTER XLVII.

THE RED CROSS.

IT is most fortunate that the busy world leaves time to some for' thinking about humanity. Woman seems to be the instrument chosen by God for preventing men from lapsing into absolute selfishness. Mad with everything else, the sight or companionship of a noble woman will ofttimes restore man to his nobler nature.

The face of Europe was, at the time of which we now speak, the battle-ground of two great races. The Society of the Red Cross was an organization devoted to humanity. Its membership was composed of noble and self-sacrificing women, who left homes of luxury to minister to the dead and dying on the battle-field.

A young woman, of surpassing beauty, was at this time gaining great fame by reason of her brave and unceasing labors among the armies. Little was known about her, beyond the fact that she was apparently an English woman, and had been very zealous in the work of the Society of the Red Cross. Her name was Geraldine Corsair. She had charge of a section of the Society, that was detailed to accompany one of the great armies and relieve all the suffering it could. Sometimes, while the battle was still raging, Geraldine Corsair could be seen ministering to some dying soldier. Oft, as the bombs thundered around her, she would be kneeling to offer a prayer for some departing spirit.

There was a young American Colonel in the army to which Geraldine was attached, who had received from the Emperor's own hands a decoration for gallantry and for many brilliant services. He was the talk of the army. He was promoted to an important command on the eve of a decisive battle. The Emperor told him that the fate of his empire depended on the fortunes of that day.

The battle raged. It was as if the volcanic fires of the earth had oped their burning mouths, and breathed out the work of hell. Whole batallions lay afield. Now comes the gallant charge; the sickening repulse, and again the rally. It was the decisive moment. Then was seen the young American, with sword drawn, gallantly leading the final charge. Following close behind the rear batallions were the members of the Red Cross Society. On, on the brave chargers went. Reinforcements trampled over the bodies of the dead and dying in their mad haste for the front. The enemy fly! There lay the long, silent lines of the dead. The groans of the wounded piteously appealed for aid. Geraldine cooled their parching tongues with the refreshing water. Anon she heard a piercing cry that came from some one on her right. She looked up and saw the young American Colonel in his dying throes. He was motioning frantically toward Geraldine. She hastened to him.

"Take this," he gasped, as he drew from his breast a letter. "Send it to her whose name is on it. Tell them how I died. My real name is *Jerome Lenardine*. Tell father ——."

He was silent. Death had come. Geraldine took the sacred missive, and though there were yet others who had dying messages for loved ones at home, yet she lingered. Let us leave Geraldine while she is finishing her God-like work, and find out some explanation of the strange words of the dying American officer.

It will be remembered that Mr. Jerome Lenardine sailed for Europe about the time of Ida Lexter's disappearance. He never returned the next season as was expected. The facts of the case were, that he had really gone to Europe to search for Ida Lexter. He firmly believed that she had gone abroad, and was concealing herself in order to escape from the doom of marrying one she did not love. It must be said for Jerome Lenardine, that although he had not a loving nature, and felt few unselfish emotions, yet he was generous. He would not have blighted the life of an innocent and confiding girl. But he had mistaken the nature of Ida Lexter. He knew not that she was the very soul of truth; that she had a heart that only a pure and confiding love could satisfy.

Jerome Lenardine felt that he had banished Ida Lexter from her home. He was touched with remorse. So he resolved that he would make the circuit of the world if necessary, in order to find her, or else learn her fate,—to find her that he might absolve her from all his claims upon her. In England he found no traces of her. Not discouraged, he commenced his search on the Continent. He advertised for her. He had a number of private detectives in his employ. After two years of fruitless search, he concluded that he would suspend his endeavors for a while. So to wear off his *ennui*, he joined the army.

The more he pondered over the character of Ida Lexter, the more was he impressed with the feeling that she was one too noble to be blighted. And her mysterious fate added a mournful interest to it all. It is highly probable that had not death overtaken the hapless Lenardine, he would have lived to be a better man. But he was not unlike that poor wretch who was taken captive by Italian Bandits, who, as the story goes, demanded of the prisoner whether or not he was a Christian. The man answered that he was.

"Then" said the leader of the bandits, "deny your Saviour, Jesus Christ, or else I'll kill you instantly." The poor man, thinking that there would be time in the future for repentance, said "Yes, I deny my Saviour, Jesus Christ."

"Then, take that," cried out the bandit as he stabbed the captive to the heart. Not unlike this ill-fated prisoner was Jerome Lenardine. Many times in his life had he denied the promptings of the better angels of his nature, trusting that he could make amends for it in the future. But his bark was wrecked in sight of a better shore, and the grim messenger came unexpectedly wafted on the very breezes of better resolves, which, alas, could now only

> "* * * cry to the sea that roared, sigh
> To the winds, whose pity, sighing back again,
> Did him but loving wrong."

"O God, receive his spirit!" devoutly prayed Geraldine -- she lingered for a moment to look upon the

> "Soldier of the Legion who in a foreign land was dead."

e eyes of Geraldine were suffused with unwonted tears. She had seen many a brave heart bled in death, but somehow this dead American strangely moved her. Muttering "poor, poor man," she gently stroked his now cold brow with her own soft hand, and then hastened on her way.

*   *   *   *   *   *   *

"What is the matter, Geraldine, are you ill?" asked one of the attendants at the headquarters of the Society of the Red Cross, the day after the great battle that has been described above. Geraldine had just examined the letter

A STARTLING DISCOVERY. 313

that had been handed her by the dying American, when immediately she turned deathly pale, and uttering a piercing cry, swooned and fell to the floor. Restoratives were applied and at length she regained consciousness. She then was removed to a quiet apartment for rest. The letter left by Jerome Lenardine to the care of Geraldine was addressed thus:

"To MISS IDA LEXTER, FORMERLY OF PHILOPOLIS,
"U. S. A."

Beneath this was written the following:

"Into whosever hands this letter falls, may it be delivered to her to whom it is addressed. Search her out, find her and tell her that I handed you this. Whatever the cost of the search, it will be paid on the presentation of this envelope to the executors of the estate of my father, the Hon. Lucius L. Lenardine, Philopolis, U. S. A. Spare no time nor toil, nor expense; for the sake of a dying man's last wish, find her, or else drop a tear for me over her grave.

"JEROME LENARDINE."

In a few days the army moved on, meanwhile the Society of the Red Cross continued its labors. But many noticed the melancholy demeanor and the changed manner of the once cheerful and happy Geraldine.

CHAPTER XLVIII.

OVER THE WATERS.

ONE balmy Summer's morning an elderly gentleman, accompanied by a young man, stepped upon the deck of an ocean steamer that was about to sail from New Cretonia for Liverpool. Their names appeared upon the register as Alfred S. Lexter and Jenkins Castleton, both of Philopolis.

Jenkins had now graduated from college, and had been admitted to the bar, where he was fast gaining fame as an advocate.

It had been determined that the search for Ida Lexter should be prosecuted in Europe by Mr. Lexter and Jenkins. None knew of their intentions except those immediately concerned.

Arriving in London they found the name of Jerome Lenardine registered as one of the visitors to the American consul two years before. Just beneath his and written in the same hand was the name of a *young lady*.

This was valuable information to the two visitors. They carefully noted the matter. They traced Mr. Lenardine as far as Paris, but there they could learn no more of him. They continually found evidence that he was associated with a young woman about whom they could learn very little. The impressions these discoveries made upon the father and lover can be more easily imagined than described. They now felt satisfied that the mystery was being cleared up.

"What is heaven with thee untrue?"

Ere long Mr. Lexter and Jenkins left Paris to visit other European capitals. Peace had come, and they were at the city where the victorious sovereign held his court.

Great preparations were being made for the reception of a brave young woman who belonged to the Red Cross Society, and who during the war had won laurels in the field of mercy more unfading than any that ever decked a warrior's brow. Her name was on every lip. With his own hands the emperor was to present her with a magnificent gold medal.

The name "Geraldine Corsair" was inscribed upon it.

Jenkins and Mr. Lexter read of the heroine and of how she would be received by the people as she passed through the streets on her way to the palace. Mr. Lexter and Jenkins purposed to go out and see the sight, and especially to get a glimpse of the noble woman.

But on the morning of the day of the reception of the heroine Mr. Lexter received an important telegram which necessitated that he should leave at once for Paris. So they hastily prepared themselves and were soon speeding on their way. They regretted much that they had to miss seeing the ovation of a grateful people to the heroine of mercy.

The heroine received the great honors that were bestowed upon her with becoming modesty. It had not been for fame that she had done so much to relieve the cruelties of war. It was from the dictates of a holy love which gives a consolation more sweet than all earthly joy beside. "Whosoever has done it unto the least of these has done it unto me." When Geraldine received the medal from the emperor's hands the acclamations of the multitude rang out; old soldiers that had seen her amid the fire and smoke of carnage ministering to the fallen, wept—

"The pretty and sweet manner of it forced
Those waters from them which they would have stopp'd."

After the ceremonies the fellow-workers with Geraldine in the Red Cross Society judged it wise that a period of perfect rest should be given to their devoted leader, in order that her wasted powers might be restored. So Geraldine accepted the invitation of the Baroness ——— to spend a while at her beautiful and romantic chateau on the shore of Lake Leman.

Geraldine sat one afternoon beneath the shade of the cooling arbor that adorned the chateau, perusing, as was often her custom, one of the great journals of the city of Paris. Her eye happened to light upon an advertisement in the "personals" which read thus:

"Wanted information in regard to a young American lady, formerly of Philopolis, U. S. A., who suddenly disappeared from her home several years ago. Her right name is *Ida Lexter*." (Here followed a description of her.) "It is thought that she is somewhere on the Continent. Any information concerning her will be thankfully received by her father, Alfred S. Lexter, or by Mr. Jenkins Castleton, whose address for the next thirty days will be the Hotel, d X——, Paris."

It was well that no one but herself was near at the moment she read this startling notice. Geraldine seemed so agitated and disturbed by the strange advertisement, that it was some moments before she could calm herself. "The hour of my destiny is come," she said, as with bated breath she read again the words of the "Personal."

The reader has no doubt by this time become well assured that Geraldine Corsair is none other than Ida Lexter, once the general favorite of Dr. Siddons' Church, in the far distant city of Philopolis,—the Ida, who in the mountain gorge, where the turbid rivulet flowed restlessly by, pledged a life-long fidelity to the sacred vows of love. Of the conflict between the commands of society and the dictates of her heart; of the deep struggles of her soul, when the alternatives of her fate were a father's curse, an unhappy marriage, or the cold folds of death self-imposed, or else flight to regions unknown, where like a drop in the fineless ocean, she could be tossed unrecognized and unknown in the sea of humanity,—of these struggles let us say no more. And here she beheld a divided duty. She had espoused the cause of humanity; she had joined the ranks; she had served the cause faithfully. On the other hand, the monitors of her heart sounded the call to the fulfillment of a vow made in bygone days. Should she leave the gentle folds of mercy, or should she fulfill the pledges of love? Oh, how her spirit was racked to the nether depths. "The genius and the mental instruments were then in council."

CHAPTER XLIX.

RESTORATION.

FOR a quarter of a century the people of the United States had enjoyed an abundance of Rule and Ruin. Thinking men had begun to ask themselves if the restoring and recuperating powers of a free Republic were ever to be applied to the body politic, now weakened and groaning under many ills.

A new generation had grown up. Young men animated by different motives than those of the war generation appeared upon the scene. Their pure and vigorous blood instilled new life into the torpid veins of the political body.

The great battle was fought while Jenkins Castleton was abroad, intent on his holy mission. But it had his full sympathy; and the cable dispatches announcing the triumphant success of the people filled his heart with gratitude.

The new political party combined the principles of progress with those of justice and peace.

"Let the dead past bury its dead" was the rule of action adopted by the new party.

"Act, act in the *living* present" was yet another cardinal principal which was cherished. The new President was the Chief Magistrate of the *Republic*, and not of any cabal or party. He was no votary at the altar of "spoils." He solved the much vexed problem of Civil Service Reform by following the very simple principle of appointing only honest and capable men to office, but the test for honesty and capability was not partizan service as it had been for twenty years or more. Reform had begun at the *head* and not at the *tail* of the government. The *source* of the civil service was purified and then the stream itself began to grow less muddy and more wholesome. The heated and bitter contests of former years were looked upon with a kind of mournful interest, something akin to the way the party broils of the Fathers of the Republic were regarded.

Old Dr. Lawrence Castleton—a characteristic Southern fossil—used to remark that "they *shot* us back into the Union and ever since they've tried to abuse us out again." But the old gentleman concluded that he would amend his past slowness by voting, in the last Presidential election it would probably be his privilege to see, the progressive ticket.

Dr. Castleton had a habit of asking the street organ-grinders whenever he met with them, if they could play "Dixie." If they did, as the old tune sounded out, the tottering frame of the once "Chairman of the Binghampton

County Vigilance Committee" would be reinvigorated; from his eyes flashed the slumbering fires of other times and other men. He was a harmless monument of the "Lost Cause." He could never forget the past. The aroma of the sweet flowers that once bedecked the gardens of his beloved Elmwood still lured him back through the vista of years. He seemed to sit again beneath the shade of the broad elms at evening-tide and watch the splendors of the setting sun as he sank into his burning bed to reappear through the gilded gates of the east. He looked up again towards a serene sky dotted with the merrily-twinkling stars that he would fain think were "the brilliant nail heads in the floor of Heaven."

The aged man was sometimes comforted by the consoling lines of the poet:

> " As the evening twilight fades away,
> The sky is filled with stars invisible by day."

Yes, just as the Doctors lamp of life was flickering, as it neared the long night of the lonely grave, the brilliant day-star of the Regenerated Republic was rising. It had not a fellow in the firmament of nations.

Its refulgent light shed down the beams of the truest Freedom that ever dazzled the longing eyes of mankind. The Republic was far on in the second century of its existence. It had borne the ordeal of fire; it had wrestled with factious foes within and envious enemies without. Its flag

K

now floated on the breezes of every clime, from the Arctic shores to Afric's burning sands. Its sails of Commerce whitened every sea. At its own hearth stones Liberty was a perpetual guest. The noble political system, conceived in the minds of Revolutionary patriots, perfected by the wisdom of unselfish statesmen, and preserved by the worthy sons of honored sires continued to bless the children of the great Republic. But how were the precious inheritances saved? What wondrous alchemy so compounded the heterogenous elements of a widely extended territory, and made them one grand and harmonious whole? Not the "eternal vigilance," but the eternal *action* of the people saved the Republic from lapsing into despotism. The people may be vigilant, but they may not *act*. They may see the danger-signals waving, but become indifferent, close their eyes, and blindly fall into the hopeless chasm of political slavery. We are told in the stories of mythology, that the Sirens were wont to sit on the seashore, play the most enchanting melodies, and sing with such sweetness that the hapless mariners sailing by forgot home and country, and were lured toward the fatal shore, where ere long the waves, as they rolled over their bones bleaching on the strand, gave the only echoes that sounded to the Sirens' melifluous but fatal song. But 'tis said that Ulysses as he neared the ever-destroying shore stopped the ears of the rowers and then lashed himself to the mast, till they had gone beyond the range of the Sirens' enchanting and resistless sounds. And so should the people of the Republic have their ears ever stopped against the political despot's alluring music. He is ever upon the shore. He has as many forms as his victims have ideals of beauty. Sometimes the despot is hydra-headed. Then the music that is heard by the unwary populace is that tuned to the strings of "Party." The soft cadences of the "bosses," as they sit in their well tapestried apartments bartering away the people's rights, are ever wafted on the morning breezes. Cæsar were no wolf, had not the Romans been but sheep! Oh, may the people stop their ears to the deadly melodies ere it be too late, and like Ulysses of old lash themselves firmly to the solid mast of Liberty, and reach at last the farther shore in safety!

CHAPTER L.

THE STORY TOLD.

"My feet are wearied and my hands are tired—
My soul oppressed,
And with desire have I long desired
Rest—only Rest."

WE left Ida Lexter (we'll call her by the familiar name) tossed between the claims of conflicting duties. Conscientious in everything, she could not now act in any but the most consistent manner. Yet had she not served long enough in the ranks of the Red Cross Society? Had she not paid the price of liberty?

* * * * * * *

When the morrow came, it found Ida in the presence of the Baroness in one of the commodious apartments of the Chateau. The Baroness bade Ida take a seat beside herself and then the two began an earnest conversation. Ida told her that circumstances over which she had no control compelled her to sever her connection with the Red Cross Society. A sacred feeling of duty had decided her to enter it, and now a duty as sacred constrained her to retire from its membership. This intelligence deeply grieved the Baroness, for she was one of the most zealous patronesses of the Society. She had seen the sterling worth, the bravery and the fidelity of Ida; and had flattered herself that the Society's future guiding star had been found.

Ida, too, was deeply moved and could not restrain her tears.

"God knows best," murmured the Baroness.

Finally Ida composed herself and informed the Baroness that she thought it best that she should start for the Capital at the earliest possible moment, and there acquaint the members of the Society with the fact that she had to leave them, perhaps forever.

It was a mournful journey for Ida. She almost shrank from the ordeal of facing her co-workers and bidding them farewell. She had become much attached to them and they to her. Many common dangers braved and the suffering of many hardships together, had woven a cord of tender sympathy around them all.

Arriving at the Capital, she hastened at once to communicate her resolves to the officers of state. They were filled with regrets.

On the day she was to leave, the Society met in one of the apartments of the Government Buildings. In the presence of the Society and its patrons Ida Lexter cast off her robes and the insignia of her position, and addressed the assembly as well as her emotions would permit her. She told them of the sorrow she felt at parting with those whom she loved so well; at leaving, perhaps forever, the companions endeared to her by co-labors on many battle-fields. But that which pained her most was the laying aside of the sacred robes, the emblems of Mercy. When she thought of how the world was hemmed in on every side by fortresses and barracks, as she beheld the grim messengers of death summoning the children of mercy-to the front—as she thought of all this the duty of serving humanity claimed all but the highest allegiance. But still she had made yet other vows which years before had been registered in heaven. She could not now inform them fully of the nature of these vows, but could she do so, she truly believed that they would, one and all, say to her, "fulfill thy sacred vows."

As Ida spoke, the subdued emotions, the suppressed feeling, and above all the calm and religious light which beamed from her countenance made the scene a most solemn one. Having given her last farewells and carrying away many tokens of the love which those with whom she had been associated bore her, Ida, accompanied by one of the Officers of the Army, started at once for the city of *Paris*.

"Any information concerning her will be thankfully received by her father, Alfred S. Lexter, or by Mr. *Jenkins Castleton*, whose address for the next thirty days will be the Hotel de X———, Paris."

Oh, for some bosom friend on whom she might lay the

burden of her thoughts! Ida was free, but how, how should she communicate with those she longed to see?

Could she confide in Major C——, her escort?

Finally she concluded that it would be necessary to inform the Major, to some extent at least, of the object of her journey.

She told him that she had some friends at the Hotel de X——, and wished to find them if possible. She requested that he should register her as "Miss Amelia Brown," as she wished to prepare a little surprise for her friends. Ida was clad in deep black and was also heavily veiled. So she felt little fear of an unexpected recognition.

Arriving at the city she was driven at once to the Hotel de X——, the Major registering her name as directed.

Ida trembled as the dinner hour approached. She was soon about to realize her dearest hopes, and yet she feared.

"It was such perfect happiness,
It must have some alloy."

Glancing over the Hotel Register which Ida had requested should be sent to her, with eager eye she looked for *two* names.

Yes, there they were!

"ALFRED S. LEXTER,
"JENKINS CASTLETON,
"U. S. A."

Ida nerved herself for the first sight of those for whom

she longed. She did not wish to cause any excitement, or to make a scene in the parlors of the Hotel—a scene which could not be understood by those who saw it.

The re-union of hearts so true was a sight too sacred to be seen by aught but those who could know and feel its joy.

At dinner a young woman in sable attire was seen entering the Dining Hall, leaning upon the arm of a young army officer. It was Ida Lexter and Major C——!

Ida looked anxiously around. She seemed to start at the sight of almost every table.

Ida bravely determined to control herself should she see her father and Jenkins in the Hall. She was, however, in spite of all her efforts much agitated.

Ah, did Jenkins Castleton but know what being sat but a few paces from him on that eventful day!

At last a gentleman with long locks of gray covering his head and with a grave countenance and dignified look caught the eye of Ida Lexter. Ida started a little at the glance.

"Had he," she thought, "father's rich, dark, raven locks, I would think it was surely he."

Alas, fair creature, that is father, but trouble has now silvered o'er those shining locks, and age in a few years has advanced a decade or more.

But who is that tall and graceful young man that sits by the aged gentleman?

Ida ceased her eating, and when the Major inquired the cause, she seemed to answer not, but was looking intently towards one of the tables.

The Major asked again if she was ill. This seemed to wake her from the reverie and she turned quickly around and said:

"I thought I saw the friends I am looking for, but I suppose I am mistaken. *One* of them seems much like the friend I wish to find, but as there are *two* of them, I would think they would dine at the *same* table."

The hoary hairs of her father, and the deep lines of trouble on his face had deceived her. She knew him not.

Ida was satisfied at least that she had seen Jenkins Castleton. So she might now prepare for the coming meeting with him.

After dinner, Ida and the Major returned to the parlor.

Ida was an expert performer on the piano, as well as an excellent singer. Her voice was peculiarly mellow and sweet.

Ida remembered that years before when she and Jenkins met at "Tyro's Glen," she had sung a selection from one of Verdi's operas to the company that gathered one evening in the parlors of the "Tyro Mountain House."

Among those who listened to her song on that evening was Jenkins Castleton. He was much impressed by it, and afterwards, when thinking of the unknown fate of Ida, he sometimes consoled himself by dwelling in memory upon the sounds of her voice as she sweetly caroled the words of the opera on that evening at the "Tyro Mountain House."

Ida thought now of this song as she sat in the drawing room of the hotel in far distant Paris. The words and sentiments of the selection were strangely appropriate to the present occasion.

She saw the guests passing by the curtained entrance on their way from the dining hall. Near the entrance to the drawing room stood a piano. The thought came to Ida that if she were now to sing again the song that Jenkins had heard at the glen in the long ago, would he not hear it as he passed in the hallway, and would it not awaken the depths of memory?

"Shall I play something for you, Major?" asked Ida, as she seated herself at the piano.

"Certainly, Miss Geraldine (he knew her only by that name), I would be pleased to hear you," answered the courteous Major.

Ida began to play and presently to sing:

" *   *   Eposso crederlo?
Ti veggo a me d' accanto!
E questo ——"

Just then Jenkins and Mr. Lexter were coming up the corridor.

"What do you hear, Jenkins," asked Mr. Lexter as he saw his companion stop suddenly and assume a most attentive attitude.

"I hear a song; I've often heard it before. Still there seems something about that voice that strangely attracts me," replied Jenkins.

Ida continued:

> "e questo un sogno, un' estasi,
> Un sovrumano incanto!
>   *   *   *   *
> Sei tu dal ceil diceso
> O in ceil son io con te?" *

Jenkins needed no more to satisfy him as to whose voice that was which sounded in his ear. He had heard it before.

With one rapturous bound he rushed into the parlor from whence came the sounds.

The sounds of music ceased, and were replaced by the responsive throbs of loving hearts re-united. Father, child and lover wept tears of joy.

The reader must let the happy scene pass before him in imagination. The pen must surrender its powers of description in despair.

It is said that the immortal genius who painted the

---

*" * * * Can I believe my eyes?
Do I see thee before me? Is it a dream?
A phantom of the wandering brain?
A wild and fearful illusion!
 * * * Say, didst thou from heaven come,
Or am I now in heaven with thee?"

Sacrifice of Iphigenia at Aulis represents the attendants and the chiefs as filled with sorrow. The tears ran down their cheeks and the air was rent with their lamentations. But there was *one* in the group who covered his head with his robe! 'Tis the father of the fair Iphigenia, as he stands by the altar where his darling child is being offered up a living sacrifice. The pencil shrank from the attempt to paint that sorrow which cannot be pictured.

So the joy of the re-union of Ida Lexter with her father and her lover after their long separation is unpicturable. The best we can do is to enrobe the scene with the mantle of imagination.

What an interesting chapter would the story of the experience of the separated lovers make, as in the freedom of unrestrained conversation they unfolded them to each other on this day in the Hotel de X———?

Major C—— had been so amazed at what had occurred in his presence, that thus far he had been unable to say a word. He seemed as much interested in their conversation as did the now happy lovers themselves.

A cable dispatch the next morning sent some joyful news to the Lexter home in far away Philopolis. It was a fortunate step of the Lexters that they did not make the disappearance of Ida public. It was known only to a few of her personal friends and to some of the congregation of Dr. Siddons' church.

CLOSING SCENES. 333

So the family felt that all their troubles were now removed. Every one was cheerful, and felt that, after all, a kind Providence had watched over their destinies.

As Ida told the fate of Jerome Lenardine to her father and Jenkins, she observed that it, from some cause, strangely moved them. Jenkins inquired if she was sure that it was none other than Jerome Lenardine. She replied that she was absolutely certain. She then produced the letter which had been handed to her upon the battle-field. Mr. Lexter at once recognized the familiar handwriting of his once favorite business and social friend.

There were some secrets which Jenkins and Mr. Lexter decided had better perish in their own breasts. One of those was the suspicion that Ida had been unfaithful to the vows she had made to Jenkins, and that they had sought for Jerome Lenardine under grave suspicions that he and Ida had fled together. Mr. Lexter deeply deplored his unrelenting opposition to the dictates of his daughter's heart. Deep down in the depths of his conscience lay a pang which ever and anon rebuked him, because his opposition to Ida's love sprang from selfish and material motives.

When Ida informed Jenkins and Mr. Lexter that the "Geraldine Corsair" they had read so much about, that the heroine of so many battle-fields was none other than the gentle Ida that once graced his own home—when he heard this, his

> "Subdued eyes, albeit unused to the melting mood,
>   Dropped tears as fast as Arabian
>   Trees their medicinal gum."

Ida requested, on her part, that when they returned home the fact that "Geraldine Corsair" and herself were one and the same should not be divulged. It was so agreed.

In due time the party began their journey homeward. Ida had laid aside her sable garments, and in her new attire looked quite herself once more—except that her character had been even more beautified by the graces that self-sacrifice and good deeds ever bestow.

*   *   *   *   *   *   *

The time is a balmy day in May. The place a church in the city of Philopolis. The great organ is sounding forth the symphonies of the "Wedding March."

The bridal procession enters. The bride, Ida Lexter, is advancing to the altar leaning on the arm of her father. Then followed Mr. Jenkins Castleton, the groom, and Mrs. Lexter.

Old Dr. Lawrence Castleton is there to give his blessing to his son. Rebecca recalls a scene in the long ago, when she was playing her part in a similar drama.

'Tis over.

After many trials Jenkins and his ever faithful Ida had at last set sail on the sea of life to realize the fond dreams of their youthful loves.

Old Dr. Lawrence Castleton was gathered to his fathers. His last request was that he be laid to rest near his beloved Elmwood, where the restless winds that once rustled through the outspreading elms of his Southern home could come again, and find a responsive spirit beneath his own head-stone.

He had lived to see his South bloom again 'neath the genial sky of a new republic. He had seen his son attain to honor and fame. He had filled the full measure of years and peacefully fell at last into his long sleep.

Rebecca lived to watch over the onward career of her sons. After many toils she found a green old age in the satisfaction that comes from the fulfillment of duty.

A visitor to the residence of Mr. Jenkins Castleton, in Philopolis, is sometimes shown two little Castletons. Some declare that they favor Mrs. Ida Castleton, their mother; others that they are much like their father. However that might be, Jenkins is proud of them because he sees in little Rebecca (for he named her so) and her brother, young Lawrence, the elements of *true* Americans. In their veins courses the blood of North and South, which, united in their persons, made them the worthy children of the New Republic.

THE END.

www.ingramcontent.com/pod-product-compliance
Lightning Source LLC
Chambersburg PA
CBHW030002240426
43672CB00007B/788